EASTON AREA PUBLIC LIB.

1901 9100 056 746 1

W9-AEI-235

NO LONGER PROPERTY
OF EASTON AREA
PUBLIC LIBRARY

EASTON AREA PUBLIC LIB.

REVERSIBLE TWO-COLOR KNITTING

REVERSIBLE TWO-COLOR KNITTING

by Jane Neighbors

CHARLES SCRIBNER'S SONS/NEW YORK

EASTON PUBLIC LIBRARY
EASTON PA

746.43
N 397r

Copyright © 1974 Jane F. Neighbors

Library of Congress Cataloging in Publication Data

Neighbors, Jane F.
    Reversible two-color knitting.

    1. Knitting—Patterns.   I. Title.
TT820.N43   746.4'3   73-1106
ISBN 0-684-13905-7

This book published simultaneously in the
United States of America and in Canada—
Copyright under the Berne Convention

All rights reserved. No part of this book
may be reproduced in any form without the
permission of Charles Scribner's Sons.

1 3 5 7 9 11 13 15 17 19 C/MD 20 18 16 14 12 10 8 6 4 2

Printed in the United States of America

APR 17 1975
EASTON PUBLIC LIBRARY
EASTON PA

ACKNOWLEDGMENTS

Most of all I appreciate the support of my husband, James E. Neighbors, Jr. and my children, Keryn Jane, Daryl Ann, J. Edward, A. Griffin, and Christopher David, all of whom have been immensely helpful and encouraging.

Thanks to John Freni and Robert Raisch of John Lane Studio for their careful photographic work; and to The Spinnerin Yarn Co., Inc. for supplying most of the yarn used throughout the book.

I am especially grateful to Barbara G. Walker for encouragement, advice, and support.

CONTENTS

List of Colored Illustrations

following page 158

PREFACE

Since you have opened this book, you must be interested in knitting. More—you must have reached that happy point when you realize that the few basics of knitting make possible an infinite variety of amazing effects. You must also wish to expand your own knitting horizons. I hope this book will help you do exactly that.

Please don't think you must be an advanced knitter to try the ideas here. Certainly a real beginner could have trouble. But are you comfortable with the basic processes such as knitting, purling and slipping stitches? Past the stage of panicking at a dropped stitch? Perhaps you have worked in stitch patterns such as cables and fancy ribs or in two-color patterns. Then you should be ready to try two-color reversibles. There should be something here for the advanced knitter, too, including suggestions on techniques to use when designing articles and even how to design your own patterns.

There are sub-headings in every chapter to guide you along the way. Nothing is so upsetting as to know a fact you need is somewhere in a book, yet not be able to find it. I'd be happy to think you will make some marginal notes of your own, too (assuming the book belongs to you, not a library or a friend). Some of my best-loved reference books are ones I have written in—neatly, I hope, but helpfully for certain.

All stitch patterns have been developed by the author. In a very few instances, which are noted, a known non-reversible stitch has been adapted for reversibility. Since the processes by which knitting is formed (knit, purl, slip, etc.) are limited, there is the probability that other knitters have developed single color or non-reversible stitch patterns comparable to some herein. However, there has apparently been no previous attempt to develop stitch patterns specifically for reversibility in two colors.

I hope you will find something new and exciting to try. Good luck!

JANE NEIGHBORS

Brick House Farm
Pleasant Valley, New York

GLOSSARY

*—an asterisk is used to mark off repeats of a pattern. It will be followed later by "rep from *" indicating the knitter starts again at the *.

⑤—A circled number is used in certain Ripple and Chain patterns to indicate a number which may be substituted for the one preceding it. If one circled number is used, the circled numbers must be substituted throughout. The result is a wider design with chains farther apart.

( )—Parentheses are used to indicate a group of stitches which must be repeated and to tell how many times. "(k1, sl 1 yif) 3 times" would mean "k1, sl 1 yif, k1, sl 1 yif, k1, sl 1 yif."

adapt to spn—Change the way the directions are written so that a pattern may be worked on single-pointed needles. Instructions are given in Chapter Six.

alternate reversible—This usually indicates patterns having a texture of two distinct parts which alternate. Where one occurs on one side the other appears on the reverse. For example, where one is raised the other is depressed, where one is knit the other is purled. Sometimes design, rather than texture, alternates.

bo1—Bind off one stitch by dropping the second stitch of the right needle over the stitch just worked.

cast on dark (or light)—indicates which of two colors should be used for casting on.

dark—indicates one of the two colors used in a pattern. (see also p. 3)

decr—decrease

double wrap—In forming the stitch (either k or p) wrap the strand of yarn twice around the needle making a double stitch. The extra wrap is dropped when the st is worked in the next row, as the directions will indicate.

dpn—double-pointed needle (or needles). Circular needle may be substituted. Note that for two-color reversible knitting, dpn or circular needles do *not* indicate that circular knitting will be done. They are used for flat knitting so that rows may begin at either end. (see also p. 3)

edge—the extreme left or right where rows begin and end in flat knitting. (see also "side" and p. 174)

incr—increase

k—knit

k2 tog—knit two sts together as one.

knit-wise—Insert needle into stitch from left side, as is done for a knit stitch. Slip sts are done this way *rarely,* when indicated.

k last st (of row)—When following row directions, after all repeats are completed one st will remain; knit it.

KLT—*Knit Left Twist:* Reach behind first st on left needle and k into front loop of second st but leave it on needle, then k first st and drop both from left needle.

KPRT—*Knit Purl Right Twist:* Reach in front and k second st on left needle, leave on needle and throw yarn to front, purl first st on left needle and drop both sts from left needle.

KRT—*Knit Right Twist:* reach in front of first st on left needle and k second st but leave on needle, then k first st and drop both from left needle.

last st—see "k last st" or "sl last st."

light—designates the lighter of the two colors being used. (see also p. 3)

maintain—indicates that a row of a two-color pattern will be worked so as to keep all sts the same color as they presently show on the needle. Following the row directions will give this effect. (see also p. 4)

mirror reversible—One side will look as the other does in the mirror. If a line of the design on one side moves up and right, then on the other side it will move up and left.

multiple of ? sts plus ?—Multiples indicate the number of sts which may be cast on for a given pattern. A multiple of 3 would mean 3, or 6, or 9, or 12, etc. "Multiple of 3 sts plus 2" would call for two more than the multiple such as 5, or 8, or 11, or 14, etc.

opposite reversible—is used when colors reverse. If one side shows a dark design on a light background, the other will show a light design on a dark background.

p—purl

p2 tog—purl two sts together as one.

PKLT—*Purl Knit Left Twist:* Reach behind the first st on left needle and purl into front of second st but leave it on needle, throw yarn to back and k into first st, drop both sts from left needle together.

PLT—*Purl Left Twist:* Carefully drop first st from left needle to front, purl second st, then pick up and purl dropped st. Instead of dropping st it may be slipped to a cabling needle or dpn temporarily.

PRT—*Purl Right Twist:* Reach in front of first st on left needle, purl second st but leave on needle, then purl first st and drop both sts from needle together.

purl-wise—Insert needle into a st from the right side as if to purl. This is the way all sts are slipped unless the directions say "knit-wise."

rep—means repeat the processes just done.

repeat—A repeat is a part of a design which is the smallest complete unit. A patterned article is made of many repeats of the design.

rnd—*round:* In circular knitting, working from a starting point around the needle and back to that point completes one round. It is the equivalent of a row in flat knitting.

row—Working all the stitches on a needle once, in one direction, completes a row.

sc—single crochet

side—always indicates a surface of the work. Do not confuse with "edge." (see also p. 174)

slide—After casting on, or after working a row, "slide" means all sts should be slid to the far end of the needle in order to start the next row at the other end with the other color. (see also p. 3)

sl 1—*slip one stitch.* This is always done purl-wise unless knit-wise is specified.

sl st—*slip stitch.* A stitch which is slipped from left needle to right without being either knit or purled.

sl 1 yib—Slip one st with the *yarn in back* of the work or on the side away from the knitter (the same place it is held for a knit st).

sl 1 yif—Slip one st with the *yarn in front* of the work or toward the knitter (the same place it is held for a purl st).

slip last st (of row)—When following row directions, after all repeats are completed, one st will remain; slip it (with yarn in back if it is a k st or yarn in front if it is a p st).

spn—single-pointed needle (or needles).

st—stitch

true reversible—is rarely exactly the same on both sides but gives that impression.

turn—At the end of a row (or occasionally after casting on) "turn" means the work should be turned around so that the next row begins with the last st just worked. This is the conventional way when using spn.

unlike reversible—The two sides are completely different. Usually one side is either plain solid color or has horizontal stripes.

yib or yif—indicates "yarn in back" or "yarn in front". See "sl 1 yib" or "sl 1 yif."

yo—*yarn over:* Before working the next st put the yarn over the right needle. Bring the yarn to the front (unless it is already there), then over the needle. Leave it in back if the next st will be knit or continue to front again to prepare for a p st next. On the next row, this yo is treated as a stitch and knit or purled unless some other directions are given.

REVERSIBLE
TWO-COLOR
KNITTING

CHAPTER ONE

INTRODUCING TWO-COLOR REVERSIBLES

All types of handicrafts are enjoying an upsurge of popularity right now. Some are new, some revivals, some have always been around but are now more evident.

Knitting is a somewhat different case. It is an ancient art which has been almost continually popular. Knitting has traditionally been one of the basics of garment making. Nearly everything we wear is either woven or knit. Although most fabric (knit or woven) has long been manufactured commercially, knitting as handwork has not waned. It is fun, simple yet challenging, and gives beautiful results.

All this might lead one to believe that there is little new that could be developed in knitting. Surely every possibility has been explored by now. How far from the truth that is! In pattern stitches alone there are so many basic types (such as rib, cable, lace, textured) that the variations are literally infinite. Possible combinations of such stitches into garments are obviously unlimited. Look at the Irish Fisherman Knits! New methods of construction are continually developed and refined. Sleeves are an example. There are set-ins, raglans, saddle-shoulders, Dolman, and more. Each can be worked in a number of different ways. Some knitting techniques go out of style then are revived. Others undoubtedly have been forgotten and rediscovered.

One advantage of knitting is that there are really so few basics (knit, purl, slip stitch, increase and decrease, etc.). These can be mastered relatively easily and combined in new ways even by someone who does not ordinarily consider herself creative or artistic. Most serious knitters become designers or inventors, often without even realizing it.

Although one-color knitting can certainly be reversible, no one seems to have found a way to use two-colors without creating a wrong side.

TRADITIONAL AND NEW METHODS OF TWO-COLOR KNITTING

In the past there have been several ways to use more than one color in a knitted garment. Fair Isle knitting carries unused colors along the back of the work. This makes a warm, double-thick fabric, but no one could call the wrong side attractive. Argyles leave unused colors hanging on bobbins until needed again. This is only adaptable to certain types of patterns. The wrong side may not be as messy as in Fair Isle, but it is certainly a wrong side. Colors are twisted together at the back, and the basis of the fabric is stockinette stitch. There are also two- or three-color stitch patterns in which color is an integral part of a design which also incorporates texture. A few of these produce an attractive, although different, reverse. However, there is always a knit side and a purl side, or unused strands move along the back, or some other complication exists to make one less attractive.

This book proposes patterns and methods which look equally well on both sides. It makes two-color knitting available for uses such as scarves and afghans where a wrong side is a terrible bother to the user. Happily, the designs are accomplished in ways which are sometimes even easier to manage than the traditional methods. The knitter does not have to carry both colors along through all her work as only one is used per row or round. No bobbins need be wound. The colors only need "twisting" together every couple of rows, if at all, so the strands don't get tangled.

All the stitch patterns presented here use two colors. The question may arise as to whether three or more could be used. Certainly that is possible but it has not been done here for several reasons. With two colors, one strand may climb each edge of the work, but three or more would make for very messy edges. This is a disadvantage in reversibles where edges show (scarves, afghans) and when there must be unobtrusive seams where they exist. When stitches are slid back and forth on the needles so that rows may begin at either end, more than two colors would tend to make directions difficult to understand, follow, and remember.

TERMINOLOGY

Skimming through the patterns, you may find several terms you don't see in other knitting books. There is a complete glossary to refer to, but discussion of a few words may be helpful.

Dark and **light** refer to the two colors used in each pattern. For clarity, the samples photographed use starkly contrasting colors to show up as black and white. Following the directions will give the same results as those illustrations. Don't forget that in most cases a different result will be produced by using the dark color in rows marked "light" and vice versa. Of course it is sometimes better to choose colors with less contrast where there is not really a dark one and a light one. When you decide which color you want for a certain part of the design, note whether that is dark or light in the picture and you will know which rows to do with the color.

Dpn means double-pointed needle. It is also used here to refer to the plural (double-pointed needles, usually in pairs) and can indicate that a circular needle may be substituted. The knitter should realize that in this book such needles are used for *flat* back-and-forth knitting, not for working around in a circle. Ordinary straight needles have points on only one end. This means a row of knitting may only begin at the edge which is at the pointed end of the needles. With dpn the dark color strand may be at one end of the needle and the light strand at the other. The knitter is able to start a row with whichever one is required. On large pieces of knitting a circular needle is used but work still proceeds from one end to the other, not around.

Some of the patterns actually can be adapted for the use of single-pointed needles and directions for doing so are given in Chapter Six. *Any* pattern may be worked around on a circular needle. An explanation of how to do so is in the same chapter.

Turn or **slide** occurs at the end of each row of directions. Turn indicates that the knitting should be turned around in order to work back in the direction you just came from (the "normal" way of proceeding). Slide means the stitches should be slid to the opposite end of the circular or double-pointed needle because that is where you will find the desired color of yarn for the next row.

Every set of directions uses turn or slide (usually the latter) after the cast on. Typical is "cast on dark, slide." It will be important to slide the stitches to the other end of the needle and begin Row 1 with the other color at the other end. If this is done, all further turn and slide instructions are merely guides. It will be obvious whether you will have to do one or the other to get to the color called for in the next row.

By the way, when you first start the second color, do not tie it on, or make any new stitches. Simply start to use that color to knit the row of stitches already on the needle. If the first stitch is a slip stitch, just slip it onto the other needle without working it and start the new color with the second stitch. The dangling end can be tied or worked in later.

Edge and **side** are often used by knitters to refer to the same things. Picture a knitted square. "Side" will be used here *only* to refer to the two knitted "faces" or "surfaces" (these two terms will also be used for the same thing). "Edge" will refer only to the place where rows begin and end. Such a place will absolutely *never* be referred to as a side of the knitting.

Maintain is a term useful in the Reversible Geometrics of Chapter Four. If a knitter understands the way these patterns are worked, she won't even have to refer to the directions when doing a row marked "maintain." She just keeps the stitches knit, purl, dark, or light as they presently appear. However, every maintain row also has complete written directions. A beginning reversible knitter may prefer to ignore the word "maintain" and work from the directions.

If other terms are not familiar, consult the Glossary. One which may be new to knitters who have not used stitch patterns is the parenthesis. "(k1, p1) 3 times" means "knit one, purl one three times" or "k1, p1, k1, p1, k1, p1."

TRYING TWO-COLOR REVERSIBLES

The simplest stitch patterns occur at the beginning of Chapter Two. Later patterns in that chapter add slip stitches and other processes. Chapter Three's patterns are merely a specific form and could really be treated as a section of Chapter Two. Nearly all these stitches are ideal for large, flat pieces such as stoles and afghans. However, don't overlook the fact that many are wonderful for sweaters and such, too. These are patterns with textural as well as color interest.

Chapter Four stitches look like dark and light colored designs on stockinette stitch. Of course they are not really, for the stockinette stitch appears on both sides. They are appropriate for jackets, sweaters, and other garments. Being dense yet smooth they are also useful for some items more frequently done by needlepoint than knitting. The color illustrations give examples. Some of the patterns may adapt better to certain uses if they are enlarged or spread out.

In deciding on a pattern to use, make a good-sized swatch for a try-out. If you have tentatively selected a Reversible Geometric, cast on about twice as many stitches as would ordinarily be called for. The other pattern types use a more conventional number of stitches to the inch.

When working any pattern keep normal tension on the yarn at all times. Do not be confused by Scandinavian or Fair Isle knitting which requires carrying strands loosely. Even slip stitches require normal treatment here.

DON'T LOSE YOUR PLACE

There are several ways to keep your place in knitting directions. My favorite is to copy the directions on a file card. Then I slide a paper clip down the edge so it always points to the row I am doing. If the pattern frequently says "repeat row 3" or 4, or whatever, use two paper clips. One marks the row reached and the other marks the required repeat row. If rows 12 and 16 both say "repeat row 4," when row 4 is finished there is no question as to whether 5, 13, or 17 should be done next.

Trying out some of these patterns requires patience. Wait until you have done several rows before you check to see if the design looks like the picture. Some can look completely wrong at first. With Reversible Geometrics the row of stitches on the needle nearly always looks wrong because both sides of the work are lined up together.

TECHNICALITIES

Throughout the book there are detailed explanations of the hows and whys of this new kind of knitting. They are there for advanced knitters, designers, and anyone who has to know how everything works.

If you don't care for technical explanations, or if they frighten you, just skip them. Every attempt has been made to write directions so clearly that they can simply be followed step by step without any analysis being needed. The articles to knit, in Chapter Five, should also be easy to do. The only exception is the Maze Wall-hanging which does require an understanding of Reversible Geometrics. Of course, after you try several such patterns you may discover that you do understand how they work. Some people prefer to learn by doing. The stitch patterns are waiting for you to do just that.

CHAPTER TWO

SIMPLE REVERSIBLES

There is nothing in this chapter which should frighten any intermediate knitter. The first section is so basic that the stitch patterns can easily be used by a beginner since they incorporate only knit and purl stitches.

These stitches are ideal for scarves, stoles, shawls, afghans and baby blankets. Reversibility is a real advantage in such items. Yet the patterns are mostly quick and easy to learn and work.

The first few stitch patterns employ one and two row bands of dark and light colors. Textural interest comes from the way knit and purl stitches are combined. At first they are used by the row, later combined in the same row. As the patterns become more complex (not necessarily more difficult) with the use of various knitting techniques, beautiful and interesting effects are achieved. Try a few, for no picture can adequately convey qualities like denseness, stretch, and depth of pattern. Some work better on large needles, some in fine yarn on small needles. Comments and suggestions are given but they are intended as guides and stimulants to the knitter's imagination, not as rules or complete catalogs of possible applications.

It would be fun to try developing your own patterns of this type. First familiarize yourself with the basics by trying out samples. Then keep one rule in mind: change colors every row or two (perhaps three). Otherwise you will find yourself carrying the unused strand too far up the edge. Better in that case to break it off and start it again later. But then you would really be working in horizontal stripes, not in two-color stitch patterns. Try combining different numbers of knit and purl rows. Use one row of light color to two of dark or vice versa. See what happens if you introduce other types of stitches or techniques. Experiment with starting both colors at the same or at opposite edges. Check your results to see how they might be improved.

Any one- or two-row pattern can be tried as a two-color reversible. Work the pattern first in one color, then repeat in the other. If you cast on with the first color on dpn, slide the stitches to the other end and start row 1 with the second color. With a two-row pattern you will find that right sides of the first color will be on one side and right sides of the second color will be on the other side, frequently with interesting results. If there are slip stitches or other special effects in the right places, the colors will blend between the rows. Otherwise, you will have a horizontal stripe effect. Generally, this book avoids patterns which are merely stripes because they are not truly two-color stitch patterns.

If you are about to embark on your first attempt at using two-color reversible knitting, be sure to read the parts of the introductory chapter which explain techniques. A few terms used in this type of knitting might otherwise be confusing.

Some of these patterns indicate that they can be adapted for working with single-pointed needles (spn). If you wish to do so, there is a discussion of the method in Chapter Six.

SIMPLE KNIT AND PURL REVERSIBLES

TWO-COLOR GARTER STITCH

opposite reversible
This simple two-color reversible is deeply textured and has a considerable amount of "give", especially vertically. It makes a soft muffler or afghan.

Use dpn or adapt for spn. Any number of sts. Cast on dark, slide.
Row 1: light—knit. Turn.
Row 2: light—knit. Slide.
Row 3: dark—knit. Turn.
Row 4: dark—knit. Slide.
      rep Rows 1–4.

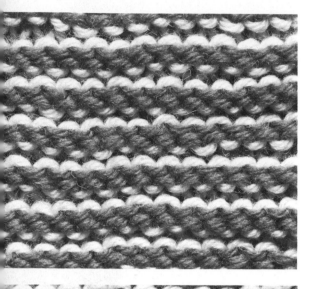

LINES AND LOOPS (left)

alternate reversible
Another deeply textured, stretchy pattern. At first glance it is a "true reversible" but of course where one side is raised the other is depressed.

Use of dpn required. Any number of sts. Cast on dark, slide.
Row 1: light—knit. Turn.
Row 2: dark—knit. Slide.
      rep Rows 1 and 2.

CROSS-RIB STRIPES (below)

alternate reversible
Use dpn or adapt for spn. Any number of sts. Cast on dark, turn.
Row 1: dark—knit. Slide.
Row 2: light—purl. Turn.
Row 3: light—knit. Slide.
Row 4: dark—knit. Turn.
Row 5: dark—knit. Slide.
Row 6: light—knit. Turn.
Row 7: light—purl. Slide.
Row 8: dark—purl. Turn.
      Rep rows 1–8.

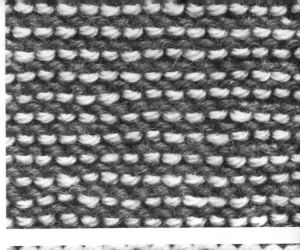

ROLL-OVER REVERSIBLE (upper pair)

upside down reversible

The back of this pattern is exactly the same as the front *except* for being upside down, hence its name. If you cast on with two lengths of yarn, leave the tail-ends hanging until you are done knitting. They will be used to indicate what row you are on. When you pick up a new color to work with and you are on the same edge as its "tail", you should knit. If the tail at that edge is the opposite color, purl.

Use of dpn required. Any number of sts. Cast on dark, slide.

Row 1: light—knit. Turn.
Row 2: dark—knit. Slide.
Row 3: light—purl. Turn.
Row 4: dark—purl. Slide.
       rep Rows 1–4.

STRAIGHT AND WAVY STRIPES (lower pair)

alternate reversible

This is similar to Cross-Rib Stripes. Note that rows seven and fourteen are exceptions to the rule of two rows of each color; that is, they are single rows of dark. Don't forget that the opposite effect of the one illustrated can be achieved by casting on with light and reversing the color of all rows.

Use of dpn required. Any number of sts. Cast on dark, slide.

Row 1: light—knit. Turn.
Row 2: light—purl. Slide.
Row 3: dark—purl. Turn.
Row 4: dark—knit. Slide.
Row 5: light—knit. Turn.
Row 6: light—purl. Slide.
Row 7: dark—purl. Turn.
Row 8: light—purl. Turn.
Row 9: light—knit. Turn.
Row 10: dark—purl. Turn.
Row 11: dark—knit. Turn.
Row 12: light—purl. Turn.
Row 13: light—knit. Turn.
Row 14: dark—purl. Slide.
       rep Rows 1–14.

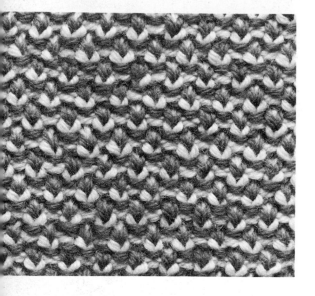

SEAGULLS (left)

true reversible
Use smaller than usual needles for this overall tweedy pattern.

Use of dpn required. Odd number of sts. Cast on dark, slide.
Row 1: light—k1, * p1, k1, rep from *. Turn.
Row 2: dark—k1, * p1, k1, rep from *. Slide.
      rep Rows 1 and 2.

KNIT TWO, PURL TWO RIBBING

These are merely the familiar ribbings done in single row or double row versions of alternating colors. They are included here only because they are useful for the ribbing which is necessary on many garments which could be made with other patterns in the book.

Double Row Method (*left*)
alternate reversible
Use dpn or adapt for spn. Multiple of 4 sts. Cast on dark, slide.
Row 1: light—* k2, p2, rep from *. Turn.
Row 2: light—rep row 1. Slide.
Rows 3 and 4: with dark, rep row 1.
      rep rows 1-4.

Single Row Method (*below*)
alternate reversible
Use of dpn required. Multiple of 4 sts. Cast on dark, slide.
Row 1: light—* k2, p2, rep from *. Turn.
Row 2: with dark, rep row 1. Slide.
      rep Rows 1 and 2.

TEXTURED HORIZONTAL STRIPES

true or alternate reversibles

To adapt any of these to spn, cast on light and in rows 3 and 4 change every k to p and every p to k.

For all four patterns: use dpn or adapt for spn. Odd number of sts. Cast on dark, slide.

Variation I
Row 1: light—k1, * p1, k1, rep from *. Turn.
Row 2: light—rep row 1. Slide.
Rows 3 and 4: with dark rep rows 1 and 2.
        rep Rows 1–4.

Variation II
Row 1: light—k1, * p1, k1, rep from *. Turn.
Row 2: light—p1, * k1, p1, rep from *. Slide.
Rows 3 and 4: with dark rep rows 1 and 2.
        rep Rows 1–4.

Variation III
Row 1: light—k1, * p1, k1, rep from *. Turn.
Row 2: light—rep row 1. Slide.
Row 3: dark—p1, * k1, p1, rep from *. Turn.
Row 4: dark—rep row 3. Slide.
        rep Rows 1–4.

Variation IV
Row 1: light—k1, * p1, k1, rep from *. Turn.
Row 2: light—p1, * k1, p1, rep from *. Slide.
Row 3: dark—rep row 2. Turn.
Row 4: dark—rep row 1. Slide.
        rep Rows 1–4.

Note: This final variation is actually a k1, p1 rib and may be used as such. Notice that the purl sts do not show in the picture. Except for the fact that there are no sl sts to hold the fabric together, this would be a member of the family of Reversible Geometrics which appear later in the book.

SINGLE KNIT ONE, PURL ONE RIB (top)

true reversible

To make the record complete, here is the other regularly formed k1, p1 rib (see the preceding Textured Horizontal Stripe Variation IV for the two-row version). Don't forget the obvious, that you can make irregular designs in ribbing with 1 row of dark, 2 of light, 1 dark or any other variation.

Use of dpn required. Odd number of sts. Cast on dark, slide.
Row 1: light—p1, * k1, p1, rep from *. Turn.
Row 2: dark—k1, * p1, k1, rep from *. Slide.
Row 3: light—k1, * p1, k1, rep from *. Turn.
Row 4: dark—p1, * k1, p1, rep from *. Slide.
      rep Rows 1–4.

SIMPLE REVERSIBLES USING SLIPPED STITCHES

SEE THE LIGHT (center and bottom)

opposite reversible

With this pattern the possible combinations are increased by introducing slipped stitches as well as plain knit and purl. The illustration shows that this particular pattern looks quite different on the two sides. A closer look reveals that what is light-colored on one is dark on the other, forming the opposite reversible. Since the eye tends to notice the light color, it overlooks the similarities. From this peculiarity comes the name.

Use dpn or adapt for spn. Odd number of sts. Cast on dark, slide.
Row 1: light—k1, * sl 1 yif, k1, rep from *. Turn.
Row 2: light—k1, * p1, k1, rep from *. Slide.
Row 3: with dark, rep row 1.
Row 4: with dark, rep row 2.
      rep Rows 1–4.

TEXTURED CHECK (*above*)

opposite reversible

Use dpn or adapt for spn. Odd number of sts. Cast on dark, slide.

Row 1: light—k1, * sl 1 yif, k1, rep from *. Turn.

Row 2: light—p1, * k1, p1, rep from *. Slide.

Rows 3 and 4: with dark rep rows 1 and 2.

      rep Rows 1–4.

TEEPEES (*below*)

opposite reversible

Use dpn or adapt for spn. Odd number of sts. Cast on dark, slide.

Row 1: light—k1, * sl 1 yif, k1, rep from *. Turn.

Row 2: light—sl 1 yif, * k1, sl 1 yif, rep from *. Slide.

Rows 3 and 4: with dark rep rows 1 and 2.

      rep Rows 1–4.

PARASOL ROWS (top)

true reversible
This pattern looks best when worked with a fairly small needle. It has textural as well as design interest but only a fair amount of stretch.

Use of dpn required. Multiple of 4 sts plus 3. Cast on dark, slide.
Row 1: light—k1, * sl 1 yif, k3, rep from * ending k1. Turn.
Row 2: dark—k3, * sl 1 yif, k3, rep from *. Slide.
    rep Rows 1 and 2.

KNOT AND SWAG (*center and below*)

opposite reversible
This is one of those patterns in which the sides look different at first glance but are actually opposite in color schemes (see note under "See The Light", page 12). It makes a cozy, thick fabric.

Use dpn or adapt for spn. Odd number of sts. Cast on dark, slide.
Row 1: light—p1, * sl 1 yif, p1, rep from *. Turn.
Row 2: light—knit. Slide.
Rows 3 and 4: with dark rep rows 1 and 2.
    rep Rows 1–4.

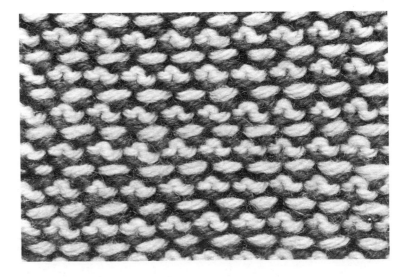

STRING OF BEADS (right)

opposite reversible

Use of dpn required. Even number of sts. Cast on dark, slide.

Row 1: light—* k1, sl 1 yif, rep from *. Turn.
Row 2: with dark, rep row 1. Slide.
Row 3: light—* sl 1 yif, k1, rep from *. Turn.
Row 4: with dark, rep row 3. Slide.
      rep Rows 1–4.

PLAIN 'N' FANCY RIB (right and below)

unlike reversible

This is useful as a k2, p2 rib if not too much stretch is needed. The sl sts hinder sideways motion and recovery. Don't forget that if you want solid *dark* ribs on one side, rather than *light* ones, you can just change all places which read "dark" to "light" and vice versa.

Use of dpn required. Multiple of 4 sts plus 2. Cast on dark, slide.

Row 1: light—p2, * k2, p2, rep from *. Turn.
Row 2: light—k2, * p2, k2, rep from *. Slide.
Row 3: dark—k2, * sl 2 yif, k2, rep from *. Turn.
Row 4: with light, rep row 1. Turn.
Row 5: with light, rep row 2. Turn.
Row 6: dark—p2, * sl 2 yib, p2. Slide.
      rep Rows 1–6.

AWN PATTERN

opposite and mirror reversible
What a nice pattern for caps, scarves, and vests. It is cozy and warm but has plenty of stretch.

Use of dpn required. Multiple of 4 sts. Cast on dark, slide.

Row 1: light—k1, * sl 1 yib, p1, k2, rep from * but end k1. Turn.

Row 2: with dark, rep row 1. Slide.

Row 3: light—k2, * sl 1 yif, k3, rep from * but end k1. Turn.

Row 4: dark—k3, * sl 1 yif, k3, rep from * but end k4. Slide.

Row 5: light—* k2, sl 1 yib, p1, rep from * but end sl 1 yib, k1. Turn.

Row 6: dark—k1, p1, k2, * sl 1 yib, p1, k2, rep from *. Slide.

Row 7: light—k1, * sl 1 yif, k3, rep from * but end k2. Turn.

Row 8: dark—k4, * sl 1 yif, k3, rep from *. Slide.

Row 9: light—k3, * sl 1 yib, p1, k2, rep from * but end k3. Turn.

Row 10: with dark rep row 9. Slide.

Row 11: with light rep row 8. Turn.

Row 12: with dark rep row 7. Slide.

Row 13: with light rep row 6. Turn.

Row 14: with dark rep row 5. Slide.

Row 15: with light rep row 4. Turn.

Row 16: with dark rep row 3. Slide.
rep Rows 1–16.

ROUGH TWEED (*right*)

opposite reversible

Here is another of those patterns which look different on the two sides although there is really only a color reverse. The dark side has a rather slanted-looking pattern. The fabric is thick, textured, and stretches easily for use in garments.

Use of dpn required. Multiple of 4 stitches. Cast on dark, slide.

Row 1: light—* k3, sl 1 yif, rep from *. Turn.

Row 2: dark—k1, * sl 1 yif, k3, rep from * but end k2. Slide.

Row 3: light—p2, * sl 1 yib, p3, rep from * but end p1. Turn.

Row 4: dark—* sl 1 yib, p3, rep from *. Slide. rep Rows 1–4.

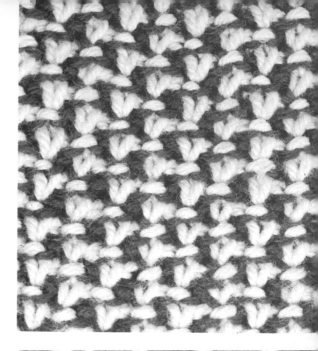

MOSS ROWS (*below*)

alternate reversible

This name derives from the fact that the dark color is woven through a moss stitch background.

Use of dpn required. Odd number of sts. Use double strand of dark yarn. Cast on light, turn.

Row 1: light—k1, * p1, k1, rep from *. Turn.

Row 2: dark—sl 1 yif, * sl 1 yib, sl 1 yif, rep from *. Slide.

Row 3: light—p1, * k1, p1, rep from *. Turn.

Row 4: light—rep row 3. Slide.

Row 5: dark—rep row 2. Turn.

Row 6: light—rep row 1. Turn. rep Rows 1–6.

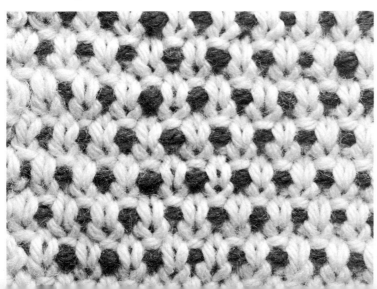

WOVEN DOTS

unclassified (almost a true reversible)

This stitch pattern is based on one in a book by Barbara G. Walker (Woven Polka Dot Pattern, *A Second Treasury of Knitting Patterns,* p. 48). It was made reversible principally by using a garter stitch base rather than a stockinette stitch. Use a double strand of the dark color yarn, or a much heavier one. This color is never actually knitted, only woven. The result is a fabric with no lateral stretch although it can be pulled at an angle or vertically.

Use of dpn required. Use double strand of dark yarn. Odd number of sts. Cast on light, turn.
Row 1: light—knit. Slide.
Row 2: double dark—sl 1 yib, * sl 1 yif, sl 1 yib. Turn.
Row 3: light—knit. Turn.
Row 4: light—knit. Turn.
Row 5: double dark—rep row 2. Slide.
Row 6: light—knit. Turn.
Row 7: light—knit. Slide.
Row 8: double dark—rep row 2. Turn.
      continue in this fashion, knitting two rows light, weaving one row dark.

Variation

This will give the same effect but is worked on spn and takes a little longer because a double strand of dark cannot be used.

Use spn. Odd number of sts. Cast on light, turn.
Row 1: light—knit.
Row 2: light—knit.
Row 3: dark—* sl 1 yib, sl 1 yif, rep from *.
Row 4: dark—k1, * sl 1 yib, sl 1 yif, rep from *.
Rows 5 and 6: light—knit.
Row 7: dark—* sl 1 yif, sl 1 yib, rep from *.
Row 8: dark—k1, * sl 1 yif, sl 1 yib, rep from *.
      rep Rows 1–8.

SIDE-SLIP STITCH

mirror reversible

Another pattern in which one color is woven rather than knit, this one must be done on dpn's because a single strand is used. This time the stranding color is the light one to serve as a reminder that colors can be reversed from what is given in the directions. It is certainly easy to count the rows worked since each line of stranding is an even-numbered row. Be certain to twist colors at the start of every dark row.

Use of dpn required. Multiple of 6 sts. Cast on dark, turn.

Row 1 and all odd-numbered rows: dark—* k1, p1, rep from *. Slide.

Row 2:   light—* sl 3 yif, sl 3 yib, rep from *. Turn.

Row 4:   light—sl 2 yib, * sl 3 yif, sl 3 yib, rep from * but end sl 1 yib. Turn.

Row 6:   light—rep row 4. Turn.

Row 8:   light—rep row 2. Turn.

Row 10:   light—sl 1 yif, * sl 3 yib, sl 3 yif, rep from * but end sl 2 yif. Turn.

Row 12:   light—rep row 8. Turn.
          rep Rows 1–8.

Zig-Zag Variation

Several variations can be worked. A large section of this one is shown to give the effect. For the pattern work 22 rows of Side-Slip Stitch (rows 1–12, then rows 1–10). Rep these 22 rows. By varying the lengths of "zigs" and "zags" you can also make a pattern like a sideways "W".

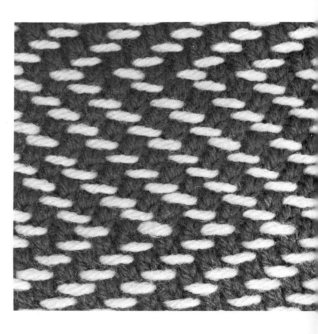

WOVEN CHECK

alternate reversible

This woven variation has the interesting effect of appearing to be done in only knit sts—on both sides. This impossibility is simulated by covering the purl backs of the sts with carefully planned weaving. It is lacking the characteristic stretch we associate with most knitting, but makes an interesting firm, flat pattern.

Use of dpn required. Multiple of 4 sts plus 2. Use *double strand* of dark yarn. Be sure to twist colors when they are at the same end. Cast on light, turn.

Row 1: light—p1, * k2, p2, rep from * but end k1. Slide.
Row 2: dark—sl 1 yif, * sl 2 yib, sl 2 yif, rep from * but end sl 1 yib. Turn.
Row 3: light—rep row 1. Slide.
Row 4: dark—rep row 2. Turn.
Row 5: light—k1, * p2, k2, rep from * but end p1. Slide.
Row 6: dark—sl 1 yib, * sl 2 yif, sl 2 yib, rep from * but end sl 1 yif. Turn.
Row 7: light—rep row 5. Slide.
Row 8: dark—rep row 6. Turn.
　　　　rep Rows 1–8.

PURL 'N' WEAVE

alternate reversible

This is a purl version of Woven Check although the effect is quite different. The dark yarn moves along in the depressions between the groups of five raised purl bumps. There is more textural interest and more "give" in this design (except laterally).

Use of dpn required. Multiple of 4 sts. Use double strand of dark yarn. Cast on light, turn.

Row 1: light—* k2, p2, rep from *. Turn.
Row 2: dark—* sl 2 yif, sl 2 yib, rep from *. Slide.
Row 3: light—rep row 1. Turn.
Row 4: light—* p2, k2, rep from *. Slide.
Row 5: dark—* sl 2 yib, sl 2 yif, rep from *. Turn.
Row 6: light—rep row 4. Turn.
　　　　rep Rows 1–6.

OVER AND OUT

alternate reversible

This pattern can be used for ribbing. Even on non-reversible sweaters, mittens, etc., a two-color cuff which can be turned up would be interesting. Note that more of one color is used than the other; the one used for casting on predominates.

Use of dpn required. Multiple of 4 sts plus 3. Cast on light, turn.

Row 1: dark—k3, * p1, k3, rep from *. Slide.
Row 2: light—k3, * sl 1 yif, k3, rep from *. Turn.
Row 3: light—p3, * k1, p3, rep from *. Slide.
Row 4: dark—k1, p1, * k3, p1, rep from *, k last st. Turn.
Row 5: light—p1, sl 1 yib, * p3, sl 1 yib, rep from *, p last st. Turn.
Row 6: light—k1, p1, * k3, p1, rep from *, k last st. Turn.
    rep Rows 1–6.

SIMPLE REVERSIBLES USING "YARN OVERS"

RICK RACK

true reversible

An easy-to-work pattern which results in an interesting design. It is more open and flexible than the illustration indicates. Try it in two similar colors (rose and pink, yellow and gold, or two greens) for an afghan. Blocking is necessary due to a diagonal curl.

Use of dpn required. Even number of sts. Cast on dark, slide.

Row 1: light—k1, * y o, k2 tog, rep from * but end k1. Turn.
Row 2: with dark rep row 1. Slide.
    rep Rows 1 and 2.

CHECK BACK (upper pair)

opposite reversible

This pattern also has a "berry" which is opposite in color on the two sides. The fairly firm yet flexible fabric makes it very useful. It is quite slow to work, however. Note that for every 2 sts cast on, there will be 3 sts after rows 1 and 3. In rows 2 and 4, the single k sts are worked into sts which are the opposite color of the one being used in that row.

Use of dpn required. Even number of sts. Cast on loosely with light, slide.
Row 1: dark—* k1, y o, sl 1 as if knitting, rep from *. Turn.
Row 2: dark—* k1, k2 tog in backs of sts, rep from *. Slide.
Row 3: with light, rep row 1. Turn.
Row 4: with light, rep row 2.
    rep Rows 1–4.

NIP AND TUCK (lower pair)

opposite reversible

This unusual-looking pattern is useful where vertical stretch should be controlled. For this reason it was selected for a belt shown later in this book. The even-numbered rows of the directions may be awkward to work, but the odd-numbered ones make up for that fact by being extremely quick since they contain no actual knitting.

Use of dpn required. Any number of sts. Cast on dark, slide.
Row 1: light—* sl 1 as if knitting, y o, rep from *. Turn.
Row 2: light—* k2 tog into back of y o and next st, rep from *. Slide.
Row 3: with dark, rep row 1. Turn.
Row 4: with dark, rep row 2. Slide.
    rep Rows 1–4.

DOUBLEBERRY

opposite reversible

Here is an attractive open pattern with dark "berries" on one side and light ones on the other. While sharply contrasting colors were chosen to show up well in the illustration, more similar colors may prove more pleasing in a garment. If the work is laid aside after a row 1, be certain the yo is not lost when beginning again.

Use of dpn required. Even number of sts. Cast on dark, turn, knit one row, slide.

Row 1: light—p2 tog, * find strand running between st just worked and next one on left needle then k1 under this strand, p2 tog, rep from *. At end of needle, y o to make 1 st. Turn.

Row 2: light—k into back of made st, k all remaining sts (there should now be the original number of sts on needle). Slide.

Row 3: dark—p1, p2 tog, k under strand as in row 1, rep from * but end p1. Turn.

Row 4: dark—knit. Slide.
　　　　rep Rows 1–4.

SIMPLE REVERSIBLES
WITH SPECIAL PROCEDURES

SHADOW BOXING

opposite reversible

Here is a "thermal" stitch pattern especially useful for afghans, mufflers, and any other applications where warmth without weight is desirable. Use rather large needles to this end. A little stretching in the blocking will help to open up the squares, but some knitters may prefer to use a triple wrap in rows 2 and 4. Be certain to keep the first st of each row loose.

Use dpn or adapt for spn. Multiple of 4 sts plus 3. Cast on light, slide.

Row 1: dark—k3, * sl 1 yib letting extra wrap drop (there will be no extra wrap in the very first row), k3, rep from *. Turn.

Row 2: dark—p1, p1 wrapping the yarn twice around needle instead of once, p1, * sl 1 yif, p1, p1 with double wrap, p1, rep from *. Slide.

Row 3: light—k1, * sl 1 yib letting extra wrap drop, k3, rep from *, ending k1. Turn.

Row 4: light—p1, sl 1 yif, p1, * p1 with double wrap, p1, sl 1 yif, p1, rep from *. Slide.
rep Rows 1–4.

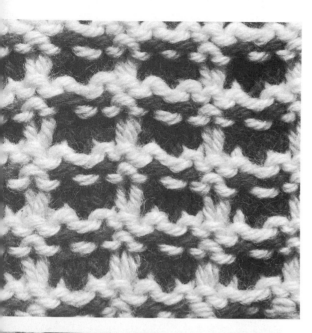

SHADOW RIB

opposite reversible

This is a two-color relative of the old continental or fisherman's rib. It has the elasticity of a true rib with extra depth or thickness which makes it delightfully puffy. After about three rows are done, the work may look as if it will never come out like the illustration. Don't worry . . . keep working. After a few more rows, if it still makes you nervous, give a little tug downwards and everything will undoubtedly go into place. As you work along making first dark-colored rows and then light-colored ones, you should see the stitches miraculously slither this way and that leaving all the knit stitches on one side in one color and the knit stitches on the other side the opposite color.

Use of dpn required. Odd number of sts. Cast on dark, turn. Preparatory row: dark—p1, * k1, p1, rep from *. Slide.

Row 1: light—sl 1 yif, * k1 into the loop in the row *below* the next st and sl that next st off left needle, p1, rep from *, end sl 1 yif. Turn.

Row 2: dark—k1, p1, * k into row below next st, p1, rep from *, k last st. Slide.

Row 3: light—sl 1 yib, * p into row below next st, k1, rep from *, end sl 1 yib. Turn.

Row 4: dark—p1, k1, * p1 into row below next st, k1, rep from *, p last st. Slide.

rep Rows 1–4.

Adaptation for Circular Knitting:

Even number of sts. Cast on dark, join in circle.

Preparatory round: dark—* k1, p1, rep from *.

Round 1: light—* k into row below next st, p1, rep from *.

Round 2: dark—* k1, p into row below next st, rep from *.

rep Rounds 1 and 2

Note: at the end of each round, leave the color strand which is finished on the outside of the work and merely pick up the new color. There will be nothing to indicate the end of the rounds where the colors were changed.

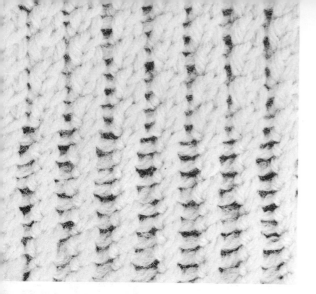

REVERSIBLE SPIRALS (upper left)

opposite reversible

Although this makes a very thick fabric, it is also flexible. There will be two layers, joined at top, bottom, and edges. Cast on plenty of stitches for it makes a gauge with almost twice as many sts per inch as most patterns.

Use dpn or adapt for spn. Multiple of 4 sts plus 2. Cast on dark, Slide.

Row 1: light—k1, * KRT, sl 2 yif, rep from *, k last st. Turn.

Row 2: light—k1, * sl 2 yib, p2, rep from *, k last st. Slide.

Row 3: with dark, rep row 1. Turn.

Row 4: with dark, rep row 2. Slide.
      rep Rows 1–4.

DOUBLE TWIST AND SWAG (lower left)

opposite reversible

This pattern is actually a variation of Reversible Spirals with more texture and more openness to it.

All directions are the same as for the preceding pattern except, wherever "p2" occurs (in rows 2 and 4) substitute "PLT".

COLONEL'S MOTIF (opposite)

alternate reversible

This may seem like a true reversible until you notice that there are more motifs on one side than the other. The pattern is related to reversible geometrics in that it uses k1, p1 rib to give the effect of two right sides. It could be used effectively for a baby blanket in white with pink or blue motifs. A sweater or jacket could have the motifs on the body but solid color sleeves.

There is a special technique involved in this pattern which is similar to the one used in "quilted" knitting. It is not difficult to work but is done in a knit form and a purl form, as follows:

p-l-str (purl-lift-strand): p1, shift knitting yarn to back in preparation for next k st. Lift light-colored strand from front of work onto right needle so that it rests between first and second sts; slip first st of right needle back onto left needle briefly, allowing strand to fall to rear of work, then immediately replace st on right needle in original position.

k-l-str (knit-lift-strand): k1, shift knitting yarn to front in preparation for next p st. Lift light-colored strand from back of work onto right needle so that it rests between first and second sts; slip first st of right needle back onto left needle briefly, allowing strand to fall to front of work, then immediately replace st on right needle in original position.

Be certain to twist the two colors when they are both at the same end of a row.

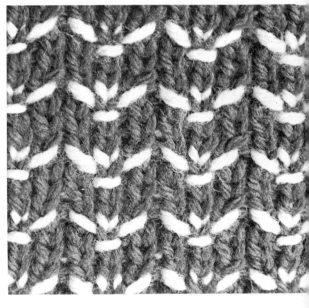

Use of dpn required. Multiple of 6 sts plus 3. Cast on dark, turn.

Preparatory Row: dark—p1, * k1, p1, rep from *. Slide.

Row 1: light—sl 1 yif, k1, * sl 5 yif, k1, rep from * but end sl 1 yif. Turn.

Row 2: dark—k1, sl 1 yif, k1, * (p1, k1) twice, sl 1 yif, k1, rep from *. Turn.

Row 3: dark—p1, k1, p1, * k1, p-l-str, (k1, p1) twice, rep from *. Turn.

Row 4: light—sl 4 yif, * k1, sl 5 yif, rep from * but end sl 4. Slide.

Row 5: dark—k1, p1, k1, * p1, sl 1 yib, (p1, k1) twice, rep from *. Turn.

Row 6: dark—p1, k-l-str, p1, * (k1, p1) twice, k-l-str, p1, rep from *. Slide.
rep Rows 1-6.

MINI-BOXES

alternate reversible

Another thermal-type pattern, this resembles Shadow Boxing. The different method of working it makes for smaller "boxes." In addition, both sides of this pattern look alike while the colors reverse in Shadow Boxing.

Use of dpn required. Odd number of sts. Cast on loosely (or with a larger needle) using light; slide.

Row 1: dark—p1, * k1, p1, rep from *. Turn.
Row 2: light—p1, * k1 into the loop in row *below* the next st and sl that next st off left needle, p1, rep from *. Slide.
Row 3: dark—k1, * p1, k1, rep from *. Turn.
Row 4: light—k into row below next st, * p1, k into row below, rep from *. Slide.
          rep Rows 1–4.

DARK AND LIGHT BALUSTERS

true reversible

Another dense, textured stitch which is a variation of the two previous ones. This one alternates rows of dark and light for a better appearance since the strand weaves from one face to the other.

Use of dpn required. Multiple of 8 sts plus 2. Cast on dark, slide.

Row 1: light—k1, * sl 2 yif, KRT, p2, sl 2 yib, rep from *, p last st. Turn.
Row 2: dark—k1, * p2, sl 2 yib, sl 2 yif, KRT, rep from *, p last st. Slide.
          rep Rows 1 and 2.

Variation

Work as above, but for every "p2" substitute "PLT". This variation is not illustrated but the effect is comparable to "Double Twist and Swag", although the colors alternate as in "Dark and Light Balusters."

TWISTED COLUMN

opposite reversible

A very thick warm garment can be made with this pattern. It tends to pull in laterally quite a bit and should be blocked to spread out somewhat. Check carefully to figure the correct gauge. Note that you must slip *two* stitches at a time, a somewhat unusual procedure. You may not find it necessary to work the preparatory rows (which are like the others except that the columns do not twist). However, if you choose to do so you will probably want to repeat them at the end before binding off.

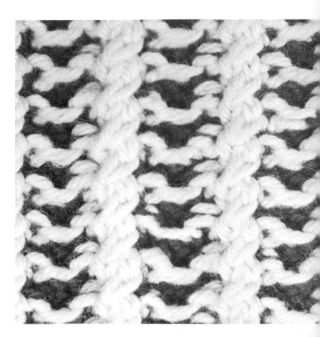

Use dpn or adapt for spn. Multiple of 6 sts plus 4. Cast on light, slide.

Preparatory row A: dark—k1, * sl 2 yif, k4, rep from * but end sl 2 yif, k1. Turn.

Preparatory row B: dark—k1, sl 2 yib, k1, * p2, k1, sl 2 yib, k1, rep from *. Slide.

Preparatory row C: light—k4, * sl 2 yif, k4, rep from *. Turn.

Preparatory row D: light—k1, p2, k1, * sl 2 yib, k1, p2, k1, rep from *. Slide.

Row 1: dark—k1, sl 2 yif, k1, * KRT, k1, sl 2 yif, k1, rep from *. Turn.

Row 2: dark—rep preparatory row B. Slide.

Row 3: light—k1, KRT, k1, * sl 2 yif, k1, KRT, k1, rep from *. Turn.

Row 4: light—rep preparatory row D. Slide.
rep Rows 1–4.

BIAS RIB

opposite and mirror reversible

The raised knit-stitch ribs of this pattern are in opposite colors on the two sides, but it is also a mirror reversible because on one side they go up to the right and on the other side they go up to the left. Use large needles for this dense fabric which would make an interesting heavy jacket or other outer wear. Be certain to twist the two colors at the beginning of each row.

Use of dpn required. Multiple of 4 sts. Cast on light, slide.

Row 1: dark—* KRT, sl 2 yif, rep from *. Turn.

Row 2: light—* KLT, sl 2 yif, rep from *. Slide.

Row 3: dark—p1, sl 2 yib, * PRT, sl 2 yib, rep from * but end p1. Turn.

Row 4: light—sl 1 yib, PLT, * sl 2 yib, PLT, rep from * but end sl 1 yib. Slide.

Row 5: dark—* sl 2 yif, KRT, rep from *. Turn.

Row 6: light—* sl 2 yif, KLT, rep from *. Slide.

Row 7: dark—sl 1 yib, PRT, * sl 2 yib, PRT, rep from * but end sl 1 yib. Turn.

Row 8: light—p1, sl 2 yib, * PLT, sl 2 yib, rep from * but end p1. Slide.

rep Rows 1–8.

GOSSAMER STITCH

alternate reversible, very nearly true
Isn't it amazing what a simple 2-row pattern can produce! Use fine yarn for the best advantage in most cases. The lacy fabric tends to fall in soft rippling folds. Its uses are almost unlimited—scarves, stoles, hats, afghans, a baby's sacque, etc.

Use of dpn required. Multiple of 6 sts plus 1. Cast on dark, slide.

Row 1: light—k1, * y o twice, k1, y o 3 times, k1, y o twice, k4, rep from *. Turn.

Row 2: dark—purl, letting all y o's drop and working only actual sts. Slide.
rep Rows 1 and 2.

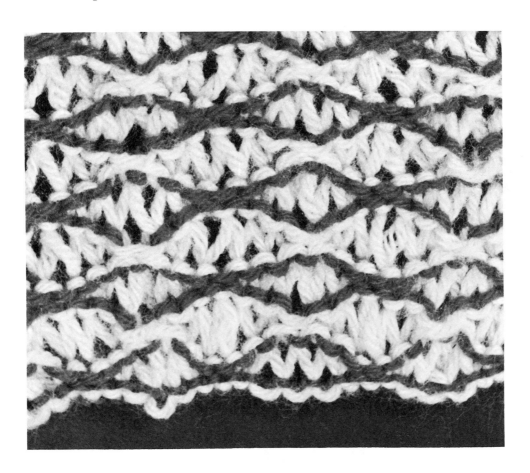

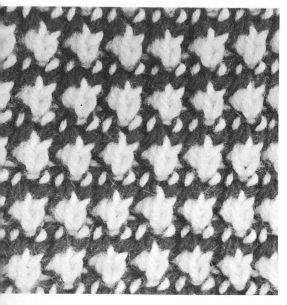

ROSEBUD ROWS

opposite reversible

This pattern is related to Doubleberry but it uses a triple increase and decrease instead of double ones. The first increase may be awkward to work, but later ones are easier. Be careful at the end of rows 2 and 4 where it is easy to make a mistake by forgetting the double decrease. There are two special operations. The first is a knit-slip-knit increase: knit but leave st on left needle; raise tip of right needle up and over and insert back into same st toward you as in a slip st but leave st on left needle; raise needle tip again and insert into back of same st and knit. Drop st from left needle. Note carefully that during this entire three step operation the yarn is kept in the back in the knit position. The recommended triple decrease: insert right needle into next two sts as if to knit but slip them together from this position; knit next st; pass the 2 sl sts over the k st.

Use dpn or adapt for spn. Odd number of sts. Cast on dark, knit 1 row, slide.

Row 1: light—p1, * k-sl-k increase, p1, rep from *. Turn.

Row 2: light—k2 tog, * p1, triple decrease, rep from * but end k2 tog. Slide.

Row 3: dark—k-sl-k increase, * p1, k-sl-k incr, rep from *. Turn.

Row 4: dark—p2 tog, * triple decr, p1, rep from * but end triple decr, p2 tog. Slide.
rep Rows 1–4.

CRAZY STRIPES

true reversible

It is unusual to find a slanted pattern which is a true rather than mirror reversible. This heavy, warm pattern tends to curl on the bias but can easily be blocked to lie flat. There are two facts which should be noted before starting. The first st in row 4 is a p st which may not seem correct but is. KPRT means knit-purl right twist and is worked: insert right needle into second st on left needle and knit; throw yarn to front and purl first st, then drop both sts from left needle together.

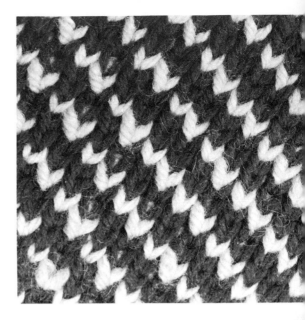

Use of dpn required. Multiple of 4 sts. Cast on dark, turn.

Preparatory row: dark—* p1, k1, rep from *. Slide.

Row 1: light—* p1, k1, sl 1 yif, sl 1 yib, rep from *. Turn.

Row 2: dark—* KPRT, rep from *. Slide.

Row 3: light—* k1, p1, sl 1 yib, sl 1 yif, rep from *. Turn.

Row 4: dark—p1, * KPRT, rep from * but end k1. Slide.

Row 5: light—* sl 1 yif, sl 1 yib, p1, k1, rep from *. Turn.

Row 6: dark—rep row 2. Slide.

Row 7: light—* sl 1 yib, sl 1 yif, k1, p1, rep from *. Turn.

Row 8: dark—rep row 4. Slide.
rep Rows 1–8.

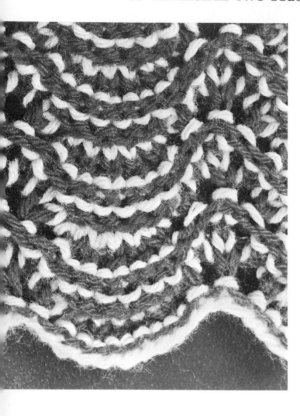

BANDED SCALLOPS

alternate reversible

Here's something different—textured, open-work, and scallops. It is difficult to acheive an attractive two-color reversible lace but this is at least somewhat lacy. In actual use, for a shawl or the lower edge of a garment, two similar colors might be preferred to the great contrast shown here. Large needles are recommended.

Use of dpn required. Multiple of 12 sts. Cast on light, slide.

Row 1: dark—purl. Turn.

Row 2: dark—(p2 tog) twice, * (y o, p1) 4 times, (p2 tog) 4 times, rep from * but end (p2 tog) twice. Slide.

Row 3: light—purl. Turn.

Row 4: dark—knit. Turn.

Row 5: dark—(k2 tog) twice, * (y o, k1) 4 times, (k2 tog) 4 times, rep from * but end (k2 tog) twice. Turn.

Row 6: light—purl. Slide.
      rep Rows 1–6.

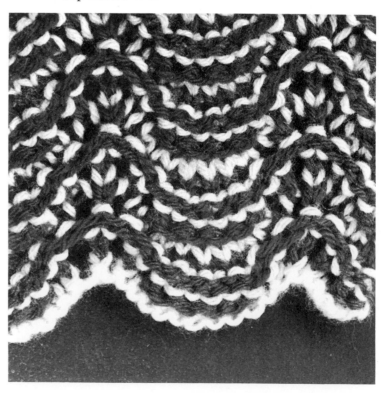

CHAPTER THREE

CHAIN PATTERNS

This chapter will deal with "variations on a theme," the theme of Ripple and Chain Stitch. The background or "ripple" of these patterns is merely knit and purl rows arranged so as to make pleasing combinations with no right side or wrong side. The "chains" are columns of stitches in one color only. This is managed by working them when using their own color but slipping them when using the contrasting color. In other words, Ripple and Chain patterns really belong to the same category as those in Chapter Two. They are given a chapter of their own because they make possible, by their nature, so many variations including patterns designed specifically for the article being created.

There are three basic Ripple and Chain stitch patterns given here. They differ in what ripple background is used. This, in turn, affects the appearance of the chain. It is also responsible for the fact that only the type I stitches can be done on single-pointed needles. (Directions for adapting to spn are in Chapter Six.) In the basic patterns, dark chains are made to appear on one side, light chains on the other. But the same color may be used on both sides or the colors may alternate on both sides. Examples are given of several such variations but more are possible. The directions are written so that the chains come quite close together. This is so that the illustrations will be clear. In many instances it will be more useful to have the chains widely spaced. Directions for pattern enlarging are given in a later section.

DESIGNING WITH RIPPLE AND CHAIN

These chain stitch patterns are ideal for designing basically rectangular articles such as mufflers, stoles, spreads, and afghans. Once the designer understands this type of stitch a great variety of possibilities will be apparent. She has only to decide how wide and long she wants the article, where the chains will be placed, and whether they will follow a straight line or some other course. Do be sure to consider, in addition to the zig-zags, diamonds, chevrons, "V" and "W" shapes, even hexagons. This last can be done by starting off in a "V", then going straight up on both sides, finishing with an inverted "V". Some interesting effects are achieved by using a pattern sideways of the way you work it. When an article is made of more than one piece, it may be useful to cover seams with a chain embroidered to match the knitted ones. This can be an integral part of the design. Don't forget that many of the patterns can be encouraged to pleat, which is useful for skirts and such.

INCREASING PATTERN SIZE

As noted before, most articles will be more attractive when the chains are placed farther apart than in the directions given. Many of those directions have options for increasing the pattern size by 2 stitches at a time. Suppose the basic example uses a multiple of 6 stitches plus 3 and the options is for a multiple of 8 plus 3. You may also use 10 plus 3. In every place where the directions increase by one stitch, you increase by one more. If they increase by two, you will add another two. Similarly, you may widen the pattern size to 12 stitches plus 3 or any other even number of stitches you wish.

Here is another way to look at it: Let "O" stand for stitches which change color according to whether light or dark is being used. Let "X" indicate the dark-colored chain stitches, and "I" be the light-colored chain stitches. Slash marks (/) are inserted to show a pattern repeat. However, there is nothing to show on which side the chains appear. That is determined by whether stitches are slipped yib or yif.

Here is one row of Ripple and Chain I explained in this way:

O/XOOIOO/XOOIOO/XO

The stitches between slash marks indicate a 6 stitch multiple; the 3 stitches at the ends balance the pattern. This gives a multiple of 6 plus 3.

Here is how the pattern might be increased:

O/XOOOOOIOOOOOO/XOOOOOOIOOOOOO/XO

By inserting extra plain stitches ("O") we have increased to a multiple of 14 stitches plus 3.

Ripple and Chain II and III work the same way except for which rows are knit and which purled. In the zig-zag stitches, however, the chains are side by side and start nearer one edge than the other, as shown here:

O/XIOOOOO/XIOOOOO/XIOOOOO/O

This uses a multiple of 7 plus 2 edge stitches. The chains are obviously ready to move first to the right in the row shown. The pattern could be enlarged to a multiple of 14 plus 2 thus:

O/XIOOOOOOOOOOOO/XIOOOOOOOOOOOO/XIOOOOOOOOOO

For a diamond design, start the chains in the center this way:

/OOOOOOOIX/XIOOOOOOO/

That is for a multiple of 9 stitches. After a light-color twist stitch row it would become:

/OOOOOOIOX/XOIOOOOOOO/

and after a dark-color twist row:

/OOOOOOIXO/OXIOOOOOO/

and so on until the diamond was as wide as desired. There would then be a row in which the light chains did not move. The dark chains would start back first.

ADVICE FOR LESS-ADVANCED KNITTERS

Several of the above paragraphs are rather complicated explanations for the intermediate knitter (the advanced one will have her own way of approaching pattern enlargement). If you are a beginner, don't be frightened of Ripple and Chain. Nothing could be easier than to cast on about thirty to forty stitches (in one of the multiples indicated in the desired pattern). Use a size 10 needle and knitting worsted. After working four or five feet, bind off. Fringe the ends. And have a nice warm muffler in your favorite color combination. It will take one four-ounce skein of each color and about ten to fifteen hours of your time depending on how speedy a knitter you are and how big you make the scarf.

STITCH PATTERNS

RIPPLE AND CHAIN I

opposite reversible

For best results, use a fairly large size needle with ripple and chain stitch patterns. This particular one tends to fall in soft pleats, which looks attractive in scarves and stoles. Further, it can be used to advantage in skirts having more sts between the "chains" at the bottom than at the top.

If you are new to pattern stitches, this is an easy one to do without constantly consulting the directions once you are used to them. You will soon learn the interval between slip stitches. Then note that when both strands of yarn are at the same end you will pick up the one which matches the majority of the sts on the needle and work a purl row. When the two strands are at opposite ends, pick up the color which has only a few sts on the needle and start a knit row with it.

The sample illustrated was knitted using the regular numbers in the directions. To make the chains farther apart, use the circled numbers instead or substitute even larger numbers.

Use dpn or adapt to spn. Multiple of 6 sts plus 3 (or ⑧ sts plus 3).
Cast on dark, slide.
Row 1: light—k1, * sl 1 yif, k5 ⑦, rep from *, but end k1. Turn.
Row 2: light—p1, * sl 1 yib, p5 ⑦, rep from * but end p1. Slide.
Row 3: dark—k4 ⑤, * sl 1 yif, k5 ⑦, rep from * but end k4 ⑤. Turn.
Row 4: dark—p4 ⑤, * sl 1 yib, p5 ⑦, rep from * but end p4 ⑤. Slide.
rep Rows 1–4.

Knit Variation (*opposite, right*)
opposite reversible
To work this variation, merely follow the preceding directions for Ripple and Chain I *except* in every place which reads "p" substitute "k". Retain all other directions in their original form, especially "sl 1 yib."

A denser fabric is achieved by this method. Note that more rows must be worked to make one inch. Also, the original Ripple and Chain I has light-colored "chains" on a dark background and vice versa but this variation is predominantly dark on one side and light on the other. You may also notice that the "chains" are not entirely in knit stitches. Can you figure out which stitches to purl in rows 2 and 4 if you wish them to be? An interesting comparison with this pattern is Shadow Boxing in Chapter Two.

RIPPLE AND CHAIN I

Light Chain Variation (*below*)

unlike reversible

As written here, the pattern will have light-colored chains on both sides. For dark chains, cast on light and use dark in rows 1 and 2, light in rows 3 and 4. The two sides look quite different from each other. Once again, directions for a wider space between chains use the number of stitches which is circled.

Use dpn or adapt to spn. Multiple of 6 sts plus 3 (or ⑧ sts plus 3).
Cast on dark, slide.
Row 1: light—k1, * p1, k5 ⑦, rep from * but end k1. Turn.
Row 2: light—p1, * k1, p5 ⑦, rep from * but end p1. Slide.
Row 3: dark—k1, sl 1 yib, k2 ③, * sl 1 yif, k2 ③, sl 1 yib, k2 ③, rep from * but end k1. Turn.
Row 4: dark—p1, sl 1 yif, p2 ③, * sl 1 yib, p2 ③, sl 1 yif, p2 ③, rep from * but end p1. Slide.
rep Rows 1–4.

ZIG-ZAG ON RIPPLE AND CHAIN I

mirror and opposite reversible.

By using twist stitches, it is possible to make the chains meander anywhere you want them on the surface of these patterns. Only a couple of examples are given here because it is at this point that the knitter's imagination should be allowed a free rein. These directions are not even "finished", for they could go on almost forever. And yet, any knitter using this sort of pattern should understand what is happening well enough that she will not even need to follow all the directions printed here. If you wish to make a large article such as an afghan, you will probably want the chains much farther apart, and you may even wish to have them move toward and away from each other. However, this example should start you thinking of possibilities and how to work them out. Refer to the glossary for twist stitch directions (KRT and KLT).

Use dpn or adapt for spn. Multiple of 7 stitches plus 2. Cast on dark, slide.

Row 1: light—k5, * KRT, sl 1 yif, k4, rep from * but end k1. Turn.

Row 2: light—p1, * sl 1 yib, p6, rep from * but end p7. Slide.

Row 3: dark—k1, * KLT, sl 1 yif, k4, rep from * but end k5. Turn.

Row 4: dark—p5, * sl 1 yib, p6, rep from * but end p3. Slide.

Row 5: light—k4, * KRT, sl 1 yif, k4, rep from * but end k2. Turn.

Row 6: light—p2, * sl 1 yib, p6, rep from *. Slide.

Row 7: dark—k2, * KLT, sl 1 yif, k4, rep from *. Turn.

Row 8: dark—p4, * sl 1 yib, p6, rep from * but end p4. Slide.

Row 9: light—k3, * KRT, sl 1 yif, k4, rep from * but end k3. Turn.

Row 10: light—p3, * sl 1 yib, p6, rep from * but end p5. Slide.

Row 11: dark—k3, * KLT, sl 1 yif, k4, rep from * but end k3. Turn.

Row 12: dark—p3, * sl 1 yib, p6, rep from * but end p5. Slide.

Row 13: light—k2, * KRT, sl 1 yif, k4, rep from *. Turn.

Row 14: light—p4, * sl 1 yib, p6, rep from * but end p4. Slide.

Row 15: dark—k4, * KLT, sl 1 yif, k4, rep from * but end k2. Turn.

Row 16: dark—p2, * sl 1 yib, p6, rep from *. Slide.

Row 17: light—k1, * KRT, sl 1 yif, k4, rep from * but end k5. Turn.

Row 18: light—p5, * sl 1 yib, p6, rep from * but end p3. Slide.

Row 19: dark—k5, * KLT, sl 1 yif, k4, rep from * but end k1. Turn.

Row 20: dark—p1, * sl 1 yib, p6, rep from * but end p7. Slide.

Row 21: light—k2, * sl 1 yif, k6, rep from *. Turn.

Row 22: light—p6, * sl 1 yib, p6, rep from * but end p2. Slide.

Row 23: dark—k5, * KRT, sl 1 yif, k4, rep from * but end k1. Turn.

Row 24: dark—p1, * sl 1 yib, p6, rep from * but end p7. Slide.

Row 25: light—k1, * KLT, sl 1 yif, k4, rep from * but end k5. Turn.

Row 26: light—p5, * sl 1 yif, p6, rep from * but end p3. Slide.

Continue in this way. Work 2 rows light (one knit, one purl) moving light chain on the knit row; then 2 rows of dark, moving dark chain on the knit row. When the dark chain gets 1 st from the edge, maintain it there through the next 2 dark rows. Then start moving light chain back with dark chain following it until the light chain is one st from the edge.

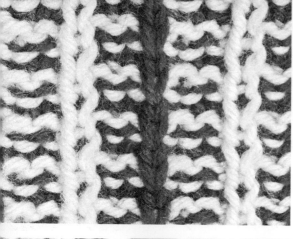

RIPPLE AND CHAIN I (*upper pair*)

Alternate Color Chain Variation

opposite background and true reversible chains

Use dpn or adapt for spn. Multiple of 8 sts plus 4 (or ⑩ plus 4). Cast on dark, slide.

Row 1: light—k1, sl 1 yib, sl 1 yif, * k3 ④, p1, k2 ③, sl 1 yib, sl 1 yif, rep from *, k last st. Turn.

Row 2: light—p1, sl 1 yib, sl 1 yif, * p2 ③, k1, p3 ④, sl 1 yib, sl 1 yif, rep from *, p last st. Slide.

Row 3: dark—k2, p1, k2 ③, * sl 1 yib, sl 1 yif, k3 ④, p1, k2 ③, rep from * but end k1. Turn.

Row 4: dark—p1, k1, p3 ④, * sl 1 yib, sl 1 yif, p2 ③, k1, p3 ④, rep from * but end p2. Slide.

rep Rows 1–4.

WOVEN RIPPLE AND CHAIN (*lower pair*)

opposite and alternate

Some may think this pattern doesn't belong in this chapter as it does not adapt well to the Ripple and Chain variations such as zig-zags. However, it is certainly another interesting variation on the theme, in this case Ripple and Chain I. Squares of this pattern, some turned sideways and perhaps in a different color combination, forming a checkerboard, would make an interesting afghan.

Use dpn or adapt to spn. Multiple of 8 sts plus 5. Cast on dark, slide.

Row 1: light—k7, * sl 1 yif, k7, rep from * but end k5. Turn.

Row 2: light—p5, * sl 1 yib, p7, rep from *. Slide.

Row 3: with dark rep row 1. Turn.

Row 4: with dark rep row 2. Slide.

Row 5: light—k3, * sl 1 yif, k7, rep from * but end k1. Turn.

Row 6: light—p1, * sl 1 yib, p7, rep from * but end p3. Slide.

Row 7: with dark rep row 5. Turn.

Row 8: with dark rep row 6. Slide.

rep Rows 1–8.

RIPPLE AND CHAIN II (upper pair)

opposite reversible

The background used here is Rollover Reversible. Since it changes color every row it is less "ridged" and the chains are more even. This pattern also shows a tendency to pleat. Numbers in circles may be used as alternates to make a wider space between chains.

Use of dpn required. Multiple of 6 sts plus 3 (or ⑧ plus 3). Cast on dark, slide.

Row 1: light—k1, * sl 1 yif, k5 ⑦, rep from * but end k1. Turn.

Row 2: dark—k4 ⑤, * sl 1 yif, k5 ⑦, rep from * but end k4 ⑤. Slide.

Row 3: light—p1, * sl 1 yib, p5 ⑦, rep from * but end p1. Turn.

Row 4: dark—p4 ⑤, * sl 1 yib, p5 ⑦, rep from * but end p4 ⑤. Slide.
     rep Rows 1–4.

Light Chain Variation (lower pair)

almost a true reversible

It is hard to categorize the type of reversible here. The chains are not back to back. There is one more on one side than the other, as in an alternate reversible. Other than that, the pattern seems almost a true reversible except for the fact that one side is flat, the other ridged.

Once again, circled numbers may be used for a wider spacing of chains. To have dark chains rather than light ones, change every dark row (and cast-on) to light and vice versa.

Use of dpn required. Multiple of 6 sts plus 3 (or ⑧ plus 3). Cast on dark, slide.

Row 1: light—k1, * p1, k5 ⑦, rep from *, but end k1. Turn.

Row 2: dark—k1, sl 1 yib, k2 ③, * sl 1 yif, k2 ③, sl 1 yib, k2 ③, rep from * but end k1. Slide.

Row 3: light—p1, * k1, p5 ⑦, rep from * but end p1. Turn.

Row 4: dark—p1, sl 1 yif, p2 ③, * sl 1 yib, p2 ③, sl 1 yif, p2 ③, rep from * but end p1. Slide.
     rep Rows 1–4.

RIPPLE AND CHAIN II (top)

Alternate Color Chain Variation
true reversible

This variation has light and dark chains alternating on both sides. The effect is quite different when they are widely spaced.

Use of dpn required. Multiple of 8 sts plus 4 (or ⑩ plus 4). Cast on dark, slide.

Row 1: light—k1, sl 1 yib, sl 1 yif, * k3 ④, p1, k2 ③, sl 1 yib, sl 1 yif, rep from *, k last st. Turn.

Row 2: dark—k2, p1, k2 ③, * sl 1 yib, sl 1 yif, k3 ④, p1, k2 ③, rep from * but end k1. Slide.

Row 3: light—p1, sl 1 yib, sl 1 yif, * p2 ③, k1, p3 ④, sl 1 yib, sl l yif, rep from *, p last st. Turn.

Row 4: dark—p1, k1, p3 ④, * sl 1 yib, sl 1 yif, p2 ③, k1, p3 ④, rep from * but end p2. Slide.
rep Rows 1–4.

Changing Chain Variation (*center and bottom*)
opposite reversible chains, true background

Here is an interesting variation which tones down the vertical effect of the chains.

Use of dpn required. Multiple of 12 sts. Cast on dark, slide.

Row 1: light—k4, * p1, k2, sl 1 yib, k2, sl 1 yif, k5, rep from * but end k1. Turn.

Row 2: with dark rep row 1. Slide.

Row 3: light—p1, * k1, p5, rep from * but end p4. Turn.

Row 4: dark—p1, * k1, p5, sl 1 yib, p2, sl 1 yif, p2, rep from * but end p1. Slide.

Row 5: light—k1, * sl 1 yib, k2, sl 1 yif, k5, p1, k2, rep from * but end k1. Turn.

Row 6: dark—k4, * p1, k5, rep from * but end k1. Slide.

Row 7: light—p1, * sl 1 yib, p2, sl 1 yif, p2, k1, p5, rep from * but end p4, Turn.

Row 8: with dark rep row 7. Slide.

Row 9: with light rep row 6. Turn.

Row 10: with dark rep row 5. Slide.

Row 11: with light rep row 4. Turn.

Row 12: with dark rep row 3. Slide.
rep Rows 1–12.

RIPPLE AND CHAIN III

opposite reversible

While the other basic Ripple and Chain patterns have a tendency to pleat, this one is almost completely lacking in it. The background here is Reversible Purl Stripes. If you wish to have the background colors reversed, merely cast on light, and use the opposite color of the one indicated here for each row. This pattern is a little more complicated than the preceding ones but is not difficult once it is under way, especially if you are already familiar with the Ripple and Chain principles. In this case two alternatives are given, circled numbers and squared numbers, so that you may see how it would be possible to increase the pattern size even more.

Use of dpn required. Multiple of 6 stitches plus 3 (or ⑧ plus 3, or ⑩ plus 3). Cast on dark, slide.

Row 1: light—k1, * sl 1 yif, k5 ⑦ ⑨, rep from * but end k1. Turn.

Row 2: dark—k4 ⑤ ⑥, * sl 1 yif, k5 ⑦ ⑨, rep from * but end k4 ⑤ ⑥. Slide.

Row 3: light—k1, sl 1 yib, k2 ③ ④, * p1, k2 ③ ④, sl 1 yib, k2 ③ ④, rep from * but end k1. Turn.

Row 4: dark—k1, p1, k2 ③ ④, * sl 1 yib, k2 ③ ④, p1, k2, ③ ④, rep from * but end k1. Slide.
rep Rows 1–4.

ZIG-ZAG ON RIPPLE AND CHAIN II

mirror and opposite reversible

While this is similar to the preceding zig-zag pattern, the chain moves faster because it can be twisted every row. This is due to the fact that colors are changed every row. Again, myriad variations are possible, but if you want the chains to slant at a sharp angle this is the preferred pattern. If you are not sure how to work the twist stitches (KLT, etc.) they are explained in the glossary.

Use of dpn required. Multiple of 7 stitches plus 2. Cast on dark, slide.

Row 1: light—k5, * KRT, sl 1 yif, k4, rep from * but end k1. Turn.

Row 2: dark—k1, * KLT, sl 1 yif, k4, rep from * but end k5. Slide.

Row 3: light—p2, * sl 1 yib, PRT, p4, rep from *. Turn.

Row 4: dark—p4, * sl 1 yib, PLT, p4, rep from * but end p2. Slide.

Row 5: light—k3, * KRT, sl 1 yif, k4, rep from * but end k3. Turn.

Row 6: dark—k3, * KLT, sl 1 yif, k4, rep from * but end k3. Slide.

Row 7: light—p4, * sl 1 yib, PRT, p4, rep from * but end p2. Turn.

Row 8: dark—p2, * sl 1 yib, PLT, p4, rep from *. Slide.

Row 9: light—k1, * KRT, sl 1 yif, k4, rep from * but end k5. Turn.

Row 10: dark—k5, * KLT, sl 1 yif, k4, rep from * but end k1. Slide.

Row 11: light—p6, * sl 1 yib, p6, rep from * but end p2. Turn.

Row 12: dark—p1, * sl 1 yib, PRT, p4, rep from * but end p5. Slide.

Row 13: with light rep row 2. Turn.

Row 14: dark—k4, * KRT, sl 1 yif, k4, rep from * but end k2. Slide.

Row 15: with light rep row 4. Turn.

Row 16: dark—p3, * sl 1 yib, PRT, p4, rep from * but end p3. Slide.

Row 17: with light rep row 6. Turn.

Row 18: dark—k2, * KRT, sl 1 yif, k4, rep from *. Slide.

Row 19: with light rep row 8. Turn.

Row 20: dark—p5, * sl 1 yib, PRT, p4, rep from * but end p1. Slide.

Row 21: with light rep row 10. Turn.

Row 22: dark—k2, * sl 1 yif, k6, rep from *. Slide.

Row 23: with light rep row 12. Turn.

Row 24: dark—p5, * sl 1 yib, PLT, p4, rep from * but end p1. Slide.

Continue in this manner. Note that in rows 11 and 22 one chain "stood still" and in the next row the other chain started leading it back. With more stitches between chains, it would take more rows before starting back. In this case there are 5 stitches between; with 6 between, row 13 would "stand still." Of course, the chains can move back any time the knitter desires.

RIPPLE AND CHAIN III

Light Chain Variation
alternate reversible

The two faces of this pattern look identical except that one has an extra chain. In the illustrated sample, the reverse has four chains. As in previous patterns, you may use the regular stitch count or substitute those in circles for a wider pattern. If you are still not comfortable working a pattern without continually referring to the directions, notice in this one that except for where the chains occur the light rows are purled and the dark ones knit.

Use of dpn required. Multiple of 6 sts plus 3 (or ⑧ plus 3). Cast on light, slide.

Row 1: dark—k1, * sl 1 yib, k2 ③, sl 1 yif, k2 ③, rep from * but end sl 1 yib, k1. Turn.

Row 2: light—p4 ⑤, * k1, p5 ⑦, rep from *, but end p4 ⑤. Slide.

Row 3: dark—k1, * sl 1 yif, k2 ③, sl 1 yib, k2 ③, rep from * but end sl 1 yif, k1. Turn.

Row 4: light—p1, * k1, p5 ⑦, rep from * but end k1, p1. Slide.

rep Rows 1–4.

Alternate Color Chain Variation
true reversible

Use of dpn required. Multiple of 8 sts plus 4 (or ⑩ plus 4). Cast on dark, slide.

Row 1: light—k1, sl 1 yib, sl 1 yif, * k3 ④, p1, k2 ③, sl 1 yib, sl 1 yif, rep from *, k last st. Turn.

Row 2: dark—k2, p1, * k2 ③, sl 1 yib, sl 1 yif, k3 ④, p1, rep from *, k last st. Slide.

rep Rows 1 and 2.

Changing Chain Variation

opposite reversible chains, true background

There is a comparable variation on Ripple and Chain II for the knitter who prefers it.

Use of dpn required. Multiple of 12 sts. Cast on dark, slide.

Row 1:   light—k4, * p1, k2, sl 1 yib, k2, sl 1 yif, k5, rep from * but end k1. Turn.

Row 2:   with dark rep row 1. Slide.

Row 3:   light—k4, * p1, k5, rep from * but end k1. Turn.

Row 4:   with dark rep row 1. Slide.

Row 5:   light—k1, * sl 1 yib, k2, sl 1 yif, k5, p1, k2, rep from * but end k1. Turn.

Row 6:   with dark rep row 3. Slide.

Row 7:   light—rep row 5. Turn.

Row 8:   with dark rep row 5. Slide.

Row 9:   light—rep row 3. Turn.

Row 10: with dark rep row 5. Slide.

Row 11: light—rep row 1. Turn.

Row 12: with dark rep row 3. Slide.

          rep Rows 1–12.

ZIG-ZAG ON RIPPLE AND CHAIN III

opposite and mirror reversible chains, true background

The purl-knit left twist (PKLT) used in this pattern is definitely awkward to perform but not difficult. It may keep some knitters from using what is really a very attractive slip-stitch effect. The zig-zag goes on more of a slant than the one on Ripple and Chain I. It is more like the Ripple and Chain II zig-zag in that way. The reason, of course, is the chains move every row (dark one row, light the next) since the background changes color every row.

Use of dpn required. Multiple of 7 sts plus 2. Cast on dark, slide.

Row 1: light—k5, * KRT, sl 1 yif, k4, rep from * but end k1. Turn.

Row 2: dark—k1, * KLT, sl 1 yif, k4, rep from * but end k5. Slide.

Row 3: light—k2, * sl 1 yib, KPRT, k4, rep from *. Turn.

Row 4: dark—k4, * sl 1 yib, PKLT, k4, rep from * but end k2. Slide.

Row 5: light—k3, * KRT, sl 1 yif, k4, rep from * but end k3. Turn.

Row 6: dark—k3, * KLT, sl 1 yif, k4, rep from * but end k3. Slide.

Row 7: light—k4, * sl 1 yib, KPRT, k4, rep from * but end k2. Turn.

Row 8: dark—k2, * sl 1 yib, PKLT, k4, rep from *. Slide.

Row 9: light—k1, * KRT, sl 1 yif, k4, rep from * but end k5. Turn.

Row 10: dark—k5, * KLT, sl 1 yif, k4, rep from * but end k1. Slide.

Row 11: light—k6, * sl 1 yib, p1, k5, rep from * but end k1. Turn.

Row 12: dark—k1, * sl 1 yib, KPRT, k4, rep from * but end k5. Slide.

Row 13: light—k1, * KLT, sl 1 yif, k4, rep from * but end k5. Turn.

Row 14: dark—k4, * KRT, sl 1 yif, k4, rep from * but end k2. Slide.

Row 15: light—k4, * sl 1 yib, PKLT, k4, rep from * but end k2. Turn.

Row 16: dark—k3, * sl 1 yib, KPRT, k4, rep from * but end k3. Slide.

Row 17: light—k3, * KLT, sl 1 yif, k4, rep from * but end k3. Turn.

Row 18: dark—k2, * KRT, sl 1 yif, k4, rep from *. Slide.

Row 19: light—k2, * sl 1 yib, PKLT, k4, rep from *. Turn.

Row 20: dark—k5, * sl 1 yib, KPRT, k4, rep from * but end k1. Slide.

Row 21: light—k5, * KLT, sl 1 yif, k4, rep from * but end k1. Turn.

Row 22: dark—k2, * sl 1 yif, k6, rep from *. Slide.

Row 23: light—k1, * sl 1 yib, KPRT, k4, rep from * but end k5. Turn.

Continue in this manner. For additional hints, see the note at the end of the directions for Zig-Zag on Ripple and Chain II.

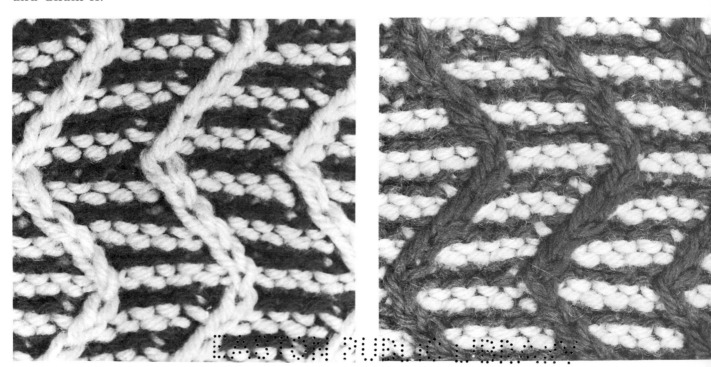

EASTON PUBLIC LIBRARY
EASTON PA

CHAPTER FOUR

REVERSIBLE GEOMETRICS

More than half the stitch patterns in this book are contained in this chapter, and with good reason. This type of stitch is so adaptable that almost any design or figure may be worked up. Of course, knitting has its limitations. Circles, for example, are never easily achieved. The fact that stitches are wider than tall imposes some limitations. And the necessity for shapes to follow stitches and rows results in geometric and stair-step effects. (Embroidery has the edge here for it can flow where it wishes.) Nonetheless, the considerable range of designs available to knitters can now be worked reversibly!

Reversible Geometrics take quite a bit more time and yarn than most knitting. This is not surprising when you consider that two separate but interlocked faces are being made. Such beautiful knitted fabrics can be made this way that the effort is often worthwhile.

BASIC TECHNIQUES

Before attempting Reversible Geometrics, less-experienced knitters should be sure they understand three basics. First, be certain you can pick up a stitch and put it on the needle in the right direction, not twisted. That is, no matter which side of the work faces you, no matter whether it is a knit or purl stitch, the strand from the "front" of the loop (the side coming over the needle toward you) should lead on to the next st on your *right*. Second, be sure you can tell a knit stitch from a purl. In these patterns, once a knit stitch always a knit stitch. If you doubt your ability to tell, work a swatch of k1, p1 ribbing but don't bind off. Spread the stitches on the needle. Notice that knit stitches flow downward in a smooth column. Each stitch, including the one on the needle, rises from the hole in the stitch below. Purl stitches present a pattern of horizontal strands. Most important, the stitch on the needle has a crosswise strand at its base. The sight of this strand should always

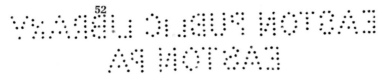
EASTON PUBLIC LIBRARY
EASTON PA

make you think "PURL!" Third, be sure you understand "sl 1 yif" and "sl 1 yib". When a knit st presents itself, if you don't knit it the directions will tell you to slip it "yib" (with the "yarn in back" of the work). A purl stitch which is not worked will be slipped "yif" (with the "yarn in front" or toward you). A general rule of knitting is to slip "purl-wise" unless told otherwise. "Purl-wise" means you insert the right needle into the stitch in the way you would if you were going to purl it. All slip stitches in this chapter are done this way. Once you understand these basics you need not fear Reversible Geometrics.

UNDERSTANDING REVERSIBLE GEOMETRICS

In reality all Reversible Geometrics are based on the same "stitch pattern." It is the colored design which varies. The stitch pattern is a k1, p1 rib with certain stitches slipped. Any knitter knows that in ribbing the knit stitches stand forward and the purl stitches recede. Of course if you turn the work around, on the opposite side those purl stitches will be the knit stitches which now stand out and what was previously considered a knit stitch has become a receding purl stitch. No matter which side of the work you look at, consider only the knit stitches as belonging to the design on that side.

The fact that ribbing can stretch out and reveal the purl stitches is no problem here. The slipped stitches will hold it together. If, for the sake of our design, we do not want to make a certain stitch in the color being used on that row, we simply slip it, leaving the stitch its former color (or to be worked in the other color on the succeeding row). The strand of yarn behind that stitch holds the adjoining stitches (which *were* worked) close together. With enough slipped stitches, the ribbing stops being ribbing and can't stretch out. Do remember that a "k" stitch becomes "sl 1 yib" and "p" becomes "sl 1 yif". The directions will tell you that but you will be happier when you can work a pattern without continually looking at the directions. The "yif" or "yib" is important so that the unused yarn will hide behind the slipped stitch. By the way, don't be frightened if you pick up a new color, ready to begin a pattern, and the very first stitch says "sl 1 yif". Just slip the stitch! There can be no "yib" or "yif" until the next time you work that row and when the color is already part of the work.

The stitch patterns in this chapter are subdivided into six groups according to the way they are worked. Occasionally a pattern is difficult to classify. In a few instances one is deliberately misplaced because it is a variation worked by a different method than the "parent" design but inserted following it.

Once you have tried several patterns and perhaps made some of the Reversible Geometric items included in Chapter Five, you should be ready to design your own articles. Be sure to consult Chapter Six first.

SHORT FORM REVERSIBLE GEOMETRICS

Short Form patterns are so useful that they make up about one third of the Reversible Geometrics in this chapter. They are true reversibles, with two kinds of exceptions. Five of the first six patterns reverse to horizontal stripes. They could have been worked differently, but making stripes on one side is an easy way to achieve reversibility and it is often useful because of being completely different. A few other short form patterns are not true reversibles because they have an element of pattern that moves left to right causing a mirror reverse; but, after all, that is so close to true that the casual observer will be fooled.

Look at some of the illustrations and you will see that most of these patterns can be viewed as being made of alternate bands—first two rows of knitting which is mostly dark, then two rows of mostly light. That is exactly how they are worked: two rows of one color (slipping some stitches to keep them the other color), then two rows of the contrasting color. More of this when we discuss designing your own patterns in Chapter Seven.

The last five patterns in this section are one-row short forms. As the name implies, each horizontal band is made of just one row, so colors alternate continually.

With the exception of those one-row patterns, and Two-sided Stripes which is only a Short Form in its variation, the patterns in this chapter can be adapted to the use of regular single-pointed needles. Simply cast on in the color named, *turn,* and start the first row. Work rows in this order: 1, 2, 4, 3, 5, 6, 8, 7. In other words, for every set of four rows, reverse the last two. Be forewarned that all the changing of colors will be done at the same edge, giving a rather untidy effect. This may be all right for some uses but is not recommended for scarves, afghans, and the like where edges are sure to be noticed.

REVERSED STRIPES (*top and center*)

unlike reversible

Even an experienced knitter will do a double-take when she first sees this one. It does the impossible—the colors run horizontally on one side and vertically on the other. The trick, of course, comes in hiding strands of yarn between the two faces. It really is an extremely easy pattern to work.

Use dpn or adapt for spn. Multiple of 4 sts plus 3. Cast on dark, slide.

Row 1: light—k1, sl 1 yif, k1, * p1, k1, sl 1 yif, k1, rep from *. Turn.

Row 2: light—p1, sl 1 yib, p1, * k1, p1, sl 1 yib, p1, rep from *. Slide.

Row 3: dark—p1, k1, p1, * sl 1 yib, p1, k1, p1, rep from *. Turn.

Row 4: dark—k1, p1, k1, * sl 1 yif, k1, p1, k1, rep from *. Slide.

rep Rows 1–4.

Variation (*below and right*)

Everything is the same with these exceptions: dpn required; work the above rows in this order— 1, 3, 2, 4. The result is that the vertical stripes are more even and the other side looks tweedy because the horizontal stripes are only one row thick.

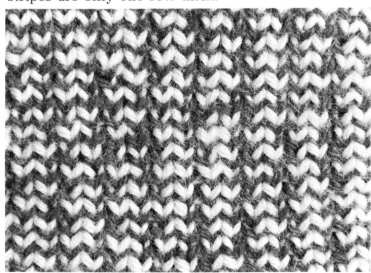

A CROSS AND ACROSS

unlike reversible

This geometric pattern is fairly easy to follow once it is established. The "cross" of the title is within a diamond. If the colors are reversed so that the cross is dark it seems to stand out more and the diamond is less apparent.

Use dpn or adapt for spn. Multiple of 8 sts plus 3. Cast on dark, slide.

Row 1:   light—* k1, sl 1 yif, (k1, p1) 3 times, rep from * but end sl 1, k1. Turn.

Row 2:   light (maintain)—* p1, sl 1 yib, (p1, k1) 3 times, rep from * but end sl 1, p1. Slide.

Row 3:   dark—(p1, k1) twice, * p1, sl 1 yib, (p1, k1) 3 times, rep from * but end (p1, k1) twice, p1. Turn.

Row 4:   dark (maintain)—(k1, p1) twice, * k1, sl 1 yif, (k1, p1) 3 times, rep from * but end (k1, p1) twice, k1. Slide.

Row 5:   light—k1, p1, k1, * sl 1 yif, k1, p1, k1, rep from *. Turn.

Row 6:   light (maintain)—p1, k1, p1, * sl 1 yib, p1, k1, p1, rep from *. Slide.

Row 7:   with dark rep row 2. Turn.

Row 8:   with dark rep row 1 (maintain). Slide.

Row 9:   with light rep row 4. Turn.

Row 10: with light rep row 3 (maintain). Slide.

Row 11: with dark rep row 2. Turn.

Row 12: with dark rep row 1 (maintain). Slide.

Row 13: light—rep row 5. Turn.

Row 14: light (maintain)—rep row 6. Slide.

Row 15: dark—rep row 3. Turn.

Row 16: dark (maintain)—rep row 4. Slide.
     rep Rows 1–16.

BIRDS-EYE

unlike reversible

If you are just trying out reversible geometrics, this is an easy pattern to begin with. If you are familiar with them, you should find this easy to work without looking at the directions once the pattern is established. The side not photographed will be striped horizontally (see A Cross and Across).

Use dpn or adapt for spn. Multiple of 4 sts plus 3. Cast on dark, slide.

Row 1: light—p1, k1, p1, * sl 1 yib, p1, k1, p1, rep from *. Turn.

Row 2: light (maintain)—k1, p1, k1, * sl 1 yif, k1, p1, k1, rep from *. Slide.

Row 3: dark—k1, * p1, k1, rep from *. Turn.

Row 4: dark (maintain)—p1, * k1, p1, rep from *. Slide.

Row 5: light—p1, sl 1 yib, p1, * k1, p1, sl 1 yib, p1, rep from *. Turn.

Row 6: light (maintain)—k1, sl 1 yif, k1, * p1, k1, sl 1 yif, k1, rep from *. Slide.

Rows 7 and 8: Rep rows 3 and 4.
    rep Rows 1–8.

LATTICE

unlike reversible

Lattice is closely related to Birds-eye. The same comments apply including the fact that both reverse to stripes.

Use dpn or adapt for spn. Multiple of 4 sts plus 1. Cast on dark, slide.

Row 1: light—k1, * p1, sl 1 yib, p1, k1, rep from *. Turn.

Row 2: light (maintain)—p1, * k1, sl 1 yif, k1, p1, rep from *. Slide.

Row 3: dark—p1, * k1, p1, rep from *. Turn.

Row 4: dark (maintain)—k1, * p1, k1, rep from *. Slide.
    rep Rows 1–4.

OFFSET STEPS

mirror reversible

This pattern presents a neat, orderly appearance without being overly regimented. Better yet, once the pattern is established it is extremely easy to follow.

Use dpn or adapt for spn. Multiple of 8 sts plus 2. Cast on light, slide.

Row 1: dark—p1, * (k1, p1) 3 times, sl 1 yib, sl 1 yif, rep from *, k last st of row. Turn.

Row 2: dark (maintain)—p1, * sl 1 yib, sl 1 yif, (k1, p1) 3 times, rep from *, k last st. Slide.

Row 3: light—p1, * (k1, p1) twice, sl 1 yib, sl 1 yif, k1, p1, rep from *, k last st. Turn.

Row 4: light (maintain)—p1, * k1, p1, sl 1 yib, sl 1 yif, (k1, p1) twice, rep from *, k last st. Slide.

Row 5: dark—rep row 2. Turn.

Row 6: dark (maintain)—rep row 1. Slide.

Row 7: light—rep row 4. Turn.

Row 8: light (maintain)—rep row 3. Slide.

Row 9: with dark rep row 4. Turn.

Row 10: with dark (maintain) rep row 3. Slide.

Row 11: with light rep row 2. Turn.

Row 12: with light (maintain) rep row 1. Slide.

Row 13: with dark rep row 3. Turn.

Row 14: with dark (maintain) rep row 4. Slide.

Row 15: with light rep row 1. Turn.

Row 16: with light (maintain) rep row 2. Slide. rep Rows 1–16.

GRID

opposite reversible

With this pattern we introduce Reversible Geometrics which have true patterns on both sides, not just stripes on one. This is an extremely easy one to follow. After working four rows, try to figure out what way the next rows will be worked before looking at the directions to check. Here is a hint to help: rows 1 and 2 are dark, 3 and 4 light; rows 2 and 4 are easy because they maintain the pattern; in rows 1 and 3 you will work all the sts except those where the contrasting color shows all the way back to the cast on.

Use dpn or adapt for spn. Multiple of 6 sts plus 5. Cast on light, slide.

Row 1: dark—k1, * p1, sl 1 yib, (p1, k1) twice, rep from * but end (p1, k1) once. Turn.

Row 2: dark (maintain)—p1, * k1, sl 1 yif, (k1, p1) twice, rep from * but end (k1, p1) once. Slide.

Row 3: light—* p1, (k1, p1) twice, sl 1 yib, rep from * but omit final sl st. Turn.

Row 4: light—(maintain)—* k1, (p1, k1) twice, sl 1 yif, rep from * but omit final sl st. Slide.
    rep Rows 1–4.

TWO-SIDED STRIPES

opposite reversible (appears true)

Here is an easy place to start working in reversible geometrics. It is exceedingly easy to do because after the first row all rows "maintain" the existing pattern (see Glossary for definition of "maintain"). The stripes are quite even because each stitch is worked once, then slipped once. A variation may be tried by working rows 1 and 3 with light yarn, then repeating those two rows with dark yarn. The result will look exactly like the vertically-striped side of Reversed Stripes with small and large stitches alternating. The reason is that some stitches are not slipped at all while others are slipped in two successive rows. The uneven look may appear more interesting to some knitters. Only this variation can be adapted to spn.

Use of dpn required. Multiple of 4 sts plus 2. Cast on dark, slide.

Row 1: light—p1, * k1, p1, sl 1 yib, sl 1 yif, rep from *, k last st of row. Turn.

Row 2: with dark (maintain)—rep row 1. Slide.

Row 3: light (maintain)—p1, * sl 1 yib, sl 1 yif, k1, p1, rep from *, k last st. Turn.

Row 4: with dark (maintain)—rep row 3. Slide.
    rep Rows 1–4.

TIERS

mirror reversible

Tiers is obviously related to Offset Steps and the knitter may choose whichever appeals to her more. Either one is quite simple to follow once the pattern is set up.

Use dpn or adapt to spn. Multiple of 10 sts plus 2. Cast on dark, slide.

Row 1: light—p1, * k1, p1, sl 1 yib, sl 1 yif, (k1, p1) 3 times, rep from *, k last st of row. Turn.

Row 2: light (maintain)—p1, * (k1, p1) 3 times, sl 1 yib, sl 1 yif, k1, p1, rep from *, k last st. Slide.

Row 3: dark—p1, * sl 1 yib, sl 1 yif, (k1, p1) 4 times, rep from *, k last st. Turn.

Row 4: dark (maintain)—p1, * (k1, p1) 4 times, sl 1 yib, sl 1 yif, rep from *, k last st. Slide.

Row 5: light—p1, * (k1, p1) twice, sl 1 yib, sl 1 yif, (k1, p1) twice, rep from *, k last st. Turn.

Row 6: light (maintain)—rep row 5. Slide.

Row 7: dark—rep row 4. Turn.

Row 8: dark (maintain)—rep row 3. Slide.

Row 9: light—rep row 2. Turn.

Row 10: light (maintain)—rep row 1. Slide.

Row 11: with dark rep row 2. Turn.

Row 12: with dark (maintain) rep row 1. Slide.

Row 13: with light rep row 4. Turn.

Row 14: with light (maintain) rep row 3. Slide.

Row 15: with dark rep row 5. Turn.

Row 16: with dark (maintain) rep row 5. Slide.

Row 17: with light rep row 3. Turn.

Row 18: with light (maintain) rep row 4. Slide.

Row 19: with dark rep row 1. Turn.

Row 20: with dark (maintain) rep row 2. Slide.
rep Rows 1–20.

CURRY COMBS

true reversible

If you were able to work Grid without referring to the directions, this one shouldn't be much more difficult. While this is classified as a true reversible, the pictures will reveal that the design is offset a little.

Use dpn or adapt for spn. Multiple of 12 sts plus 2. Cast on light, slide.

Row 1: dark—k1, p1, * (k1, p1) 3 times, sl 1 yib, p1, k1, sl 1 yif, k1, p1, rep from *. Turn.

Row 2: dark (maintain)—k1, p1, * sl 1 yib, p1, k1, sl 1 yif, (k1, p1) 4 times, rep from *. Slide.

Rows 3 and 4: with light rep rows 1 and 2 (Row 4 is a maintain row).
rep Rows 1–4.

STUMBLING BLOCKS

mirror reversible

The name refers to the *appearance* of the pattern. It is an easy pattern to learn.

Use dpn or adapt to spn. Multiple of 12 sts plus 2. Cast on dark, slide.

Row 1: light—p1, * (k1, p1) twice, (sl 1 yib, sl 1 yif) twice, (k1, p1) twice, rep from *, k last st of row. Turn.

Row 2: light (maintain)—p1, * (k1, p1) twice, (sl 1 yib, sl 1 yif) twice, (k1, p1) twice, rep from *, k last st. Slide.

Row 3: dark—p1, * (sl 1 yib, sl 1 yif) twice, (k1, p1) 4 times, rep from *, sl last st. Turn.

Row 4: dark (maintain)—sl 1, * (k1, p1) 4 times, (sl 1 yib, sl 1 yif) twice, rep from *, k last st. Slide.

Rows 5 and 6: with light rep rows 3 and 4.

Rows 7 and 8: with dark rep rows 1 and 2.

Row 9: with light rep row 4. Turn. (This is not a maintain row.)

Row 10: with light (maintain) rep row 3. Slide.

Row 11: dark—rep row 4 (not maintain). Turn.

Row 12: dark (maintain) rep row 3. Slide.
rep Rows 1–12.

Z-PATTERN

mirror reversible (appears true)
Once the knitter has worked one repeat of this pattern she should be able to do the rest without referring to the directions. That is, assuming she understands the basics of how reversible geometrics are done!

Use dpn or adapt for spn. Multiple of 16 sts plus 2. Cast on light, slide.

Row 1: dark—p1, * (k1, p1) 3 times, sl 1 yib, sl 1 yif, rep from *, k last st of row. Turn.

Row 2: dark (maintain)—p1, * sl 1 yib, sl 1 yif, (k1, p1) 3 times, rep from *, k last st. Slide.

Row 3: light—p1, * (k1, p1) 7 times, sl 1 yib, sl 1 yif, rep from *, k last st. Turn.

Row 4: light (maintain)—p1, * sl 1 yib, sl 1 yif, (k1, p1) 7 times, rep from *, k last st. Slide.

Row 5: dark—p1, * k1, p1, sl 1 yib, sl 1 yif, (k1, p1) 3 times, sl 1 yib, sl 1 yif, (k1, p1) twice, rep from *, k last st. Turn.

Row 6: dark (maintain)—p1, * (k1, p1) twice, sl 1 yib, sl 1 yif, (k1, p1) 3 times, sl 1 yib, sl 1 yif, k1, p1, rep from *, k last st. Slide.

Row 7: light—p1, * (k1, p1) 3 times, sl 1 yib, sl 1 yif, (k1, p1) 4 times, rep from *, k last st. Turn.

Row 8: light (maintain)—p1, * (k1, p1) 4 times, sl 1 yib, sl 1 yif, (k1, p1) 3 times, rep from *, k last st. Slide.

rep Rows 1–8.

STAGGERED FEET (top, opposite)

true reversible
An appealing horizontal effect is created by these zany bands. Perhaps to some people it may only look as though a tractor had run back and forth. It is an easy pattern to work.

Use dpn or adapt for spn. Multiple of 8 sts plus 2. Cast on light, slide.

Row 1: dark—p1, (k1, p1) 3 times, sl 1 yib, sl 1 yif, rep from *, k last st of row. Turn.

Row 2: dark (maintain)—p1, * sl 1 yib, sl 1 yif, (k1, p1) 3 times, rep from *, k last st. Slide.

Row 3: light—p1, * (k1, p1) twice, sl 1 yib, sl 1 yif, k1, p1, rep from *, k last st. Turn.

Row 4: light (maintain)—p1, * k1, p1, sl 1 yib, sl 1 yif, (k1, p1) twice, rep from *, k last st. Slide.

Row 5: dark—* p1, k1, rep from *. Turn.

Row 6: dark—rep row 5. Slide.

Row 7: light—p1, * sl 1 yib, sl 1 yif, (k1, p1) 3 times, rep from *, k last st. Turn.

Row 8: light (maintain)—p1, * (k1, p1) 3 times, sl 1 yib, sl 1 yif, rep from *, k last st. Slide.

Row 9: with dark rep row 4. Turn.

Row 10: with dark (maintain) rep row 3. Slide.

Rows 11 and 12: with light rep row 5, twice.

        rep Rows 1–12.

INSCRUTABLE PAGODAS *(center and bottom)*

unlike reversible

Is it possible to explain the ridiculous name of this simple pattern? It was developed late one evening as the television sets were showing Nixon's return from China. One side looks rather like pagodas and since the other side is completely unexpected the pattern is inscrutable. It is an easy reversible geometric, very interesting in knitting worsted.

Use dpn or adapt for spn. Multiple of 8 sts plus 3. Cast on light, slide.

Row 1: dark—* k1, sl 1 yif, (k1, p1) 3 times, rep from * but end sl 1 yif, k1. Turn.

Row 2: dark—* p1, sl 1 yib, (p1, k1) 3 times, rep from * but end sl 1 yib, p1. Slide.

Row 3: light—(p1, k1) twice, * p1, sl 1 yib, (p1, k1) 3 times, rep from * but omit final k st. Turn.

Row 4: light—(k1, p1) twice, * k1, sl 1 yif, (k1, p1) 3 times, rep from * but omit final p st. Slide.

        rep Rows 1–4.

PEDESTALS

true reversible
Another of those patterns which are easy to follow after one repeat has been worked!

Use dpn or adapt for spn. Multiple of 12 sts plus 2. Cast on light, slide.

Row 1: dark—p1, * (k1, p1) 3 times, sl 1 yib, sl 1 yif, (k1, p1) twice, rep from *, k last st of row. Turn.

Row 2: dark (maintain)—p1, * (k1, p1) twice, sl 1 yib, sl 1 yif, (k1, p1) 3 times, rep from *, k last st. Slide.

Row 3: light—p1, * (k1, p1) 5 times, sl 1 yib, sl 1 yif, rep from *, k last st. Turn.

Row 4: light (maintain)—p1, * sl 1 yib, sl 1 yif, (k1, p1) 5 times, rep from *, k last st. Slide.

Row 5: dark—p1, k1, rep from *. Turn.

Row 6: dark (maintain)—rep row 5. Slide.

Rows 7 and 8: with light rep rows 5 and 6.

Row 9: with dark rep row 4. Turn.

Row 10: with dark (maintain) rep row 3. Slide.

Row 11: with light rep row 2. Turn.

Row 12: with light (maintain) rep row 1. Slide.

Rows 13 and 14: with dark rep rows 5 and 6.

Rows 15 and 16: with light rep rows 5 and 6.

rep Rows 1–16.

Stairstep Variation

mirror reversible

Although the end result looks a little more complicated, this variation is as easy to follow as the basic version of Pedestals.

Use dpn or adapt for spn. Multiple of 24 sts plus 2. Cast on light, slide.

Row 1: dark—p1, * (k1, p1) 11 times, sl 1 yib, sl 1 yif, rep from *, k last st of row. Turn.

Row 2: dark (maintain)—p1, * sl 1 yib, sl 1 yif, (k1, p1) 11 times, rep from *, k last st. Slide.

Row 3: light—p1, * (k1, p1) 9 times, sl 1 yib, sl 1 yif, (k1, p1) twice, rep from *, k last st. Turn.

Row 4: light (maintain)—p1, * (k1, p1) twice, sl 1 yib, sl 1 yif, (k1, p1) 9 times, rep from *, k last st. Slide.

Row 5: dark—p1, * (k1, p1) 5 times, sl 1 yib, sl 1 yif, (k1, p1) 6 times, rep from *, k last st. Turn.

Row 6: dark (maintain)—p1, * (k1, p1) 6 times, sl 1 yib, sl 1 yif, (k1, p1) 5 times, rep from *, k last st. Slide.

Row 7: light—p1, * (k1, p1) 3 times, sl 1 yib, sl 1 yif, (k1, p1) 8 times, rep from *, k last st. Turn.

Row 8: light (maintain)—p1, * (k1, p1) 8 times, sl 1 yib, sl 1 yif, (k1, p1) 3 times, rep from *, k last st. Slide.

rep Rows 1–8.

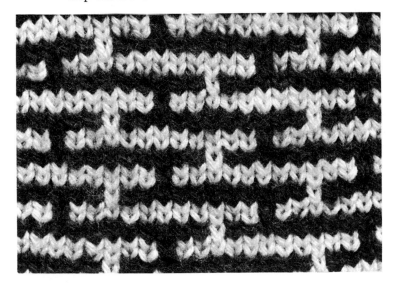

SNAKE WALK

mirror reversible

Both sides of this are shown to illustrate how difficult it is to classify some types of reversibles. To call this one a "mirror reversible" is academic. If a dark line threads left, right, left, right on one side, it will go right, left, right, left on the other. However, the effect is such that the pattern could as effectively be called "true reversible."

Use dpn or adapt. Multiple of 14 sts plus 2. Cast on light, slide.

Row 1:   dark—sl 1 yif, * (k1, p1) 4 times, sl 1 yib, sl 1 yif, k1, p1, sl 1 yib, sl 1 yif, rep from *, k last st of row. Turn.

Row 2:   dark (maintain)—p1, * sl 1 yib, sl 1 yif, k1, p1, sl 1 yib, sl 1 yif, (k1, p1) 4 times, rep from *, sl last st. Slide.

Row 3:   light—sl 1 yif, * k1, p1, sl 1 yib, sl 1 yif, (k1, p1) 4 times, sl 1 yib, sl 1 yif, rep from *, k last st. Turn.

Row 4:   light (maintain)—p1, * sl 1 yib, sl 1 yif, (k1, p1) 4 times, sl 1 yib, sl 1 yif, k1, p1, rep from *, sl last st. Slide.

Row 5:   dark—sl 1 yif, * k1, p1, sl 1 yib, sl 1 yif, (k1, p1) 4 times, sl 1 yib, sl 1 yif, rep from *, k last st. Turn.

Row 6:   dark (maintain)—p1, * sl 1 yib, sl 1 yif, (k1, p1) 4 times, sl 1 yib, sl 1 yif, k1, p1, rep from *, sl last st. Slide.

Row 7:   light—sl 1 yif, * (k1, p1) 4 times, sl 1 yib, sl 1 yif, k1, p1, sl 1 yib, sl 1 yif, rep from *, k last st. Turn.

Row 8:   light (maintain)—p1, * sl 1 yib, sl 1 yif, k1, p1, sl 1 yib, sl 1 yif, (k1, p1) 4 times, rep from *, sl last st. Slide.

Row 9:   dark—p1, * (k1, p1, sl 1 yib, sl 1 yif) twice, (k1, p1) 3 times, rep from * k last st. Turn.

Row 10: dark (maintain)—sl 1 yif, * (k1, p1) 3 times, (sl 1 yib, sl 1 yif, k1, p1) twice, rep from *, k last st. Slide.

Row 11: light—sl 1 yif, * (k1, p1) 4 times, sl 1 yib, sl 1 yif, k1, p1, sl 1 yib, sl 1 yif, rep from *, k last st. Turn.

Row 12: light (maintain)—p1, * sl 1 yib, sl 1 yif, k1, p1, sl 1 yib, sl 1 yif, (k1, p1) 4 times, rep from *, sl last st. Slide.

Row 13: dark—sl 1 yif, * k1, p1, sl 1 yib, sl 1 yif, (k1, p1) 4 times, sl 1 yib, sl 1 yif, rep from *, k last st. Turn.

Row 14: dark (maintain)—p1, * sl 1 yib, sl 1 yif, (k1, p1) 4 times, sl 1 yib, sl 1 yif, k1, p1, rep from *, sl last st. Slide.

Row 15: light—sl 1 yif, * k1, p1, sl 1 yib, sl 1 yif, (k1, p1) 4 times, sl 1 yib, sl 1 yif, rep from *, k last st. Turn.

Row 16: light (maintain)—p1, * sl 1 yib, sl 1 yif, (k1, p1) 4 times, sl 1 yib, sl 1 yif, k1, p1, rep from *, sl last st. Slide.
rep Rows 1–16.

STAIRWAY

mirror reversible

A strange optical illusion is created when this design is viewed from the right direction. Once a knitter understands how to design these reversible geometrics she can adapt this one for the length of step which suits her purposes.

Use dpn or adapt to spn. Multiple of 16 sts plus 2. Cast on light, slide.

Row 1:   dark—p1, * (k1, p1) 7 times, sl 1 yib, sl 1 yif, rep from *, k last st of row. Turn.

Row 2:   dark (maintain)—p1, * sl 1 yib, sl 1 yif, (k1, p1) 7 times, rep from *, k last st. Slide.

Rows 3 and 4: with light rep rows 1 and 2.

Row 5:   dark—p1, * k1, p1, sl 1 yib, sl 1 yif, (k1, p1) 6 times, rep from *, k last st. Turn.

Row 6:   dark (maintain)—p1, * (k1, p1) 6 times, sl 1 yib, sl 1 yif, k1, p1, rep from *, k last st. Slide.

Row 7:   light—p1, * (k1, p1) 5 times, sl 1 yib, sl 1 yif, (k1, p1) twice, rep from *, k last st. Turn.

Row 8:   light (maintain)—p1, * (k1, p1) twice, sl 1 yib, sl 1 yif, (k1, p1) 5 times, rep from *, k last st. Slide.

Row 9:   dark—p1, * (k1, p1) 3 times, sl 1 yib, sl 1 yif, (k1, p1) 4 times, rep from *, k last st. Turn.

Row 10: dark (maintain)—p1, * (k1, p1) 4 times, sl 1 yib, sl 1 yif, (k1, p1) 3 times, rep from *, k last st. Slide.

Rows 11 and 12: with light rep rows 9 and 10.

Rows 13 and 14: with dark rep rows 7 and 8.

Rows 15 and 16: with light rep rows 5 and 6.

      rep Rows 1–16.

PARQUET

mirror reversible

Use dpn or adapt for spn. Multiple of 16 sts plus 2.
Cast on light. slide.

Row 1: dark—p1, * k1, p1, sl 1 yib, sl 1 yif, rep from *, k last st of row. Turn.

Row 2: dark (maintain)—p1, * sl 1 yib, sl 1 yif, k1, p1, rep from *, k last st. Slide.

Row 3: light—p1, * (k1, p1) 5 times, sl 1 yib, sl 1 yif, (k1, p1) twice, rep from *, k last st. Turn.

Row 4: light (maintain)—p1, * (k1, p1) twice, sl 1 yib, sl 1 yif, (k1, p1) 5 times, rep from *, k last st. Slide.

Row 5: dark—p1, * (k1, p1, sl 1 yib, sl 1 yif) twice, (k1, p1) 4 times, rep from *, k last st. Turn.

Row 6: dark (maintain)—p1, * (k1, p1) 4 times, (sl 1 yib, sl 1 yif, k1, p1) twice, rep from *, k last st. Slide.

Row 7: light—rep row 3. Turn.

Row 8: light (maintain)—rep row 4. Slide.

Row 9: dark—rep row 1. Turn.

Row 10: dark (maintain)—rep row 2. Slide.

Row 11: light—p1, * k1, p1, sl 1 yib, sl 1 yif, (k1, p1) 6 times, rep from *, k last st. Turn.

Row 12: light (maintain)—p1, * (k1, p1) 6 times, sl 1 yib, sl 1 yif, k1, p1, rep from *, k last st. Slide.

Row 13: dark—p1, * (k1, p1) 5 times, sl 1 yib, sl 1 yif, k1, p1, sl 1 yib, sl 1 yif, rep from *, k last st. Turn.

Row 14: dark (maintain)—p1, * sl 1 yib, sl 1 yif, k1, p1, sl 1 yib, sl 1 yif, (k1, p1) 5 times, rep from *, k last st. Slide.

Row 15: light—p1, * k1, p1, sl 1 yib, sl 1 yif, (k1, p1) 6 times, rep from *, k last st. Turn.

Row 16: light (maintain)—p1, * (k1, p1) 6 times, sl 1 yib, sl 1 yif, k1, p1, rep from *, k last st. Slide. rep Rows 1–16.

KEY

mirror reversible

Here is a classic border design. The piece illustrated was worked: * sl 1 yif, k1, rep from * for eight rows in white only before the pattern was started. After the border was completed the rest was knit the same way, making a smooth, heavy fabric. The bottom edge has a tendency to scallop which is more pronounced the nearer the design is to it. In this case it has almost disappeared.

Use dpn or adapt for spn. Multiple of 18 sts plus 2. Cast on light, slide immediately or after last solid color preparatory row.

Row 1: dark—p1, * (k1, p1) 8 times, sl 1 yib, sl 1 yif, rep from *, k last st. Turn.

Row 2: dark (maintain)—p1, * sl 1 yib, sl 1 yif, (k1, p1) 8 times, rep from *, k last st. Slide.

Row 3: light—p1, * k1, p1, sl 1 yib, sl 1 yif, (k1, p1) 6 times, sl 1 yib, sl 1 yif, rep from *, k last st. Turn.

Row 4: light (maintain)—p1, * sl 1 yib, sl 1 yif, (k1, p1) 6 times, sl 1 yib, sl 1 yif, k1, p1, rep from *, k last st. Slide.

Row 5: dark—p1, * k1, p1, sl 1 yib, sl 1 yif, (k1, p1) 4 times, sl 1 yib, sl 1 yif, k1, p1, sl 1 yib, sl 1 yif, rep from *, k last st. Turn.

Row 6: dark (maintain) p1, * (sl 1 yib, sl 1 yif, k1, p1) twice, (k1, p1) 3 times, sl 1 yib, sl 1 yif, k1, p1, rep from *, k last st. Slide.

Row 7: light—p1, * (k1, p1, sl 1 yib, sl 1 yif) twice, k1, p1, (k1, p1, sl 1 yib, sl 1 yif) twice, rep from *, k last st. Turn.

Row 8: light (maintain)—p1, * (sl 1 yib, sl 1 yif, k1, p1) twice, k1, p1, (sl 1 yib, sl 1 yif, k1, p1) twice, rep from *, k last st. Slide.

Row 9: with dark rep row 7. Turn.

Row 10: with dark (maintain) rep row 8. Slide.

Row 11: light—p1, * k1, p1, sl 1 yib, sl 1 yif, (k1, p1) twice, (sl 1 yib, sl 1 yif, k1, p1) twice, sl 1 yib, sl 1 yif, rep from *, k last st. Turn.

Row 12: light (maintain)—p1, * (sl 1 yib, sl 1 yif, k1, p1) 3 times, k1, p1, sl 1 yib, sl 1 yif, k1, p1, rep from *, k last st. Slide.

Row 13: dark—p1, * (k1, p1, sl 1 yib, sl 1 yif) twice, (k1, p1) 4 times, sl 1 yib, sl 1 yif, rep from *, k last st. Turn.

Row 14: dark (maintain)—p1, * sl 1 yib, sl 1 yif, (k1, p1) 4 times, (sl 1 yib, sl 1 yif, k1, p1) twice, rep from *, k last st. Slide.

Row 15: light—p1, * (k1, p1) 6 times, sl 1 yib, sl 1 yif, k1, p1, sl 1 yib, sl 1 yif, rep from *, k last st. Turn.

Row 16: light (maintain)—p1, * sl 1 yib, sl 1 yif, k1, p1, sl 1 yib, sl 1 yif, (k1, p1) 6 times, rep from *, k last st. Slide.

Row 17: dark—p1, * k1, p1, sl 1 yib, sl 1 yif, (k1, p1) 7 times, rep from *, k last st. Turn.

Row 18: dark (maintain)—p1, * (k1, p1) 7 times, sl 1 yib, sl 1 yif, k1, p1, rep from *, k last st. Slide.

Do not repeat. Work a few solid rows of light color (as explained in introduction to pattern) and then do another band of KEY, or work rest of project in solid color or some other pattern.

ROW OF BOXES

alternate reversible

The other side of this would appear to be the same but closer inspection reveals that a dotted dark-colored band backs up each solid light-colored one. Of course, if you prefer to have the dotted bands (or Rows of Boxes) in light with dark lines between, reverse all color directions.

Use dpn or adapt for spn. Multiple of 4 sts plus 1. Cast on dark, slide.

Row 1: light—p1, * k1, p1, sl 1 yib, p1, rep from *. Turn.

Row 2: light (maintain)—k1, * sl 1 yif, k1, p1, k1, rep from *. Slide.

Row 3: dark—k1, * p1, k1, rep from *. Turn.

Row 4: dark (maintain)—p1, * k1, p1, rep from *. Slide.

Row 5: light—p1, * k1, sl 1 yif, k1, p1, rep from *. Turn.

Row 6: light (maintain)—k1, * p1, sl 1 yib, p1, k1, rep from *. Slide.

Row 7: dark—rep row 3. Turn.

Row 8: dark (maintain)—rep row 4. Slide.
rep Rows 1–8.

CHINESE PUZZLE

mirror reversible

This is actually a shortened (and not opposite reversible) form of Philena's Border (page 88) repeated over and over. Compare the pictures of the two patterns.

Use dpn or adapt to spn. Multiple of 12 plus 2 sts. Cast on dark, slide.

Row 1: light—p1, * (k1, p1) twice, sl 1 yib, sl 1 yif, (k1, p1) 3 times, rep from *, k last st. Turn.

Row 2: light (maintain)—p1, * (k1, p1) 3 times, sl 1 yib, sl 1 yif, (k1, p1) twice, rep from *, k last st. Slide.

Row 3: dark—p1, * (k1, p1) twice, (sl 1 yib, sl 1 yif, k1, p1) twice, rep from *, k last st. Turn.

Row 4: dark (maintain) p1, * (k1, p1, sl 1 yib, sl 1 yif) twice, (k1, p1) twice, rep from *, k last st. Slide.

Row 5: light—p1, * sl 1 yib, sl 1 yif, (k1, p1) 5 times, rep from *, k last st. Turn.

Row 6: light (maintain)—p1, * (k1, p1) 5 times, sl 1 yib, sl 1 yif, rep from *, k last st. Slide.

Row 7: dark—p1, * (sl 1 yib, sl 1 yif, k1, p1) twice, (k1, p1) twice, rep from *, k last st. Turn.

Row 8: dark (maintain)—p1, * (k1, p1) twice, (k1, p1, sl 1 yib, sl 1 yif) twice, rep from * k last st. Slide.

Row 9: light—p1, * sl 1 yib, sl 1 yif, (k1, p1) 3 times, sl 1 yib, sl 1 yif, k1, p1, rep from *, k last st. Turn.

Row 10: light (maintain)—p1, * k1, p1, sl 1 yib, sl 1 yif, (k1, p1) 3 times, sl 1 yib, sl 1 yif, rep from *, k last st. Slide.

Row 11: dark—p1, * sl 1 yib, sl 1 yif, (k1, p1) 3 times, sl 1 yib, sl 1 yif, k1, p1, rep from *, k last st. Turn.

Row 12: dark (maintain)—p1, * k1, p1, sl 1 yib, sl 1 yif, (k1, p1) 3 times, sl 1 yib, sl 1 yif, rep from *, k last st. Slide.

Row 13: light—p1, * (k1, p1) 4 times, sl 1 yib, sl 1 yif, k1, p1, rep from *, k last st. Turn.

Row 14: light (maintain)—p1, * k1, p1, sl 1 yib, sl 1 yif, (k1, p1) 4 times, rep from *, k last st. Slide.

Row 15: dark—p1, * (k1, p1) twice, (sl 1 yib, sl 1 yif, k1, p1) twice, rep from *, k last st. Turn.

Row 16: dark (maintain)—p1, * (k1, p1, sl 1 yib, sl 1 yif) twice, (k1, p1) twice, rep from *, k last st. Slide.

rep Rows 1–16.

CHAIN LINKS

true reversible

This pattern can be used as a border by working only rows 1–10. Of course, it would generally only be considered for use on something knit in this "Geometric Reversible" form, but the rest of the article could be in a solid color or some other pattern.

Use dpn or adapt for spn. Multiple of 12 sts plus 2. Cast on light, slide.

Row 1: dark—p1, * sl 1 yib, sl 1 yif, (k1, p1) 5 times, rep from *, k last st. Turn.

Row 2: dark (maintain)—p1, * (k1, p1) 5 times, sl 1 yib, sl 1 yif, rep from *, k last st. Slide.

Row 3: light—p1, * sl 1 yib, sl 1 yif, (k1, p1) 3 times, sl 1 yib, sl 1 yif, k1, p1, rep from *, k last st. Turn.

Row 4: light (maintain)—p1, * k1, p1, sl 1 yib, sl 1 yif, (k1, p1) 3 times, sl 1 yib, sl 1 yif, rep from *, k last st. Slide.

Row 5: dark—p1, * (k1, p1) 3 times, sl 1 yib, sl 1 yif, (k1, p1) twice, rep from *, k last st. Turn.

Row 6: dark (maintain)—p1, * (k1, p1) twice, sl 1 yib, sl 1 yif, (k1, p1) 3 times, rep from *, k last st. Slide.

Rows 7 and 8: light—rep rows 3 and 4.

Rows 9 and 10: dark—rep rows 1 and 2.

Row 11: light—* p1, k1, rep from *. Turn.

Row 12: light (maintain)—rep row 11. Slide.

Rows 13 and 14: dark—rep rows 5 and 6.

Row 15: light—p1, * (k1, p1, sl 1 yib, sl 1 yif) twice, (k1, p1) twice, rep from *, k last st. Turn.

Row 16: light (maintain)—p1, * (k1, p1) twice, (sl 1 yib. sl 1 yif, k1, p1) twice, rep from *, k last st. Slide.

Rows 17 and 18: dark—rep rows 1 and 2.

Rows 19 and 20: light—rep rows 15 and 16.

Rows 21 and 22: dark—rep rows 13 and 14.

Rows 23 and 24: light—rep rows 11 and 12.

rep Rows 1–24.

GRILLWORK

true reversible

Use dpn or adapt for spn. Multiple of 24 sts plus 2.
Cast on dark, slide.

Row 1: light—p1, * k1, p1, sl 1 yib, sl 1 yif, (k1, p1) 4 times, sl 1 yib, sl 1 yif, (k1, p1) 4 times, sl 1 yib, sl 1 yif, rep from *, k last st. Turn.

Row 2: light—p1, * sl 1 yib, sl 1 yif, (k1, p1) 4 times, sl 1 yib, sl 1 yif, (k1, p1) 4 times, sl 1 yib, sl 1 yif, k1, p1, rep from *, k last st. Slide.

Row 3: dark—p1, * (k1, p1) 3 times, sl 1 yib, sl 1 yif, rep from *, k last st. Turn.

Row 4: dark (maintain)—p1, * sl 1 yib, sl 1 yif, (k1, p1) 3 times, rep from *, k last st. Slide.

Row 5: light—p1, * (k1, p1) 3 times, sl 1 yib, sl 1 yif, (k1, p1) 5 times, sl 1 yib, sl 1 yif, (k1, p1) twice, rep from *, k last st. Turn.

Row 6: light (maintain) p1, * (k1, p1) twice, sl 1 yib, sl 1 yif, (k1, p1) 5 times, sl 1 yib, sl 1 yif, (k1, p1) 3 times, rep from *, k last st. Slide.

Row 7: dark—p1, * k1, p1, sl 1 yib, sl 1 yif, (k1, p1) 3 times, sl 1 yib, sl 1 yif, (k1, p1) 3 times, sl 1 yib, sl 1 yif, (k1, p1) twice, rep from *, k last st. Turn.

Row 8: dark (maintain)—p1, * (k1, p1) twice, sl 1 yib, sl 1 yif, (k1, p1) 3 times, sl 1 yib, sl 1 yif, (k1, p1) 3 times, sl 1 yib, sl 1 yif, k1, p1, rep from *, k last st. Slide.

Row 9: light—p1, * k1, p1, sl 1 yib, sl 1 yif, (k1, p1) 3 times, sl 1 yib, sl 1 yif, rep from *, k last st. Turn.

Row 10: light (maintain)—p1, * sl 1 yib, sl 1 yif, (k1, p1) 3 times, sl 1 yib, sl 1 yif, k1, p1, rep from * k last st. Slide.

Rows 11 and 12: dark—rep rows 3 and 4.
Rows 13 and 14: light—rep rows 5 and 6.
Rows 15 and 16: dark—rep rows 3 and 4.
Rows 17 and 18: light—rep rows 9 and 10.
Rows 19 and 20: dark—rep rows 7 and 8.
Rows 21 and 22: light—rep rows 5 and 6.
Rows 23 and 24: dark—rep rows 3 and 4.

rep Rows 1–24.

SQUARE DEAL

true reversible

Do you see dark crosses in this pattern? Look again; there are also interlocking boxes in white. These show up a little better in dark, so if you prefer that, cast on light and reverse all color directions. Whichever you do, both sides will be the same.

Use dpn or adapt for spn. Multiple of 16 sts plus 2. Cast on dark, slide.

Row 1: light—p1, * (k1, p1) 4 times, sl 1 yib, sl 1 yif, (k1, p1) 3 times, rep from *, k last st. Turn.

Row 2: light (maintain)—p1, * (k1, p1) 3 times, sl 1 yib, sl 1 yif, (k1, p1) 4 times, rep from *, k last st. Slide.

Row 3: dark—p1, * sl 1 yib, sl 1 yif, k1, p1, rep from *, sl last st. Turn.

Row 4: dark (maintain)—sl 1, * k1, p1, sl 1 yib, sl 1 yif, rep from *, k last st. Slide.

Row 5: light—p1, * sl 1 yib, sl 1 yif, (k1, p1) 7 times, rep from *, sl last st. Turn.

Row 6: light (maintain)—sl 1, * (k1, p1) 7 times, sl 1 yib, sl 1 yif, rep from *, k last st. Slide.

Row 7: dark—p1, * (k1, p1) twice, sl 1 yib, sl 1 yif, k1, p1, sl 1 yib, sl 1 yif, (k1, p1) 3 times, rep from *, k last st. Turn.

Row 8: dark (maintain)—p1, * (k1, p1) 3 times, (sl 1 yib, sl 1 yif, k1, p1) twice, k1, p1, rep from *, k last st. Slide.

Rows 9 and 10: rep rows 5 and 6.

Rows 11 and 12: rep rows 3 and 4.

Rows 13 and 14: rep rows 1 and 2.

Row 15: dark—p1, * sl 1 yib, sl 1 yif, (k1, p1) 5 times, sl 1 yib, sl 1 yif, k1, p1, rep from *, sl last st. Turn.

Row 16: dark (maintain)—sl 1, * k1, p1, sl 1 yib, sl 1 yif, (k1, p1) 5 times, sl 1 yib, sl 1 yif, rep from *, k last st. Slide.

rep Rows 1–16.

BROKEN BOXES

true reversible

Use dpn or adapt for spn. Multiple of 24 sts plus 2.
Cast on light, slide.

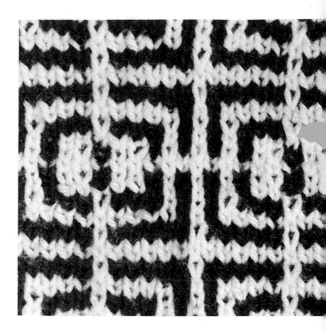

Row 1:   dark—sl 1 * (k1, p1, sl 1 yib, sl 1 yif) twice,
sl 1 yib, sl 1 yif, k1, p1, (sl 1 yib, sl 1 yif) twice,
(k1, p1, sl 1 yib, sl 1 yif) twice, rep from *, k
last. Turn.

Row 2:   dark (maintain)—p1, * (sl 1 yib, sl 1 yif, k1, p1)
twice, (sl 1 yib, sl 1 yif) twice, k1, p1, (sl 1 yib,
sl 1 yif) twice, k1, p1, sl 1 yib, sl 1 yif, k1, p1,
rep from *, sl last st. Slide.

Row 3:   light—sl 1, * (k1, p1, sl 1 yib, sl 1 yif) twice,
(k1, p1) 5 times, sl 1 yib, sl 1 yif, k1, p1, sl 1
yib, sl 1 yif, rep from *, k last st. Turn.

Row 4:   light (maintain)—p1, * (sl 1 yib, sl 1 yif, k1, p1)
twice, (k1, p1) 4 times, (sl 1 yib, sl 1 yif, k1,
p1) twice, rep from *. Slide.

Row 5:   dark—sl 1, * k1, p1, sl 1 yib, sl 1 yif, (k1, p1)
3 times, sl 1 yib, sl 1 yif, (k1, p1) 3 times, sl 1
yib, sl 1 yif, k1, p1, sl 1 yib, sl 1 yif, rep from
*, k last st. Turn.

Row 6:   dark (maintain)—p1, * (sl 1 yib, sl 1 yif, k1, p1)
twice, (k1, p1) twice, sl 1 yib, sl 1 yif, (k1, p1)
3 times, sl 1 yib, sl 1 yif, k1, p1, rep from *,
sl last st. Slide.

Row 7:   light—sl 1, * k1, p1, sl 1 yib, sl 1 yif, (k1, p1)
9 times, sl 1 yib, sl 1 yif, rep from *, k last
st. Turn.

Row 8:   light (maintain) p1, * sl 1 yib, sl 1 yif, (k1, p1)
9 times, sl 1 yib, sl 1 yif, k1, p1, rep from *,
sl last st. Slide.

Row 9:   dark—sl 1, * (k1, p1) 5 times, sl 1 yib, sl 1 yif,
rep from *, k last st. Turn.

Row 10: dark (maintain)—p1, * sl 1 yib, sl 1 yif, (k1, p1)
5 times, rep from *, sl last st. Slide.

Row 11: light—* p1, k1, rep from *. Turn.

Row 12: light (maintain)—rep row 11. Slide.

Rows 13 and 14: dark—rep rows 9 and 10.

Rows 15 and 16: light—rep rows 7 and 8.

Rows 17 and 18: dark—rep rows 5 and 6.

Rows 19 and 20: light—rep rows 3 and 4.

Rows 21 and 22: dark—rep rows 1 and 2.

Rows 23 and 24: light—rep rows 11 and 12.

rep Rows 1–24.

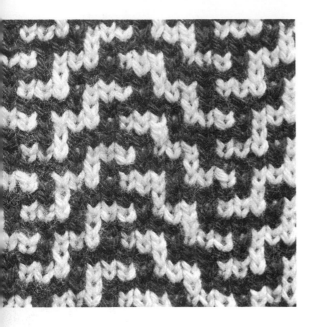

CRAZY MAZE

true reversible

At first glance, it is difficult to believe that this intricate-looking pattern is achieved by an eight-row repeat, especially considering that it takes two rows to make one line of design.

Use dpn or adapt for spn. Multiple of 24 sts plus 2. Cast on light, slide.

Row 1: dark—p1, * sl 1 yib, sl 1 yif, (k1, p1) 5 times, rep from *, k last st. Turn.

Row 2: dark (maintain)—p1, * (k1, p1) 5 times, sl 1 yib, sl 1 yif, rep from *, k last st. Slide.

Row 3: light—p1, * (k1, p1) twice, sl 1 yib, sl 1 yif, (k1, p1) 3 times, sl 1 yib, sl 1 yif, (k1, p1) 3 times, sl 1 yib, sl 1 yif, k1, p1, rep from *, k last st. Turn.

Row 4: light (maintain)—p1, * k1, p1, sl 1 yib, sl 1 yif, (k1, p1) 3 times, sl 1 yib, sl 1 yif, (k1, p1) 3 times, sl 1 yib, sl 1 yif, (k1, p1) twice, rep from *, k last st. Slide.

Row 5: dark—p1, * (k1, p1) twice, sl 1 yib, sl 1 yif, (k1, p1) 5 times, sl 1 yib, sl 1 yif, (k1, p1) 3 times, rep from *, k last st. Turn.

Row 6: dark (maintain)—p1, * (k1, p1) 3 times, sl 1 yib, sl 1 yif, (k1, p1) 5 times, sl 1 yib, sl 1 yif, (k1, p1) twice, rep from *, k last st. Slide.

Row 7: light—p1, * sl 1 yib, sl 1 yif, (k1, p1) 3 times, rep from *, k last st. Turn.

Row 8: light (maintain)—p1, * (k1, p1) 3 times, sl 1 yib, sl 1 yif, rep from *, k last st. Slide.
   rep Rows 1–8.

FEATHER STRIPES (*top, opposite*)

true reversible

The appearance of this pattern is more irregular than the actual design would indicate because the slip stitches pull others slightly out of shape. Remember to twist colors when both are at the same end, especially before starting row number 2.

Use of dpn required. Multiple of 8 sts. Cast on light, slide.

Row 1: dark—* (k1, p1) 3 times, sl 1 yib, sl 1 yif, rep from *. Turn.

Row 2: light—* (k1, p1) twice, sl 1 yib, sl 1 yif, k1, p1, rep from *. Slide.

Row 3: dark—* sl 1 yib, sl 1 yif, (k1, p1) 3 times, rep from *. Turn.

Row 4: light—* k1, p1, sl 1 yib, sl 1 yif, (k1, p1) twice, rep from *. Slide.

   rep Rows 1–4.

IRREGULAR TWEED (*lower right*)

true reversible

Despite the name this is actually a regular pattern but the design is unobtrusive. It creates fascinating visual effects from various angles. It may be difficult to figure out how to start any given row without referring to the directions but it is fortunately only a 4-row pattern.

Use of dpn required. Multiple of 12 sts. Cast on light, slide.

Row 1: dark—* k1, sl 1 yif, k1, p1, sl 1 yib, p1, rep from *. Turn.

Row 2: light—* k1, p1, sl 1 yib, p1, k1, sl 1 yif, (k1, p1) 3 times, rep from *. Slide.

Row 3: dark—* sl 1 yib, p1, k1, sl 1 yif, k1, p1, rep from *. Turn.

Row 4: light—* sl 1 yib, p1, k1, sl 1 yif, (k1, p1) 4 times, rep from *. Slide.

   rep Rows 1–4.

HERRINGBONE

true reversible

This large, bold pattern is good for articles when you want to "knock their eyes out." In related colors (tan and brown, for example) it is a little more subtle but not really quiet.

Use dpn or adapt for spn. Multiple of 20 sts plus 2. Cast on light, slide.

Row 1:   dark—p1, * sl 1 yib, sl 1 yif, (k1, p1) twice, sl 1 yib, sl 1 yif, k1, p1, rep from *, k last st of row. Turn.

Row 2:   dark (maintain)—p1, * k1, p1, sl 1 yib, sl 1 yif, (k1, p1) twice, sl 1 yib, sl 1 yif, rep from *, k last st. Slide.

Row 3:   light—p1, * (k1, p1, k1, p1, sl 1 yib, sl 1 yif) 3 times, k1, p1, rep from *, k last st. Turn.

Row 4:   light (maintain)—p1, * k1, p1, (sl 1 yib, sl 1 yif, k1, p1, k1, p1) 3 times, rep from *, k last st. Slide.

Row 5:   dark—p1, * (k1, p1) twice, sl 1 yib, sl 1 yif, (k1, p1) 3 times, sl 1 yib, sl 1 yif, (k1, p1) twice, sl 1 yib, sl 1 yif, rep from *, k last st. Turn.

Row 6:   dark (maintain)—p1, * sl 1 yib, sl 1 yif, (k1, p1) twice, sl 1 yib, sl 1 yif, (k1, p1) 3 times, sl 1 yib, sl 1 yif, (k1, p1) twice, rep from *, k last st. Slide.

Row 7:   with light rep row 2. Turn.

Row 8:   with light (maintain) rep row 1. Slide.

Row 9:   with dark rep row 4. Turn.

Row 10: with dark (maintain) rep row 3. Slide.

Row 11: with light rep row 6. Turn.

Row 12: with light (maintain) rep row 5. Slide. rep Rows 1–12.

BIAS STRIPES

mirror reversible

Try this in related tweedy colors. The pattern is the perfect example of a design which is easy to work but takes quite a number of rows. If you are trying to learn to work patterns without having to slavishly follow the directions, do the first two rows or more and thereafter keep several thoughts in mind: Remember you will alternate colors, one row dark, one row light and the color of the majority of the sts on the needle is the one you have just finished. Each row is k1, p1 except where the pattern is broken by a slip stitch (yib instead of a k st, or yif instead of a p st). Every two sts worked is followed by one st slipped, but you must know which two to work. Do those which are on the needle in the color you are using; work those which show 2 rows of the contrasting color; slip those which have just changed to the contrasting color. There are other ways of figuring this, but these suggestions may get you started.

Use of dpn required. Multiple of 6 sts. Cast on light, slide.

Row 1: dark—* k1, p1, sl 1 yib, p1, k1, sl 1 yif, rep from *. Turn.

Row 2: light—* k1, sl 1 yif, k1, p1, sl 1 yib, p1, rep from *. Slide.

Row 3: dark—rep row 1. Turn.

Row 4: with light rep row 1. Slide.

Row 5: with dark rep row 2. Turn.

Row 6: with light rep row 1. Slide.

Row 7: dark—* sl 1 yib, p1, k1, sl 1 yif, k1, p1, rep from *. Turn.

Row 8: light—rep row 2. Slide.

Row 9: dark—rep row 7. Turn.

Row 10: with light rep row 7. Slide.

Row 11: with dark rep row 2. Turn.

Row 12: with light rep row 7. Slide.
rep Rows 1–12.

DOUBLE DIAMONDS

true reversible

Double Diamonds makes a design every bit as lively as Herringbone from which it is derived. Every row of this pattern occurs in that one.

Use dpn or adapt for spn. Multiple of 20 sts plus 2. Cast on dark, slide.

Row 1: light—p1, * (k1, p1, k1, p1, sl 1 yib, sl 1 yif) 3 times, k1, p1, rep from *, k last st of row. Turn.

Row 2: light (maintain)—p1, * k1, p1, (sl 1 yib, sl 1 yif, k1, p1, k1, p1) 3 times, rep from *, k last st. Slide.

Row 3: dark—p1, * (k1, p1) twice, sl 1 yib, sl 1 yif, (k1, p1) 3 times, sl 1 yib, sl 1 yif, (k1, p1) twice, sl 1 yib, sl 1 yif, rep from *, k last st. Turn.

Row 4: dark (maintain)—p1, * sl 1 yib, sl 1 yif, (k1, p1) twice, sl 1 yib, sl 1 yif, (k1, p1) 3 times, sl 1 yib, sl 1 yif, (k1, p1) twice, rep from *, k last st. Slide.

Row 5: light—p1, * k1, p1, sl 1 yib, sl 1 yif, (k1, p1) twice, sl 1 yib, sl 1 yif, rep from *, k last st. Turn.

Row 6: light (maintain)—p1, * sl 1 yib, sl 1 yif, (k1, p1) twice, sl 1 yib, sl 1 yif, k1, p1, rep from *, k last st. Slide.

Row 7: with dark rep row 2. Turn.

Row 8: with dark (maintain) rep row 1. Slide.

Row 9: with light rep row 4. Turn.

Row 10: with light (maintain) rep row 3. Slide.

Row 11: with dark rep row 6. Turn.

Row 12: with dark (maintain) rep row 5. Slide.

Rows 13–18: rep rows 1–6.

Row 19: with dark rep row 2. Turn.

Row 20: with dark (maintain) rep row 1. Slide.

Row 21: with light rep row 4. Turn.

Row 22: with light (maintain) rep row 3. Slide.

Row 23: with dark rep row 2. Turn.

Row 24: with dark (maintain) rep row 1. Slide.

Rows 25 and 26: rep rows 5 and 6.

Rows 27 and 28: rep rows 3 and 4.

Rows 29 and 30: rep rows 1 and 2.
Row 31: with dark rep row 6. Turn.
Row 32: with dark (maintain) rep row 5. Slide.
Row 33: with light rep row 4. Turn.
Row 34: with light (maintain) rep row 3. Slide.
Row 35: with dark rep row 2. Turn.
Row 36: with dark (maintain) rep row 1. Slide.
Row 37: with light rep row 5. Turn.
Row 38: with light (maintain) rep row 6. Slide.
Rows 39 and 40: rep rows 3 and 4.
       rep Rows 1–40.

SEED DESIGN

opposite reversible
The effect of this is very much like Tweed and Solid except that there is no solid color side. Smallish needles are recommended.

Use of dpn required. Multiple of 4 sts. Cast on dark, slide.
Row 1: light—* k1, p1, k1, sl 1 yif, rep from *. Turn.
Row 2: dark—k1, * sl 1 yif, k1, p1, k1, rep from * but end k1, p1. Slide.
Row 3: light—k1, p1, * sl 1 yib, p1, k1, p1, rep from * but end sl 1 yib, p1. Turn.
Row 4: dark—* sl 1 yib, p1, k1, p1, rep from *. Slide.
      rep Rows 1–4.

 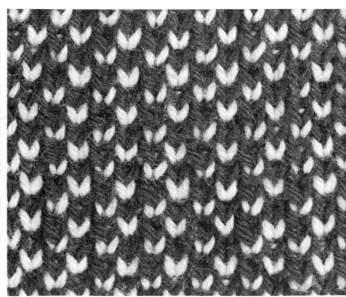

DOTTED DIAMONDS

true reversible

Use of dpn required. Multiple of 20 sts plus 2. Cast on dark, slide.

Row 1: light—p1, * sl 1 yib, sl 1 yif, (k1, p1) twice, sl 1 yib, sl 1 yif, (k1, p1) twice, sl 1 yib, sl 1 yif, (k1, p1) 3 times, rep from *, k last st. Turn.

Row 2: dark—p1, * k1, p1, sl 1 yib, sl 1 yif, (k1, p1) twice, sl 1 yib, sl 1 yif, (k1, p1) 3 times, sl 1 yib, sl 1 yif, k1, p1, rep from *, k last st. Slide.

Row 3: light—p1, * sl 1 yib, sl 1 yif, k1, p1, sl 1 yib, sl 1 yif, (k1, p1) twice, rep from *, k last st. Turn.

Row 4: with dark rep row 1. Slide.

Row 5: light—p1, * k1, p1, sl 1 yib, sl 1 yif, (k1, p1) 3 times, sl 1 yib, sl 1 yif, (k1, p1) twice, sl 1 yib, sl 1 yif, k1, p1, rep from *, k last st. Turn.

Row 6: with dark rep row 3. Slide.

Row 7: light—p1, * (k1, p1) 3 times, sl 1 yib, sl 1 yif, (k1, p1) twice, sl 1 yib, sl 1 yif, (k1, p1) twice, sl 1 yib, sl 1 yif, rep from *, k last st. Turn.

Row 8: dark—p1, * (k1, p1) twice, sl 1 yib, sl 1 yif, k1, p1, sl 1 yib, sl 1 yif, rep from *, k last st. Slide.

Row 9: light—rep row 5. Turn.

Row 10: with dark rep row 7. Slide.

Row 11: light—rep row 3. Turn.

Row 12: with dark rep row 5. Slide.

Row 13: light—rep row 1. Turn.

Row 14: with dark rep row 3. Slide.

Row 15: with light rep row 2. Turn.

Row 16: dark—rep row 8. Slide.

rep Rows 1–16.

LONG FORM REVERSIBLE GEOMETRICS

In the introduction to short-form stitches it was pointed out that two rows of knitting make a band of pattern by slipping stitches which must retain the previous color. In long form, for each two rows you see four rows are worked, two in dark and two in light. This opens new pattern possibilities which are discussed in Chapter Seven.

As a result of the way they are made, long forms take longer to do, use more yarn, but present a beautifully smooth stockinette stitch appearance.

Generally, the two colors of yarn don't have to be twisted at the beginnings of rows with these patterns.

BASKETWEAVE

opposite reversible
After working one set of directions, the knitter who understands reversible geometrics shouldn't have much trouble following this one. It is slightly easier in that way than the variation which follows.

Use of dpn required. Multiple of 20 sts. Cast on light, slide.

Row 1: dark—* (k1, sl 1 yif) twice, (sl 1 yib, p1, k1, sl 1 yif) twice, (k1, sl 1 yif) 4 times, rep from *. Turn.

Row 2: light—* (k1, sl 1 yif) 5 times, (sl 1 yib, p1, k1, sl 1 yif) twice, k1, sl 1 yif, rep from *. Slide.

Row 3: dark (maintain)—* (sl 1 yib, p1) 5 times, (k1, sl 1 yif, sl 1 yib, p1) twice, sl 1 yib, p1, rep from *. Turn.

Row 4: light (maintain)—* (sl 1 yib, p1) twice, (k1, sl 1 yif, sl 1 yib, p1) twice, (sl 1 yib, p1) 4 times, rep from *. Slide.

Row 5: dark—* (k1, sl 1 yif) 7 times, sl 1 yib, p1, k1, sl 1 yif, sl 1 yib, p1, rep from *. Turn.

Row 6: light—* (sl 1 yib, p1, k1, sl 1 yif) twice, (k1, sl 1 yif) 6 times, rep from *. Slide.

Row 7: dark (maintain)—* (k1, sl 1 yif, sl 1 yib, p1) twice, (sl 1 yib, p1) 6 times, rep from *. Turn.

Row 8: light (maintain)—* (sl 1 yib, p1) 7 times, k1, sl 1 yif, sl 1 yib, p1, k1, sl 1 yif, rep from *. Slide.

Row 9: dark—* k1, sl 1 yif, (sl 1 yib, p1) 5 times, (k1, sl 1 yif, sl 1 yib, p1) twice, rep from *. Turn.

Row 10: light—* (sl 1 yib, p1, k1, sl 1 yif) twice, (sl 1 yib, p1) 5 times, k1, sl 1 yif, rep from *. Slide.

Row 11: dark (maintain)—* (k1, sl 1 yif, sl 1 yib, p1) twice, (k1, sl 1 yif) 5 times, sl 1 yib, p1, rep from *. Turn.

Row 12: light (maintain)—* sl 1 yib, p1, (k1, sl 1 yif) 5 times, (sl 1 yib, p1, k1, sl 1 yif) twice, rep from *. Slide.

Rows 13–16: rep rows 5–8.

Rows 17–20: rep rows 9–12.

Rows 21–24: rep rows 5–8.

Rows 25–28: rep rows 1–4.

Row 29: dark—* (sl 1 yib, p1, k1, sl 1 yif) 3 times, (sl 1 yib, p1) 4 times, rep from *. Turn.

Row 30: light—* (sl 1 yib, p1) 4 times, (k1, sl 1 yif, sl 1 yib, p1) 3 times, rep from *. Slide.

Row 31: dark (maintain)—* (k1, sl 1 yif) 4 times, (sl 1 yib, p1, k1, sl 1 yif) 3 times, rep from *. Turn.

Row 32: light (maintain)—* (k1, sl 1 yif, sl 1 yib, p1) 3 times, (k1, sl 1 yif) 4 times, rep from *. Slide.

Rows 33–36: rep rows 1–4.

Rows 37–40: rep rows 29–32.

rep Rows 1–40.

Variation

opposite reversible

This pattern is based on Basketweave but note that only those rows marked "maintain" here are meant as such. Those marked "maintain" in the original may not be in this case. This form is a little more difficult because some bands of color are made of single rows and some are made of double rows.

Use of dpn required. Multiple of 20 sts. Cast on light, slide.

Rows 1 and 2: work rows 1 and 2 of Basketweave.

Rows 3 and 4: work rows 7 and 8 of Basketweave.

Rows 5–8: work rows 9–12 of Basketweave.

Rows 9 and 10: work rows 5 and 6 of Basketweave.

Rows 11 and 12: work rows 11 and 12 of Basketweave.

Rows 13 and 14: (both rows maintain)—work rows 9 and 10 of Basketweave.

Rows 15 and 16: work rows 7 and 8 of Basketweave.

Rows 17 and 18: work rows 1 and 2 of Basketweave.

Rows 19 and 20: work rows 31 and 32 of Basketweave.

Rows 21 and 22: (both rows maintain)—work rows 29 and 30 of Basketweave.

Rows 23 and 24: work rows 3 and 4 of Basketweave.

Rows 25–28: work rows 29–32 of Basketweave.

rep Rows 1–28.

PHILENA'S BORDER

opposite and mirror reversible

This interesting border design was originally a nineteenth century embroidery stamp. The intricate effect is achieved in a repeat of only six stitches. Another pattern, Chinese Puzzle (page 72), is really an overall design based on this border. To work this comparably (but as an opposite reversible which Chinese Puzzle is not), after the 36 rows are finished begin again at row 5 and rep 5–36 as many times as desired.

Use of dpn required. Multiple of 12 sts. Cast on light, slide.

Preparatory row A: dark—* k1, sl 1 yif, rep from *. Turn.

Preparatory row B: with light rep row A. Slide.

Preparatory row C: dark—* sl 1 yib, p1, rep from *. Turn.

Preparatory row D: with light rep row C. Slide.
    rep rows A–D as many times as desired before pattern.

Row 1: dark—* (sl 1 yib, p1) twice, k1, sl 1 yif, (sl 1 yib, p1) 3 times, rep from *. Turn.

Row 2: light—* (sl 1 yib, p1) 3 times, k1, sl 1 yif, (sl 1 yib, p1) twice, rep from *. Slide.

Row 3: dark (maintain)—* (k1, sl 1 yif) 3 times, sl 1 yib, p1, (k1, sl 1 yif) twice, rep from *. Turn.

Row 4: light (maintain)—* (k1, sl 1 yif) twice, sl 1 yib, p1, (k1, sl 1 yif) 3 times, rep from *. Slide.

Row 5: dark—* (k1, sl 1 yif, sl 1 yib, p1) twice, (k1, sl 1 yif) twice, rep from *. Turn.

Row 6: light—* (k1, sl 1 yif) twice, (sl 1 yib, p1, k1, sl 1 yif) twice, rep from *. Slide.

Row 7: dark (maintain)—* (sl 1 yib, p1) twice, (k1, sl 1 yif, sl 1 yib, p1) twice, rep from *. Turn.

Row 8: light (maintain)—* (sl 1 yib, p1, k1, sl 1 yif) twice, (sl 1 yib, p1) twice, rep from *. Slide.

Row 9: dark—* k1, sl 1 yif, (sl 1 yib, p1) 5 times, rep from *. Turn.

Row 10: light—* (sl 1 yib, p1) 5 times, k1, sl 1 yif, rep from *. Slide.

Row 11: dark (maintain)—* (k1, sl 1 yif) 5 times, sl 1 yif, p1, rep from *. Turn.

Row 12: light (maintain)—* sl 1 yib, p1, (k1, sl 1 yif) 5 times, rep from *. Slide.

Row 13: dark—* (k1, sl 1 yif) twice, (k1, sl 1 yif, sl 1 yib, p1) twice, rep from *. Turn.

Row 14: light—* (sl 1 yib, p1, k1, sl 1 yif) twice, (k1, sl 1 yif) twice, rep from *. Slide.

Row 15: dark (maintain)—* (k1, sl 1 yif, sl 1 yib, p1) twice, (sl 1 yib, p1) twice, rep from *. Turn.

Row 16: light (maintain)—* (sl 1 yib, p1) twice, (sl 1 yib, p1, k1, sl 1 yif) twice, rep from *. Slide.

Row 17: dark—* k1, sl 1 yif, (sl 1 yib, p1) 3 times, k1, sl 1 yif, sl 1 yib, p1, rep from *. Turn.

Row 18: light—* sl 1 yib, p1, k1, sl 1 yif (sl 1 yib, p1) 3 times, k1, sl 1 yif, rep from *. Slide.

Row 19: dark (maintain)—* k1, sl 1 yif, sl 1 yib, p1, (k1, sl 1 yif) 3 times, sl 1 yib, p1, rep from *. Turn.

Row 20: light (maintain)—* sl 1 yib, p1, (k1, sl 1 yif) 3 times, sl 1 yib, p1, k1, sl 1 yif, rep from *. Slide.

Row 21: dark—* k1, sl 1 yif, sl 1 yib, p1 (k1, sl 1 yif) 3 times, sl 1 yib, p1, rep from *. Turn.

Row 22: light—* sl 1 yib, p1, (k1, sl 1 yif) 3 times, sl 1 yib, p1, k1, sl 1 yif, rep from *. Slide.

Row 23: dark (maintain)—* k1, sl 1 yif, (sl 1 yib, p1) 3 times, k1, sl 1 yif, sl 1 yib, p1, rep from *. Turn.

Row 24: light (maintain)—* sl 1 yib, p1, k1, sl 1 yif, (sl 1 yib, p1) 3 times, k1, sl 1 yif, rep from *. Slide.

Row 25: dark—* (sl 1 yib, p1) 4 times, k1, sl 1 yif, sl 1 yib, p1, rep from *. Turn.

Row 26: light—* sl 1 yib, p1, k1, sl 1 yif, (sl 1 yib, p1) 4 times, rep from *. Slide.

Row 27: dark (maintain)—* k1, sl 1 yif, sl 1 yib, p1 (k1, sl 1 yif) 4 times, rep from *. Turn.

Row 28: light (maintain)—* (k1, sl 1 yif) 4 times, sl 1 yib, p1, k1, sl 1 yif, rep from *. Slide.

Row 29: dark—* (k1, sl 1 yif, sl 1 yib, p1) twice, (k1, sl 1 yif) twice, rep from *. Turn.

Row 30: light—* (k1, sl 1 yif) twice, (sl 1 yib, p1, k1, sl 1 yif) twice, rep from *. Slide.

Row 31: dark (maintain)—* (sl 1 yib, p1) twice, (k1, sl 1 yif, sl 1 yib, p1) twice, rep from *. Turn.

Row 32: light (maintain)—* (sl 1 yib, p1, k1, sl 1 yif) twice, (sl 1 yib, p1) twice, rep from *. Slide.

Row 33: dark—* (sl 1 yib, p1) twice, k1, sl 1 yif, (sl 1 yib, p1) 3 times, rep from *. Turn.

Row 34: light—* (sl 1 yib, p1) 3 times, k1, sl 1 yif, (sl 1 yib, p1) twice, rep from *. Slide.

Row 35: dark (maintain)—* (k1, sl 1 yif) 3 times, sl 1 yib, p1, (k1, sl 1 yif) twice, rep from *. Turn.

Row 36: light (maintain)—* (k1, sl 1 yif) twice, sl 1 yib, p1, (k1, sl 1 yif) 3 times, rep from *. Slide.

Continue solid color after border by repeating preparatory rows A–D as many times as desired. After a D row, finish as follows:

Finishing row I: with dark, rep row A. Turn.

Finishing row II: dark—* k1, sl 1 yif, rep from *. Turn.

Finishing row III: dark—rep row I or A. Turn.

Bind off: k1, sl 1 yif, bind off 1, * k1, bind off 1, sl 1 yif, bind off 1, rep from *.

If desired, finishing rows and bind off may be done in light color instead.

HEARTS PATTERN

opposite reversible

Although this is a fairly complicated pattern to work since it is difficult to figure it out without using directions, at least there is the consolation that half the rows are "maintain" ones.

Use of dpn required. Multiple of 16 sts plus 2. Cast on light, slide.

Row 1: dark—sl 1, * sl 1 yib, p1, k1, sl 1 yif, rep from *, sl last st. Turn.

Row 2: light—p1, * k1, sl 1 yif, sl 1 yib, p1, rep from *, sl last st. Slide.

Row 3: dark (maintain)—rep row 1. Turn.

Row 4: light (maintain)—rep row 2. Slide.

Row 5: dark—p1, * (sl 1 yib, p1) twice, (k1, sl 1 yif, sl 1 yib, p1) twice, (sl 1 yib, p1) twice, rep from *, sl last st. Turn.

Row 6: light—p1, * (sl 1 yib, p1) 3 times, (k1, sl 1 yif, sl 1 yib, p1) twice, sl 1 yib, p1, rep from *, sl last st. Slide.

Row 7: dark (maintain)—sl 1, * (k1, sl 1 yif) 3 times, (sl 1 yib, p1, k1, sl 1 yif) twice, k1, sl 1 yif, rep from *, k last st. Turn.

Row 8: light (maintain—sl 1, * (k1, sl 1 yif) twice, (sl 1 yib, p1, k1, sl 1 yif) twice, (k1, sl 1 yif) twice, rep from *, k last st. Slide.

Row 9: dark—p1, * sl 1 yib, p1, k1, sl 1 yif, (sl 1 yib, p1) 3 times, k1, sl 1 yif, (sl 1 yib, p1) twice, rep from *, sl last st. Turn.

Row 10: light—p1, * (sl 1 yib, p1) twice, k1, sl 1 yif, (sl 1 yib, p1) 3 times, k1, sl 1 yif, sl 1 yib, p1, rep from *, sl last st. Slide.

Row 11: dark (maintain)—sl 1, * (k1, sl 1 yif) twice, sl 1 yib, p1, (k1, sl 1 yif) 3 times, sl 1 yib, p1, k1, sl 1 yif, rep from *, k last st. Turn.

Row 12: light (maintain)—sl 1, * k1, sl 1 yif, sl 1 yib, p1, (k1, sl 1 yif) 3 times, sl 1 yib, p1, (k1, sl 1 yif) twice, rep from *, k last st. Slide.

Row 13: dark—p1, * k1, sl 1 yif, (sl 1 yib, p1) 5 times, k1, sl 1 yif, sl 1 yib, p1, rep from *, k last st. Turn.

Row 14: light—sl * sl 1 yib, p1, k1, sl yif, (sl 1 yib, p1) 5 times, k1, sl 1 yif, rep from *, sl last st. Slide.

Row 15: dark (maintain)—p1, * k1, sl 1 yif, sl l yib, p1, (k1, sl 1 yif) 5 times, sl 1 yib, p1, rep from *, k last st. Turn.

Row 16: light (maintain)—sl 1, * sl 1 yib, p1, (k1, sl 1 yif) 5 times, sl 1 yib, p1, k1, sl 1 yif, rep from *, sl last st. Slide.

rep Rows 1–16.

HOUNDSTOOTH

mirror reversible

At first glance, this pattern and the following variation are identical but there are important differences. There are more rows to the inch in the variation, although stitch gauges are the same. The variation is an opposite reversible with light-colored figures backing up dark-colored ones, although this is only apparent on careful scrutiny. The variation makes a smoother fabric because there are never more than two slip stitches in a row. Why, then, are both sets of directions given? The variation is harder to follow. The knitter must decide which form is more suitable.

Use of dpn required. Multiple of 8 sts plus 2. Cast on dark, *turn* and start at the same end.

Row 1: light—p1, * (k1, p1) twice, sl 1 yib, sl 1 yif, k1, p1, rep from *, k last st of row. Slide.

Row 2: dark—p1, * (sl 1 yib, sl 1 yif) twice, k1, p1, sl 1 yib, sl 1 yif, rep from *, k last st. Turn.

Row 3: light (maintain)—p1, * k1, p1, sl 1 yib, sl 1 yif, (k1, p1) twice, rep from *, k last st. Slide.

Row 4: dark (maintain)—p1, * sl 1 yib, sl 1 yif, k1, p1, (sl 1 yib, sl 1 yif) twice, rep from *, k last st. Turn.

Row 5: light—p1, * (sl 1 yib, sl 1 yif) 3 times, k1, p1, rep from *, k last st. Slide.

Row 6: dark—p1, * (k1, p1) 3 times, sl 1 yib, sl 1 yif, rep from *, k last st. Turn.

Row 7: light (maintain)—p1, * k1, p1, (sl 1 yib, sl 1 yif) 3 times, rep from *, k last st. Slide.

Row 8: dark (maintain)—p1, * sl 1 yib, sl 1 yif, (k1, p1) 3 times, rep from *, k last st. Turn.

Row 9: light—rep row 7. Slide.

Row 10: dark—rep row 8. Turn.

Row 11: light (maintain)—rep row 5. Slide.

Row 12: dark (maintain)—rep row 6. Turn.

Row 13: light—rep row 3. Slide.

Row 14: dark—rep row 4. Turn.

Row 15: light (maintain)—rep row 1. Slide.

Row 16: dark (maintain)—rep row 2. Turn.
rep Rows 1–16.

Variation

opposite and mirror reversible
See note with Houndstooth pattern.

Use of dpn required. Multiple of 8 sts. Cast on dark, *turn* and start at same end.

Row 1: light—* (k1, sl 1 yif) twice, sl 1 yib, p1, k1, sl 1 yif, rep from *. Slide.

Row 2: dark—* (sl 1 yib, p1) twice, k1, sl 1 yif, sl 1 yib, p1, rep from *. Turn.

Row 3: light (maintain)—* sl 1 yib, p1, k1, sl 1 yif, (sl 1 yib, p1) twice, rep from *. Slide.

Row 4: dark (maintain)—* k1, sl 1 yif, sl 1 yib, p1, (k1, sl 1 yif) twice, rep from *. Turn.

Row 5: light—* (sl 1 yib, p1) 3 times, k1, sl 1 yif, rep from *. Slide.

Row 6: dark—* (k1, sl 1 yif) 3 times, sl 1 yib, p1, rep from *. Turn.

Row 7: light (maintain)—* sl 1 yib, p1, (k1, sl 1 yif) 3 times, rep from *. Slide.

Row 8: dark (maintain)—* k1, sl 1 yif, (sl 1 yib, p1) 3 times, rep from *. Turn.

Row 9: light—* k1, sl 1 yif, (sl 1 yib, p1) 3 times, rep from *. Slide.

Row 10: dark—* sl 1 yib, p1, (k1, sl 1 yif) 3 times, rep from *. Turn.

Row 11: light (maintain)—* (k1, sl 1 yif) 3 times, sl 1 yib, p1, rep from *. Slide.

Row 12: dark (maintain)—* (sl 1 yib, p1) 3 times, k1, sl 1 yif, rep from *. Turn.

Row 13: light—* k1, sl 1 yif, sl 1 yib, p1, (k1, sl 1 yif) twice, rep from *. Slide.

Row 14: dark—* sl 1 yib, p1, k1, sl 1 yif, (sl 1 yib, p1) twice, rep from *. Turn.

Row 15: light (maintain)—* (sl 1 yib, p1) twice, k1, sl 1 yif, sl 1 yib, p1, rep from *. Slide.

Row 16: dark (maintain)—* (k1, sl 1 yif) twice, sl 1 yib, p1, k1, sl 1 yif, rep from *. Turn.
rep Rows 1–16.

HALF-SQUARE PINWHEELS

true reversible

Once you understand these stitches well enough, you could enlarge this design and make a knitted quilt which looks like an old-fashioned patchwork one. Interestingly, the design is worked like an opposite reversible, which results in a true reversible.

Use of dpn required. Multiple of 16 sts plus 2. Cast on light, slide.

Row 1: dark—p1 * k1, sl 1 yif, (sl 1 yib, p1) 3 times, (k1, sl 1 yif) 3 times, sl 1 yib, p1, rep from *, k last st. Turn.

Row 2: light—p1, * sl 1 yib, p1, (k1, sl 1 yif) 3 times, (sl 1 yib, p1) 3 times, k1, sl 1 yif, rep from *, k last st. Slide.

Row 3: dark (maintain)—rep row 1. Turn.

Row 4: light (maintain)—rep row 2. Slide.

Row 5: dark—p1, * (k1, sl 1 yif) twice, (sl 1 yib, p1) twice, rep from *, k last st. Turn.

Row 6: light—p1, * (sl 1 yib, p1) twice, (k1, sl 1 yif) twice, rep from *, k last st. Slide.

Row 7: dark (maintain)—rep row 5. Turn.

Row 8: light (maintain)—rep row 6. Slide.

Row 9: dark—p1, * (k1, sl 1 yif) 3 times, sl 1 yib, p1, k1, sl 1 yif, (sl 1 yib, p1) 3 times, rep from *, k last st. Turn.

Row 10: light—p1, * (sl 1 yib, p1) 3 times, k1, sl 1 yif, sl 1 yib, p1, (k1, sl 1 yif) 3 times, rep from *, k last st. Slide.

Row 11: dark (maintain)—rep row 9. Turn.

Row 12: light (maintain)—rep row 10. Slide.

Row 13: with dark rep row 10. Turn.

Row 14: with light rep row 9. Slide.

Row 15: with dark (maintain) rep row 10. Turn.

Row 16: with light (maintain) rep row 9. Slide.

Row 17: with dark rep row 6. Turn.

Row 18: with light rep row 5. Slide.

Row 19: with dark (maintain) rep row 6. Turn.

Row 20: with light (maintain) rep row 5. Slide.

Row 21: with dark rep row 2. Turn.

Row 22: with light rep row 1. Slide.

Row 23: with dark rep row 2. Turn.

Row 24: with light rep row 1. Slide.

rep Rows 1–24.

VARIED HERRINGBONE

true reversible

Rows 21 and 22 of this pattern are optional. In the illustration, the lower half was done with these rows included. The upper part of the sample omits them.

Use of dpn required. Multiple of 8 sts plus 2. Cast on light, slide.

Row 1: dark—p1, * k1, p1, (sl 1 yib, sl 1 yif) 3 times, rep from *, k last st. Turn.

Row 2: light—p1, * (k1, p1) 3 times, sl 1 yib, sl 1 yif, rep from *, k last st. Slide.

Row 3: dark (maintain)—p1, * (sl 1 yib, sl 1 yif) 3 times, k1, p1, rep from *, k last st. Turn.

Row 4: light (maintain)—p1, * sl 1 yib, sl 1 yif, (k1, p1) 3 times, rep from *, k last st. Slide.

Row 5: dark—p1, * sl 1 yib, sl 1 yif, k1, p1, rep from *, k last st. Turn.

Row 6: with light rep row 5. Slide.

Row 7: dark (maintain)—p1, * k1, p1, sl 1 yib, sl 1 yif, rep from *, k last st. Turn.

Row 8: with light (maintain)—rep row 7. Slide.

Row 9: dark—p1, * (sl 1 yib, sl 1 yif) twice, k1, p1, sl 1 yib, sl 1 yif, rep from *, k last st. Turn.

Row 10: light—p1, * k1, p1, sl 1 yib, sl 1 yif, (k1, p1) twice, rep from *, k last st. Slide.

Row 11: dark (maintain)—p1, * sl 1 yib, sl 1 yif, k1, p1, (sl 1 yib, sl 1 yif) twice, rep from *, k last st. Turn.

Row 12: light (maintain)—p1, * (k1, p1) twice, sl 1 yib, sl 1 yif, k1, p1, rep from *, k last st. Slide.

Rows 13–16: rep rows 1–4.

Row 17: with dark rep row 12. Turn.

Row 18: with light (maintain) rep row 11. Slide.

Row 19: with dark (maintain) rep row 10. Turn.

Row 20: with light (maintain) rep row 9. Slide.

Optional

Row 21: dark—* p1, k1, rep from *. Turn.

Row 22: dark—rep row 21. Slide.

Row 23: with dark rep row 4. Turn.

Row 24: with light rep row 3. Slide.

Row 25: with dark (maintain) rep row 2. Turn.

Row 26: with light (maintain) rep row 1. Slide.

Rows 27–30: rep rows 9–12.

rep these 28 or 30 rows.

COMBINATION FORM REVERSIBLE GEOMETRICS

The title tells the story. In these patterns short form is used whenever possible. In some places the pattern requires long form. Don't worry about it. Simply follow the directions.

BRICKS

opposite reversible

Use of dpn required. Multiple of 12 sts plus 2. Cast on light, slide.

Row 1: dark—p1, * (k1, sl 1 yif) 4 times, sl 1 yib, p1, k1, sl 1 yif, rep from *, k last st. Turn.

Row 2: light—p1, * k1, sl 1 yif, sl 1 yib, p1, (k1, sl 1 yif) 4 times, rep from *, k last st. Slide.

Row 3: dark (maintain)—p1, * sl 1 yib, p1, k1, sl 1 yif, (sl 1 yib, p1) 4 times, rep from *, k last st. Turn.

Row 4: light (maintain)—p1, * (sl 1 yib, p1) 4 times, k1, sl 1 yif, sl 1 yib, p1, rep from *, k last st. Slide.

Row 5: dark—p1, * sl 1 yib, p1, rep from *, k last st. Turn.

Row 6: with light rep row 5. Slide.

Row 7: dark—p1, * (sl 1 yib, p1) 4 times, k1, sl 1 yif, sl 1 yib, p1, rep from *, k last st. Turn.

Row 8: light—p1, * sl 1 yib, p1, k1, sl 1 yif, (sl 1 yib, p1) 4 times, rep from *, k last st. Slide.

Row 9: dark (maintain)—p1, * k1, sl 1 yif, sl 1 yib, p1, (k1, sl 1 yif) 4 times, rep from *, k last st. Turn.

Row 10: light (maintain)—p1, * (k1, sl 1 yif) 4 times, sl 1 yib, p1, k1, sl 1 yif, rep from *, k last st. Slide.

Row 11: dark—p1, k1, * sl 1 yif, k1, rep from *. Turn.

Row 12: with light, rep row 11. Slide.

rep Rows 1–12.

HOURGLASS AND DIAMOND

true reversible

Some patterns reverse colors from side to side. This interesting design reverses from band to band. First the diamonds are dark and the hourglasses are light. Above that the diamonds are light and the hourglasses dark. Watch the colors of the rows.

Use of dpn required. Multiple of 12 sts plus 2. Cast on dark, slide.

Row 1: light—p1, * (k1, p1) twice, sl 1 yib, sl 1 yif, (k1, p1) 3 times, rep from *, k last st of row. Turn.

Row 2: light (maintain)—p1, * (k1, p1) 3 times, sl 1 yib, sl 1 yif, (k1, p1) twice, rep from *, k last st. Slide.

Row 3: dark—p1, * (sl 1 yib, sl 1 yif) twice, (k1, p1) 3 times, sl 1 yib, sl 1 yif, rep from *, k last st. Turn.

Row 4: light (maintain)—p1, * k1, p1, (sl 1 yib, sl 1 yif) 3 times, (k1, p1) twice, rep from *, k last st. Slide.

Row 5: dark—p1, * (k1, p1) 5 times, sl 1 yib, sl 1 yif, rep from *, k last st. Turn.

Row 6: dark (maintain)—p1, * sl 1 yib, sl 1 yif, (k1, p1) 5 times, rep from *, k last st. Slide.

Row 7: light—p1, * (k1, p1) twice, (sl 1 yib, sl 1 yif) 3 times, k1, p1, rep from *, k last st. Turn.

Row 8: dark (maintain)—p1, * sl 1 yib, sl 1 yif, (k1, p1) 3 times, (sl 1 yib, sl 1 yif) twice, rep from *, k last st. Slide.

Row 9: light—rep row 1. Turn.

Row 10: light—* p1, k1, rep from *. Slide.

Row 11: with dark rep row 2. Turn.

Row 12: with dark (maintain) rep row 1. Slide.

Row 13: with light rep row 8. Turn.

Row 14: with dark (maintain) rep row 7. Slide.

Row 15: with light rep row 6. Turn.

Row 16: with light (maintain) rep row 5. Slide.

Row 17: with dark rep row 4. Turn.

Row 18: with light (maintain) rep row 3. Slide.

Row 19: with dark rep row 2. Turn.

Row 20: with dark rep row 10. Slide.

rep Rows 1–20.

FLEUR DE LYS

true reversible

Watch this pattern. It is a combination form. Although the rows are worked alternately in dark and light, that does not mean the pattern changes every other row. The use of "maintain" rows will give you the best clue. Row 1 is filled in and reinforced by being repeated exactly with the light color but row 3 is solid dark and no light is worked. Row 4 in light and 5 in dark are the same pattern. Six is mostly light with dark remaining only in an occasional slip stitch. Seven and 8 are essentially the same as 4 and 5 but worked from the opposite direction. Row 9 is again all dark. Ten and 11 form a pair. Twelve is worked singly. If all this confuses you, go ahead and try out the pattern anyway. Most knitters will have noticed that a miniature cross will look like a fleur de lys if turned upside down so this pattern is named with the idea that it will be used inverted. If you prefer to have the other side show dark fleur de lys on a light background, use the following variation.

Use of dpn required. Multiple of 8 sts plus 2. Cast on light, slide.

Row 1:   dark—p1, * sl 1 yib, sl 1 yif, (k1, p1) 3 times, rep from *, k last st. Turn.

Row 2:   light (maintain)—p1, * (sl 1 yib, sl 1 yif) 3 times, k1, p1, rep from *, k last st. Slide.

Row 3:   dark—* p1, k1, rep from *. Turn.

Row 4:   light—p1, * (sl 1 yib, sl 1 yif) twice, k1, p1, sl 1 yib, sl 1 yif, rep from *, k last st. Slide.

Row 5:   dark (maintain)—p1, * (k1, p1) twice, sl 1 yib, sl 1 yif, k1, p1, rep from *, k last st. Turn.

Row 6:   light—p1, * (k1, p1) 3 times, sl 1 yib, sl 1 yif, rep from *, k last st. Slide.

Row 7:   dark—p1, * k1, p1, sl 1 yib, sl 1 yif, (k1, p1) twice, rep from *, k last st. Turn.

Row 8:   light (maintain)—p1, * (sl 1 yib, sl 1 yif) twice, k1, p1, sl 1 yib, sl 1 yif, rep from *, k last st. Slide.

Row 9:   dark—rep row 3. Turn.

Row 10: light—rep row 2. Slide.

Row 11: with dark (maintain) rep row 6. Turn.

Row 12: with light rep row 5. Slide.
          rep Rows 1–12.

Variation

opposite reversible

This variation is worked in a different manner from the original design. Each row of the design is actually made by two rows of knitting, one to make the dark part, one for the light. This is really the "spot form" by which most motifs are worked. It is included here because it is a variation of another pattern and it seems more appropriate to have them together.

Use of dpn required. Multiple of 8 sts. Cast on light, slide.

Row 1: dark—* sl 1 yib, p1 (k1, sl 1 yif) 3 times, rep from *. Turn.

Row 2: light—* (k1, sl 1 yif) 3 times, sl 1 yib, p1, rep from *. Slide.

Row 3: dark—* sl 1 yib, p1, rep from *. Turn.

Row 4: with light rep row 3. Slide.

Row 5: dark—* (k1, sl 1 yif) twice, sl 1 yib, p1, k1, sl 1 yif, rep from *. Turn.

Row 6: light—*k1, sl 1 yif, sl 1 yib, p1 (k1, sl 1 yif) twice, rep from *. Slide.

Row 7: with dark rep row 2. Turn.

Row 8: with light rep row 1. Slide.

Row 9: dark—rep row 5. Turn.

Row 10: light—rep row 6. Slide.

Row 11: dark—rep row 3. Turn.

Row 12: with light rep row 3. Slide.

Row 13: dark—rep row 1. Turn.

Row 14: light—rep row 2. Slide.

Row 15: with dark rep row 6. Turn.

Row 16: with light rep row 5. Slide.
rep Rows 1–16.

CORNERED CROSSES

true reversible

Use of dpn required. Multiple of 16 sts plus 2. Cast on light, slide.

Row 1: dark—sl 1 * k1, p1, (sl 1 yib, sl 1 yif) 5 times, k1, p1, sl 1 yib, sl 1 yif, rep from *, k last st. Turn.

Row 2: light—sl 1 * k1, p1, sl 1 yib, sl 1 yif, (k1, p1) 5 times, sl 1 yib, sl 1 yif, rep from *, k last st. Slide.

Row 3: dark (maintain)—p1, * sl 1 yib, sl 1 yif, k1, p1, (sl 1 yib, sl 1 yif) 5 times, k1, p1, rep from *, sl last st. Turn.

Row 4: light (maintain)—p1, * sl 1 yib, sl 1 yif, (k1, p1) 5 times, sl 1 yib, sl 1 yif, k1, p1, rep from * sl last st. Slide.

Row 5: dark—sl 1 * (k1, p1) twice, (sl 1 yib, sl 1 yif) 3 times, (k1, p1) twice, sl 1 yib, sl 1 yif, rep from *, k last st. Turn.

Row 6: dark (maintain)—p1, * sl 1 yib, sl 1 yif, (k1, p1) twice, (sl 1 yib, sl 1 yif) 3 times, (k1, p1) twice, rep from *, sl last st. Slide.

Row 7: light—* p1, k1, rep from *. Turn.

Row 8: light (maintain)—rep row 7. Slide.

Row 9: dark—rep row 5. Turn.

Row 10: dark (maintain)—rep row 6. Slide.

Rows 11–14: rep rows 1–4.

Row 15: dark—p1, * (sl 1 yib, sl 1 yif) twice, (k1, p1, sl 1 yib, sl 1 yif) twice, (sl 1 yib, sl 1 yif) twice, rep from *, sl last st. Turn.

Row 16: light—p1, * (k1, p1) 3 times, (sl 1 yib, sl 1 yif, k1, p1) twice, k1, p1, rep from *, k last st. Slide.

Row 17: dark (maintain)—sl 1 yif, * (sl 1 yib, sl 1 yif) 3 times, (k1, p1, sl 1 yib, sl 1 yif) twice, sl 1 yib, sl 1 yif, rep from *, sl last st. Turn.

Row 18: light (maintain)—p1, * (k1, p1) twice, (sl 1 yib, sl 1 yif, k1, p1) twice, (k1, p1) twice, rep from *, k last st. Slide.

Row 19: dark—sl 1 yif, * sl 1 yib, sl 1 yif, (k1, p1) twice, sl 1 yib, sl 1 yif, (k1, p1) twice, (sl 1 yib, sl 1 yif) twice, rep from *, sl last st. Turn.

Row 20: dark (maintain)—p1, * (sl 1 yib, sl 1 yif) twice, (k1, p1) twice, sl 1 yib, sl 1 yif, (k1, p1) twice, sl 1 yib, sl 1 yif, rep from *, sl last st. Slide.

Rows 21 and 22: rep rows 7 and 8.

Rows 23 and 24: rep rows 19 and 20.

Rows 25-28: rep rows 15-18.

rep Rows 1-28.

PYRAMIDS

true reversible

This pattern is quite easy to follow once you get used to it. Be careful of colors. Light and dark do not alternate in a regular pattern of every row or every other row.

Use of dpn required. Multiple of 12 sts plus 2. Cast on light, slide.

Row 1: dark—p1, * (k1, p1) 5 times, sl 1 yib, sl 1 yif, rep from *, k last st of row. Turn.

Row 2: dark (maintain)—p1, * sl 1 yib, sl 1 yif, (k1, p1) 5 times, rep from *, k last st. Slide.

Row 3: light—p1, * (k1, p1) twice, (sl 1 yib, sl 1 yif) 3 times, k1, p1, rep from *, k last st. Turn.

Row 4: dark (maintain)—p1, * sl 1 yib, sl 1 yif, (k1, p1) 3 times, (sl 1 yib, sl 1 yif) twice, rep from *, k last st. Slide.

Row 5: light—p1, * (k1, p1) twice, sl 1 yib, sl 1 yif, (k1, p1) 3 times, rep from *, k last st. Turn.

Row 6: light—* p1, k1, rep from *. Slide.

Row 7: dark—p1, * (k1, p1) 3 times, sl 1 yib, sl 1 yif, (k1, p1) twice, rep from *, k last st. Turn.

Row 8: with dark rep row 5. Slide.

Row 9: with light rep row 4. Turn.

Row 10: with dark (maintain) rep row 3. Slide.

Row 11: with light rep row 2. Turn.

Row 12: with light rep row 6. Slide.

rep Rows 1-12.

SCALLOP PATTERN OR BORDER

true reversible

Be careful of color changes here. Sometimes a color is used for one row, sometimes for two. You may work eight rows only and have a border of a dark scalloped line, or do sixteen and have dark-light-dark, or work continually for an all-over pattern as shown. In the first row, do pull the yarn fairly tight after each section of slip stitches because there are so many of them.

Use of dpn required. Multiple of 8 sts. Cast on light, slide.

Row 1: dark—* k1, p1, (sl 1 yib, sl 1 yif) 3 times, rep from *. Turn.

Row 2: light (maintain)—* (k1, p1) 3 times, sl 1 yib, sl 1 yif, rep from *. Slide.

Row 3: dark—* k1, p1, sl 1 yib, sl 1 yif, (k1, p1) twice, rep from *. Turn.

Row 4: dark—* k1, p1, rep from *. Slide.

Row 5: with light rep row 1. Turn.

Row 6: with dark rep row 2. Slide.

Row 7: with light rep row 3. Turn.

Row 8: with light rep row 4. Slide.

rep Rows 1–8.

Variation

true reversible

A slight change in method makes wider scallops and a smoother "stockinette" look. This is actually done in "spot form" but is included here rather than its rightful section because it is a variation. Preparatory information such as number of sts is the same as for the original (above). Rows 1–3 are also the same, so we begin with . . .

Row 4:   light (maintain)—* (sl 1 yib, sl 1 yif) twice, k1, p1, sl 1 yib, sl 1 yif, rep from *. Slide.

Row 5:   dark—* k1, p1, rep from *. Turn.

Row 6:   dark (maintain)—rep row 5. Slide.

Row 7:   light—* (sl 1 yib, sl 1 yif) 3 times, k1, p1, rep from *. Turn.

Row 8:   dark (maintain)—* sl 1 yib, sl 1 yif, (k1, p1) 3 times, rep from *. Slide.

Row 9:   light—* (k1, p1) twice, sl 1 yib, sl 1 yif, k1, p1, rep from *. Turn.

Row 10: dark (maintain)—* sl 1 yib, sl 1 yif, k1, p1, (sl 1 yib, sl 1 yif) twice, rep from *. Slide.

Rows 11 and 12: with light rep row 5, twice. (Row 12 maintains).

rep Rows 1–12.

PLAIN AND FANCY REVERSIBLE GEOMETRICS

The following nine patterns are in a separate category because they all reverse to a solid color. This can be a very handy feature. For example, picture a ladies' reversible jacket which can be worn with the solid color side out but cuffs and collar folding over to show a pattern. When the jacket is reversed to the figured side, the collar and cuffs are solid.

If you are interested in understanding the construction of the patterns, picture a bricklayer making a garden wall two bricks thick, using dark bricks and light bricks. First he lays a double row of dark bricks, end-to-end (casting on). The next row will be light bricks, but they will be laid only on the south side of the wall. Then a row of dark bricks is laid only on the north side so that both sides are again of even height. The third course will also use only dark bricks but some will lie sideways over both north and south layers, tying the two walls together. Where they are not laid over the front layer the light bricks already in that spot must be stood on end to fill the gap (this is like slipping a light-colored stitch, thus stretching it to be two rows tall). The way in which the bricklayer arranges this third layer will determine the light and dark pattern on the south wall. The north row will only show dark bricks.

Like most analogies, this one is imperfect. It does show that these patterns are done in 3-row segments. It also shows us that no matter which side of the wall we view, every two courses of bricks (or two rows of stitches) which we see was actually made of three courses laid (three rows knit). In knitting we must really do 6-row patterns. Once the light-colored yarn has been worked in one direction, the next time its turn comes it must go back the other way, resulting in slightly different instructions. The fortunate bricklayer doesn't have that complication. If you wish to design your own solid-reverse patterns, keep the 6-row double-wall principle in mind.

A suggestion for those experimenting with these patterns: If you wish, at any time after completing a 3- or 6-row portion you may switch to a true reversible or opposite reversible pattern, then back to the original one. That way you will have areas of pattern on the solid side.

After reading this complicated explanation of theory, you will be pleased to know that these patterns are very simple to knit. Finally, to comment on the obvious, they will use about twice as much of one color as the other.

LINED AND SOLID

unlike reversible

Keep in mind that the Solid Reverse patterns will show on the solid side the color which you use to cast on. Most of these are written up "cast on dark" although the knitter may, of course, reverse colors. This example was made with a light cast on and, therefore, a light-colored solid side. If you prefer to use it with a dark solid side the stripes will look the same anyway.

Use of dpn required. Odd number of sts. Cast on light, slide.

Row 1: dark—sl 1 yif, * k1, sl 1 yif, rep from *. Turn.
Row 2: light—k1, * sl 1 yif, k1, rep from *. Turn.
Row 3: light—p1, * k1, p1, rep from *. Turn.
Row 4: dark—sl 1 yib, * p1, sl 1 yib, rep from *. Slide.
Row 5: light—rep row 2. Turn.
Row 6: light—rep row 3. Slide.
          rep Rows 1–6.

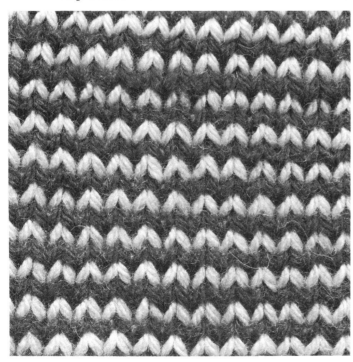

STRIPED TWEED AND SOLID

unlike reversible

As in some of the other patterns which reverse to solid colors, the "tweed" look is actually single rows of stripes. Don't forget that since you cast on with dark yarn here the reverse will be dark. If you change all color directions the reverse will be light and the vertical stripes on the tweed side will be dark, of course. This is an easy pattern to follow.

Use of dpn required. Multiple of 8 sts plus 7. Cast on dark, slide.

Row 1: light—sl 1 yif, * k1, sl 1 yif, rep from *. Turn.
Row 2: dark—k1, * sl 1 yif, k1, rep from *. Turn.
Row 3: dark—* p1, (k1, p1) 3 times, sl 1 yib, rep from *, omitting final sl st. Turn.
Row 4: light—sl 1 yib, * p1, sl 1 yib, rep from *. Slide.
Row 5: dark—rep row 2. Turn.
Row 6: dark—rep row 3. Slide.
　　　　rep Rows 1–6.

DOTTED BANDS AND SOLID

unlike reversible

Use of dpn required. Multiple of 4 sts plus 1. Cast on dark, slide.

Row 1: light—sl 1 yif, * k1, sl 1 yif, rep from *. Turn.
Row 2: dark (maintain)—k1, * sl 1 yif, k1, rep from *. Turn.
Row 3: dark—p1, * k1, p1, sl 1 yib, p1, rep from *. Turn.
Row 4: light—sl 1 yib, * p1, sl 1 yib, rep from *. Slide.
Row 5: dark—rep row 2. Turn.
Row 6: dark—p1, * k1, p1, rep from *. Slide.
　　　　rep Rows 1–6.

TWEED AND SOLID

unlike reversible

Use of dpn required. Multiple of 4 sts plus 1. Cast on dark, slide.

Row 1: light—sl 1 yif, * k1, sl 1 yif, rep from *. Turn.
Row 2: dark—k1, * sl 1 yif, k1, rep from *. Turn.
Row 3: dark—p1, * sl 1 yib, p1, k1, p1, rep from *. Turn.
Row 4: light—sl 1 yib, * p1, sl 1 yib, rep from *. Slide.
Row 5: dark—rep row 2. Turn.
Row 6: dark—p1, * k1, p1, sl 1 yib, p1, rep from *. Slide.
    rep Rows 1–6.

BROKEN CHECK

unlike reversible

What do you see in this pattern? A sort of check, humped-up cats or foxes sitting and glaring sideways, heads with a strange hair-do, or just blobs? All these have been found in this knitted Rorschach test. The reverse is just a solid light color.

Use of dpn required. Multiple of 12 sts plus 1. Cast on light, slide.

Row 1: dark—(sl 1 yif, k1) twice, sl 1 yif, sl 1 yib, rep from *, sl last st. Turn.
Row 2: light—k1, * sl 1 yif, k1, rep from *. Turn.
Row 3: light—* (p1, k1) 3 times, p1, sl 1 yib, (p1, k1) twice, rep from *, p last st. Turn.
Row 4: dark—* sl 1 yib, p1, sl 1 yib, sl 1 yif, (sl 1 yib, p1) twice, sl 1 yib, sl 1 yif, sl 1 yib, p1, rep from *, sl last st. Slide.
Row 5: light—rep row 2. Turn.
Row 6: light—p1, * sl 1 yib, p1 (k1, p1) 5 times, rep from *. Slide.
    rep Rows 1–6.

FLECKED AND SOLID

unlike reversible

The other side of this pattern is shown to confirm the fact that a dark-colored cast-on results in a dark-colored solid side for this type of reversible geometric.

Use of dpn required. Multiple of 8 sts plus 7. Cast on dark, slide.

Row 1: light—sl 1 yif, * k1, sl 1 yif, rep from *. Turn.
Row 2: dark—k1, * sl 1 yif, k1, rep from *. Turn.
Row 3: dark—p1, (k1, p1) 3 times, * sl 1 yib, p1, (k1, p1) 3 times, rep from *. Turn.
Row 4: light—sl 1 yib, * p1, sl 1 yib, rep from *. Slide.
Row 5: dark—rep row 2. Turn.
Row 6: dark—p1, k1, p1, * sl 1 yib, p1, (k1, p1) 3 times, rep from * but end (k1, p1) *once.* Slide.
rep Rows 1–6.

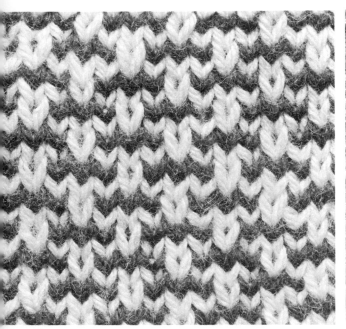

DIAGONAL TWEED AND SOLID

unlike reversible

Use of dpn required. Multiple of 10 sts plus 1. Cast on dark, slide.

Row 1: light—sl 1 yif, * k1, sl 1 yif, rep from *. Turn.

Row 2: dark—k1, * sl 1 yif, k1, rep from *. Turn.

Row 3: dark—p1, * (k1, p1) 4 times, sl 1 yib, p1, rep from *. Turn.

Row 4: light—sl 1 yib, * p1, sl 1 yib, rep from *. Slide.

Row 5: dark—rep row 2. Turn.

Row 6: dark—p1, * (k1, p1) 3 times, sl 1 yib, p1, k1, p1, rep from *. Slide.

Row 7: light—rep row 1. Turn.

Row 8: dark—rep row 2. Turn.

Row 9: dark—p1, * (k1, p1) twice, sl 1 yib, p1, (k1, p1) twice, rep from *. Turn.

Row 10: light—rep row 4. Slide.

Row 11: dark—rep row 2. Turn.

Row 12: dark—p1, * k1, p1, sl 1 yib, p1, (k1, p1) 3 times, rep from *. Slide.

Row 13: light—rep row 1. Turn.

Row 14: dark—rep row 2. Turn.

Row 15: dark—p1, * sl 1 yib, p1, (k1, p1) 4 times, rep from *. Turn.

Row 16: light—rep row 4. Slide.

Rows 17 and 18: dark—rep rows 2 and 3.

Row 19: light—rep Row 1.

Rows 20 and 21: dark—rep rows 5 and 6.

Row 22: light—rep row 4.

Rows 23 and 24: dark—rep rows 8 and 9.

Row 25: light—rep row 1.

Rows 26 and 27: dark—rep rows 11 and 12.

Row 28: light—rep row 4.

Rows 29 and 30: dark—rep rows 14 and 15.

rep Rows 1–30.

Note: Some knitters may find it easier to use the following approach to the pattern. Work rows 1–16, then repeat rows 2–16 with the exception that whenever there is a light-colored row like number 1, it will be done like row 4 and every light-colored row like number 4 will instead be done like number 1.

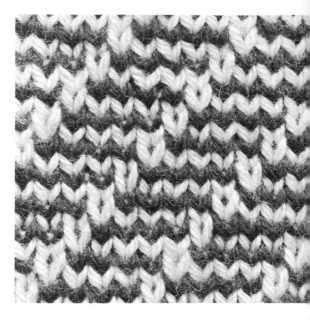

FIGURED AND SOLID

unlike reversible

This pattern is more difficult to follow than some others which reverse to a solid color because some of the design is worked in the light-colored rows.

Use of dpn required. Multiple of 12 sts plus 1. Cast on dark, slide.

Row 1: light—sl 1 yif, * k1, sl 1 yif, sl 1 yib, sl 1 yif, (k1, sl 1 yif) 4 times, rep from *. Turn.

Row 2: dark—k1, * sl 1 yif, k1, rep from *. Turn.

Row 3: dark—p1, * (k1, p1) 3 times, sl 1 yib, p1, k1, p1, sl 1 yib, p1, rep from *. Turn.

Row 4: light—sl 1 yib, * p1, sl 1 yib, sl 1 yif, sl 1 yib, (p1, sl 1 yib,) 4 times, rep from *. Slide.

Row 5: dark—rep row 2. Turn.

Row 6: dark—p1, * sl 1 yib, p1, k1, p1, sl 1 yib, p1, (k1, p1) 3 times, rep from *. Slide.

Row 7: light—sl 1 yif, * (k1, sl 1 yif) 4 times, sl 1 yib, sl 1 yif, k1, sl 1 yif, rep from *. Turn.

Row 8: dark—rep row 2. Turn.

Row 9: dark—p1, * (k1, p1) 3 times, sl 1 yib, p1, k1, p1, sl 1 yib, p1, rep from *. Turn.

Row 10: light—sl 1 yib, * (p1, sl 1 yib) 4 times, sl 1 yif, sl 1 yib, p1, sl 1 yib, rep from *. Slide.

Row 11: dark—rep row 2. Turn.

Row 12: dark—rep row 3. Slide.

Row 13: light—rep row 7. Turn.

Row 14: dark—rep row 2. Turn.

Row 15: dark—rep row 6. Turn.

Row 16: light—rep row 4. Slide.

Row 17: dark—rep row 2. Turn.

Row 18: dark—rep row 9. Slide.

rep Rows 1–18.

DIAMOND TWEED AND SOLID

unlike reversible

Use of dpn required. Multiple of 12 sts plus 1. Cast on dark, slide.

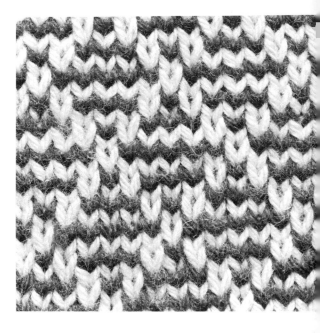

Row 1:   light—sl 1 yif, * k1, sl 1 yif, rep from *. Turn.

Row 2:   dark—k1, * sl 1 yif, k1, rep from *. Turn.

Row 3:   dark—p1, * sl 1 yib, (p1, k1) 5 times, p1, rep from *. Turn.

Row 4:   light—sl 1 yib, * p1, sl 1 yib, rep from *. Slide.

Row 5:   dark—rep row 2. Turn.

Row 6:   dark—p1, * k1, p1, sl 1 yib, (p1, k1) 3 times, p1, sl 1 yib, p1, rep from *. Slide.

Row 7:   light—rep row 1. Turn.

Row 8:   dark—rcp row 2. Turn.

Row 9:   dark—p1, * (k1, p1) twice, (sl 1 yib, p1, k1, p1) twice, rep from *. Turn.

Row 10: light—rep row 4. Slide.

Row 11: dark—rep row 2. Turn.

Row 12: dark—p1, * (k1, p1) 3 times, sl 1 yib, (p1, k1) twice, p1, rep from *. Slide.

Row 13: light—rep row 1. Turn.

Row 14: dark—rep row 2. Turn.

Row 15: dark—p1, * (k1, p1) twice, sl 1 yib, p1, k1, p1, sl 1 yib, p1, k1, p1, rep from *. Turn.

Row 16: light—rep row 4. Slide.

Row 17: dark—rep row 2. Turn.

Row 18: dark—p1, * k1, p1, sl 1 yib, (p1, k1) 3 times, p1, sl 1 yib, p1, rep from *. Slide.

rep Rows 1–18.

SPOT FORM REVERSIBLE GEOMETRICS

These patterns are worked in two-row segments which appear as one row in the finished work. First one color is used, then the remaining stitches are filled in with the other color. It is excellent for designs which are spotty. It can also be used for odd and irregular shapes because it can be continually changing. Most spot forms are opposite reversibles so that not too many stitches will have to be slipped in a row.

CHECKERBOARD

true reversible

In this pattern all rows "maintain" except 1, 2, 7, 8.

Use of dpn required. Multiple of 8 sts plus 2. Cast on light, slide.

Row 1: dark—k1, * (k1, sl 1 yif) twice, (sl 1 yib, p1) twice, rep from *, p last st. Turn.

Row 2: light—k1, * (sl 1 yib, p1) twice, (k1, sl 1 yif) twice, rep from *, p last st. Slide.

Row 3: dark—rep row 1. Turn. ⎤
Row 4: light—rep row 2. Slide. ⎟ These are
Row 5: dark—rep row 1. Turn. ⎥ "maintain" rows.
Row 6: light—rep row 2. Slide. ⎦

Row 7: with dark, rep row 2. Turn.

Row 8: with light—rep row 1. Slide.

Row 9: with dark, rep row 2. Turn. ⎤ These are
Row 10: with light, rep row 1. Slide. ⎟ "maintain" rows.
Row 11: with dark, rep row 2. Turn. ⎥
Row 12: with light, rep row 1. Slide. ⎦

  rep Rows 1–12.

MIXED BLOCKS

opposite reversible

Use of dpn required. Multiple of 16 sts plus 2. Cast on dark, slide.

Row 1:   light—* sl 1 yif, k1, rep from *. Turn.

Row 2:   with dark rep row 1. Slide.

Row 3:   light—sl 1 yif, * sl 1 yib, p1 (k1, sl 1 yif) 3 times, (sl 1 yib, p1, k1, sl 1 yif) twice, rep from *, sl last st. Turn.

Row 4:   dark—p1, * (k1, sl 1 yif, sl 1 yib, p1) twice, (k1, sl 1 yif) 3 times, sl 1 yib, p1, rep from *, k last st. Slide.

Row 5:   light (maintain)—sl 1 yif, * (sl 1 yib, p1, k1, sl 1 yif) twice, (sl 1 yib, p1) 3 times, k1, sl 1 yif, rep from *, sl last st. Turn.

Row 6:   dark (maintain)—p1, * k1, sl 1 yif, (sl 1 yib, p1) 3 times, (k1, sl 1 yif, sl 1 yib, p1) twice, rep from *, k last st. Slide.

Row 7:   light—* p1, sl 1 yib, rep from *. Turn.

Row 8:   with dark rep row 7. Slide.

Row 9:   light—sl 1 yif, * (sl 1 yib, p1) 3 times, (k1, sl 1 yif, sl 1 yib, p1) twice, k1, sl 1 yif, rep from *, sl last st. Turn.

Row 10: dark—p1, * (k1, sl 1 yif, sl 1 yib, p1) twice, k1, sl 1 yif, (sl 1 yib, p1) 3 times, rep from *, k last st. Slide.

Row 11: light (maintain)—sl 1 yif, * (sl 1 yib, p1, k1, sl 1 yif) twice, sl 1 yib, p1, (k1, sl 1 yif) 3 times, rep from *, sl last st. Turn.

Row 12: dark (maintain)—p1, * (k1, sl 1 yif) 3 times, (sl 1 yib, p1, k1, sl 1 yif) twice, sl 1 yib, p1, rep from *, k last st. Slide.

        rep Rows 1–12.

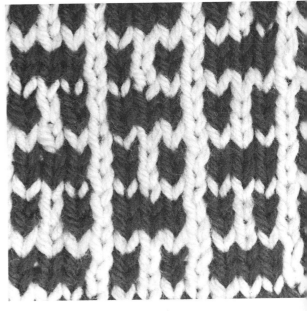

CROSS PATCH

opposite reversible

This is one of the easiest Spot Forms to learn to work without directions once the pattern is established.

Use of dpn required. Multiple of 8 sts. Cast on dark, slide.

Row 1: light—* k1, sl 1 yif, (sl 1 yib, p1) 3 times, rep from *. Turn.

Row 2: dark—* (sl 1 yib, p1) 3 times, k1, sl 1 yif, rep from *. Slide.

Row 3: light—* sl 1 yib, p1, k1, sl 1 yif, (sl 1 yib, p1) twice, rep from *. Turn.

Row 4: dark—* (sl 1 yib, p1) twice, k1, sl 1 yif, sl 1 yib, p1, rep from *. Slide.

Row 5: light (maintain)—* (k1, sl 1 yif) twice, sl 1 yib, p1, k1, sl 1 yif, rep from *. Turn.

Row 6: dark (maintain)—* k1, sl 1 yif, sl 1 yib, p1, (k1, sl 1 yif) twice, rep from *. Slide.

Row 7: light—* (k1, sl 1 yif) 3 times, sl 1 yib, p1, rep from *. Turn.

Row 8: dark—* sl 1 yib, p1, (k1, sl 1 yif) 3 times, rep from *. Slide.

Row 9: light—* sl 1 yib, p1, rep from *. Turn.

Row 10: with dark rep row 9. Slide.

Row 11: light (maintain)—* k1, sl 1 yif, rep from *. Turn.

Row 12: with dark (maintain) rep row 11. Slide.
     rep Rows 1–12.

TILES

opposite reversible

Tiles pattern is just a fancy argyle-like diamond. Be sure to notice that directions are not given for even-numbered rows. For these, merely repeat, with dark, exactly what was done in the preceding light row.

Use of dpn required. Multiple of 22 sts plus 2. Cast on dark, slide.

Row 1: light—p1, * sl 1 yib, p1, (k1, sl 1 yif) 9 times, sl 1 yib, p1, rep from *, sl last st. Turn.

Row 2 and all other even-numbered rows: with dark rep row just worked. Slide.

Row 3: light—p1, * sl 1 yib, p1, k1, sl 1 yif, (sl 1 yib, p1) 7 times, k1, sl 1 yif, sl 1 yib, p1, rep from *, sl last st. Turn.

Row 5: light (maintain)—sl 1 yif, * k1, sl 1 yif, sl 1 yib, p1, (k1, sl 1 yif) 7 times, sl 1 yib, p1, k1, sl 1 yif, rep from *, k last st. Turn.

Row 7: light—p1, * (sl 1 yib, p1) twice, (k1, sl 1 yif) twice, (sl 1 yib, p1) 3 times, (k1, sl 1 yif) twice, (sl 1 yib, p1) twice, rep from *, sl last st. Turn.

Row 9: light—sl 1 yif, * (k1, sl 1 yif) 3 times, sl 1 yib, p1, (k1, sl 1 yif) 3 times, sl 1 yib, p1 (k1, sl 1 yif) 3 times, rep from *, k last st. Turn.

Row 11: light—p1, * (sl 1 yib, p1) 4 times, k1, sl 1 yif, sl 1 yib, p1, k1, sl 1 yif, (sl 1 yib, p1) 4 times, rep from *, sl last st. Turn.

Row 13: light (maintain)—sl 1 yif, * (k1, sl 1 yif) 4 times, sl 1 yib, p1, k1, sl 1 yif, sl 1 yib, p1, (k1, sl 1 yif) 4 times, rep from *, k last st. Turn.

Row 15: light—p1, * (sl 1 yib, p1) 5 times, k1, sl 1 yif, (sl 1 yib, p1) 5 times, rep from *, sl last st. Turn.

Row 17: with light rep row 13.

Row 19: with light rep row 11.

Row 21: with light rep row 9.

Row 23: with light rep row 7.

Row 25: with light rep row 5.

Row 27: with light rep row 3.
　　　　rep Rows 1–28.

BLOCK BUSTER

mirror reversible
The bold Block Buster pattern looks especially attractive in bright colors. As you work a sample swatch, keep in mind that the size of the blocks can be increased or decreased according to what you will be making.

Use of dpn required. Multiple of 16 sts plus 2. Cast on light, slide.

Row 1: dark—p1, * (k1, sl 1 yif) 4 times, (sl 1 yib, p1) 4 times, rep from *, k last st of row. Turn.

Row 2: light—p1, * (sl 1 yib, p1) 4 times, (k1, sl 1 yif) 4 times, rep from *, k last st. Slide.

Rows 3, 5, 7, 9: dark—rep row 1. ⎫ These rows
Rows 4, 6, 8, 10: light—rep row 2. ⎬ all maintain
                                      ⎭ the pattern

Row 11: dark—p1, * (sl 1 yib, p1) twice, (k1, sl 1 yif) 4 times, (sl 1 yib, p1) twice, rep from *, sl last st yib. Turn.

Row 12: light—p1, * (sl 1 yib, p1) twice, (k1, sl 1 yif) 4 times, (sl 1 yib, p1) twice, rep from *, sl last st yib. Slide.

Rows 13, 15, 17, 19: dark—rep row 11. ⎫ These are
Rows 14, 16, 18, 20: light—rep row 12. ⎬ "maintain" rows.
rep Rows 1–20.

SUNSPOTS

opposite reversible (appears true)

Use of dpn required. Multiple of 8 sts. Cast on dark, slide.

Row 1:   light—* (sl 1 yib, p1) twice, k1, sl 1 yif, sl 1 yib, p1, rep from *. Turn.

Row 2:   dark—* sl 1 yib, p1, k1, sl 1 yif, (sl 1 yib, p1) twice, rep from *. Slide.

Row 3:   light—* (sl 1 yib, p1) 3 times, k1, sl 1 yif, rep from *. Turn.

Row 4:   dark—* k1, sl 1 yif, (sl 1 yib, p1) 3 times, rep from *. Slide.

Row 5:   light—* k1, sl 1 yif, rep from *. Turn.

Row 6:   with dark rep row 5. Slide.

Row 7:   light—rep row 3. Turn.

Row 8:   dark—rep row 4. Slide.

Row 9:   light—rep row 1. Turn.

Row 10: dark—rep row 2. Slide.

Row 11: light—rep row 5. Turn.

Row 12: with dark rep row 5. Slide.

   rep Rows 1–12.

TINY ARGYLE

Spot Form

opposite reversible

This pattern should be compared with the following one. In the illustrations this one was worked on small needles and knitting worsted while the other was done with sport yarn. The resulting diamonds are approximately the same width but the "spot form" ones are shorter than the others, nearly the same height as their width. This pattern has only one-half as many rows to be worked yet is more difficult to follow. If you prefer to use this form use smaller-than-usual needles for the type of yarn because every stitch will be slipped, pulling it to almost twice its normal size.

Use of dpn required. Multiple of 8 sts plus 2. Cast on light, slide.

Row 1: dark—p1, * k1, sl 1 yif, sl 1 yib, p1, rep from *, k last st of row. Turn. (Note: the two colors of yarn need not be twisted at the ends of the rows in this pattern.)

Row 2: light—p1, * sl 1 yib, p1, k1, sl 1 yif, rep from *, k last st. Slide.

Row 3: dark—p1, * sl 1 yib, p1, (k1, sl 1 yif) 3 times, rep from *, k last st. Turn.

Row 4: light—p1, * (k1, sl 1 yif) 3 times, sl 1 yib, p1, rep from *, k last st. Slide.

Row 5: dark—rep row 1. Turn.

Row 6: light—rep row 2. Slide.

Row 7: dark—p1, * (k1, sl 1 yif) twice, sl 1 yib, p1, k1, sl 1 yif, rep from *, k last st. Turn.

Row 8: light—p1, * k1, sl 1 yif, sl 1 yib, p1, (k1, sl 1 yif) twice, rep from *, k last st. Slide.
    rep Rows 1–8.

Long Form

Before trying this one, read the notes on the previous pattern. This version takes more time and more yarn but is tidier looking because it has fewer slip stitches.

Use of dpn required. Multiple of 8 sts plus 2. Cast on light, slide.

Row 1: dark—p1, * k1, sl 1 yif, sl 1 yib, p1, rep from *, k last st of row. Turn.

Row 2: light—p1, * sl 1 yib, p1, k1, sl 1 yif, rep from *, k last st. Slide.

Row 3: dark (maintain)—rep row 1. Turn.

Row 4: light (maintain)—rep row 1. Slide.

Row 5: dark—p1, * (sl 1 yib, p1) 3 times, k1, sl 1 yif, rep from *, k last st. Turn.

Row 6: light—p1, * k1, sl 1 yif, (sl 1 yib, p1) 3 times, rep from *, k last st. Slide.

Row 7: dark (maintain)—p1, * sl 1 yib, p1, (k1, sl 1 yif) 3 times, rep from *, k last st. Turn.

Row 8: light (maintain)—p1, * (k1, sl 1 yif) 3 times, sl 1 yib, p1, rep from *, k last st. Slide.

Row 9: dark—rep row 1. Turn.

Row 10: light—rep row 2. Slide.

Row 11: dark (maintain)—rep row 1. Turn.

Row 12: light (maintain)—rep row 2. Slide.

Row 13: dark—p1, * sl 1 yib, p1, k1, sl 1 yif, (sl 1 yib, p1) twice, rep from *, k last st. Turn.

Row 14: light—p1, * (sl 1 yib, p1) twice, k1, sl 1 yif, sl 1 yib, p1, rep from *, k last st. Slide.

Row 15: dark (maintain)—p1, * (k1, sl 1 yif) twice, sl 1 yib, p1, k1, sl 1 yif, rep from *, k last st. Turn.

Row 16: light (maintain)—p1, * k1, sl 1 yif, sl 1 yib, p1, (k1, sl 1 yif) twice, rep from *, k last st. Slide. rep Rows 1–16.

ENCHAINED

opposite reversible

Use of dpn required. Multiple of 12 sts. Cast on dark, slide.

Row 1: light—* (k1, sl 1 yif) 3 times, sl 1 yib, p1, (k1, sl 1 yif) twice, rep from *. Turn.

Row 2: dark—* (k1, sl 1 yif) twice, sl 1 yib, p1, (k1, sl 1 yif) 3 times, rep from *. Slide.

Row 3: light—* sl 1 yib, p1, (k1, sl 1 yif) 3 times, (sl 1 yib, p1) twice, rep from *. Turn.

Row 4: dark—* (sl 1 yib, p1) twice, (k1, sl 1 yif) 3 times, sl 1 yib, p1, rep from *. Slide.

Row 5: light—* k1, sl 1 yif, (sl 1 yib, p1) 5 times, rep from *. Turn.

Row 6: dark—* (sl 1 yib, p1) 5 times, k1, sl 1 yif, rep from *. Slide.

Row 7: light—* k1, sl 1 yif, sl 1 yib, p1, rep from *. Turn.

Row 8: dark—* sl 1 yib, p1, k1, sl 1 yif, rep from *. Slide.

Row 9: light (maintain)—rep row 7. Turn.

Row 10: dark (maintain)—rep row 8. Slide.

Row 11: light—* k1, sl 1 yif, (sl 1 yib, p1) 3 times, k1, sl 1 yif, sl 1 yib, p1, rep from *. Turn.

Row 12: dark—* sl 1 yib, p1, k1, sl 1 yif, (sl 1 yib, p1) 3 times, k1, sl 1 yif, rep from *. Slide.

Row 13: light—* (sl 1 yib, p1) 3 times, k1, sl 1 yif, (sl 1 yib, p1) twice, rep from *. Turn.

Row 14: dark—* (sl 1 yib, p1) twice, k1, sl 1 yif, (sl 1 yib, p1) 3 times, rep from *. Slide.

Row 15: light (maintain)—* (k1, sl 1 yif) twice, sl 1 yib, p1, (k1, sl 1 yif) 3 times, rep from *. Turn.

Row 16: dark (maintain)—* (k1, sl 1 yif) 3 times, sl 1 yib, p1, (k1, sl 1 yif) twice, rep from *. Slide.

Row 17: light—* k1, sl 1 yif, sl 1 yib, p1, (k1, sl 1 yif) 3 times, sl 1 yib, p1, rep from *. Turn.

Row 18: dark—* sl 1 yib, p1, (k1, sl 1 yif) 3 times, sl 1 yib, p1 k1, sl 1 yif, rep from *. Slide.

Row 19: light—rep row 7. Turn.

Row 20: dark—rep row 8. Slide.

Row 21: light (maintain)—rep row 7. Turn.

Row 22: dark (maintain)—rep row 8. Slide.

Row 23: light—* (k1, sl 1 yif) 5 times, sl 1 yib, p1, rep from *. Turn.

Row 24: dark—* sl 1 yib, p1, (k1, sl 1 yif) 5 times, rep from *. Slide.

Row 25: light—* (k1, sl 1 yif) twice, (sl 1 yib, p1) 3 times, k1, sl 1 yif, rep from *. Turn.

Row 26: dark—* k1, sl 1 yif, (sl 1 yib, p1) 3 times, (k1, sl 1 yif) twice, rep from *. Slide.

Row 27: light—* (sl 1 yib, p1) twice, k1, sl 1 yif, (sl 1 yib, p1) 3 times, rep from *. Turn.

Row 28: dark—* (sl 1 yib, p1) 3 times, k1, sl 1 yif, (sl 1 yib, p1) twice, rep from *. Slide.

rep Rows 1–28.

BIRDS-EYE STRIPES

alternate reversible

Use of dpn required. Multiple of 4 sts. Cast on dark, slide.

Row 1: light—* k1, sl 1 yif, rep from *. Turn.

Row 2: with dark rep row 1. Slide.

Row 3: light (maintain)—* sl 1 yib, p1, rep from *. Turn.

Row 4: with dark (maintain) rep row 3. Slide.

Row 5: light—* k1, sl 1 yif, sl 1 yib, p1, rep from *. Turn.

Row 6: dark—* sl 1 yib, p1, k1, sl 1 yif, rep from *. Slide.

Row 7: with light rep row 6. Turn.

Row 8: with dark rep row 5. Slide.

Row 9: light—rep row 3. Turn.

Row 10: with dark rep row 3. Slide.

Row 11: light (maintain)—rep row 1. Turn.

Row 12: with dark (maintain)—rep row 1. Slide.

Row 13: with light rep row 6. Turn.

Row 14: with dark rep row 5. Slide.

Row 15: light—rep row 5. Turn.

Row 16: dark—rep row 6. Slide.

rep Rows 1–16.

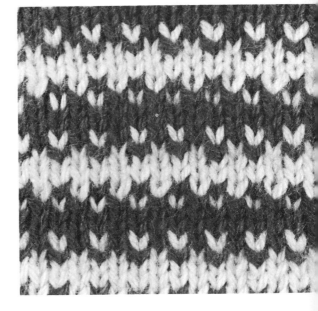

DIAMOND AND ZIG-ZAG BANDS

opposite reversible

This pattern is related to Scallop Pattern. It is easier to follow than most Spot Forms. To do a single border use rows 1–12, or do 1–24 for a double border. Chapter Six explains how to put them on a solid color opposite reversible background.

Use of dpn required. Multiple of 8 sts. Cast on dark, slide.

Row 1: light—* k1, sl 1 yif, sl 1 yib, p1 (k1, sl 1 yif) twice, rep from *. Turn.

Row 2: dark—* (k1, sl 1 yif) twice, sl 1 yib, p1, k1, sl 1 yif, rep from *. Slide.

Row 3: light—* sl 1 yib, p1, (k1, sl 1 yif) 3 times, rep from *. Turn.

Row 4: dark—* (k1, sl 1 yif) 3 times, sl 1 yib, p1, rep from *. Slide.

Row 5: light—* sl 1 yib, p1, rep from *. Turn.

Row 6: with dark rep row 5. Slide.

Row 7: with light rep row 2. Turn.

Row 8: with dark rep row 1. Slide.

Row 9: with light rep row 4. Turn.

Row 10: with dark rep row 3. Slide.

Row 11: light—rep row 5. Turn.

Row 12: with dark rep row 5. Slide.

Row 13: with light rep row 4. Turn.

Row 14: with dark rep row 3. Slide.

Row 15: with light rep row 2. Turn.

Row 16: with dark rep row 1. Slide.

Row 17: light—rep row 5. Turn.

Row 18: with dark rep row 5. Slide.

Row 19: light—rep row 3. Turn.

Row 20: dark—rep row 4. Slide.

Row 21: light—rep row 1. Turn.

Row 22: dark—rep row 2. Slide.

Row 23: light—rep row 5. Turn.

Row 24: with dark rep row 5. Slide.

rep Rows 1–24.

FLECKED BANDS

opposite reversible

Use of dpn required. Multiple of 4 sts. Cast on dark, slide.

Row 1: light—* k1, sl 1 yif, rep from *. Turn.
Row 2: with dark rep row 1. Slide.
Row 3: light—rep row 1. Turn.
Row 4: with dark rep row 1. Slide.
Row 5: light (maintain)—* sl 1 yib, p1, rep from *. Turn.
Row 6: with dark (maintain) rep row 5. Slide.
Row 7: light—rep row 5. Turn.
Row 8: with dark rep row 5. Slide.
Row 9: light—* k1, sl 1 yif, sl 1 yib, p1, rep from *. Turn.
Row 10: dark—* sl 1 yib, p1, k1, sl 1 yif, rep from *. Slide.
Row 11: with light rep row 10. Turn.
Row 12: with dark rep row 9. Slide.
Row 13: light—rep row 9. Turn.
Row 14: dark—rep row 10. Slide.
Row 15: light—rep row 5. Turn.
Row 16: with dark rep row 5. Slide.
Row 17: light—rep row 5. Turn.
Row 18: with dark rep row 5. Slide.
Row 19: light (maintain)—rep row 1. Turn.
Row 20: with dark (maintain) rep row 1. Slide.
Row 21: light—rep row 1. Turn.
Row 22: with dark rep row 1. Slide.
Row 23: light—rep row 9. Turn.
Row 24: dark—rep row 10. Slide.
Row 25: with light rep row 10. Turn.
Row 26: with dark rep row 9. Slide.
Row 27: light—rep row 9. Turn.
Row 28: dark—rep row 10. Slide.
       rep Rows 1–28.

ARGYLE CHECK (top and center)

opposite reversible

It may take a while for this pattern to become familiar enough so that you can work it without directions. Understanding it will help—it is actually a checkerboard in which solid squares alternate with checkered squares. The result looks like diagonal tweed bands.

Use of dpn required. Multiple of 24. Cast on dark, slide.

Row 1: light—* (k1, sl 1 yif) 3 times, (sl 1 yib, p1, k1, sl 1 yif) twice, k1, sl 1 yif, (k1, sl 1 yif, sl 1 yib, p1) twice, rep from *. Turn.

Row 2: dark—* (sl 1 yib, p1, k1, sl 1 yif) twice, (k1, sl 1 yif) twice, rep from *. Slide.

Row 3: light—* sl 1 yib, p1, k1, sl 1 yif, (sl 1 yib, p1) 5 times, k1, sl 1 yif, (sl 1 yib, p1) 4 times, rep from *. Turn.

Row 4: dark—* (sl 1 yib, p1) 4 times, k1, sl 1 yif, (sl 1 yib, p1) 5 times, k1, sl 1 yif, sl 1 yib, p1, rep from *. Slide.

Rows 5–8: rep rows 1–4.
Row 9: with light rep row 2. Turn.
Row 10: with dark rep row 1. Slide.
Row 11: with light rep row 4. Turn.
Row 12: with dark rep row 3. Slide.
Rows 13–16: rep rows 9–12.
      rep Rows 1–16.

TWEED AND SOLID BARS (bottom and opposite, top)

opposite reversible

This pattern and Flecked bands will give a similar effect, one vertically and the other horizontally. Some clues for following the pattern: For solid bars always maintain the color (work sts already in the color you are using and slip the contrasting sts). For tweed bars there are 3 pairs of sts per bar. When using dark, work those which are presently light and slip the dark ones. When using light, work the two outside ones on the side toward you, work the middle st on the side away from you, slip the others.

Use of dpn required. Multiple of 10 sts plus 4. Cast on light, slide.

Row 1: dark—(k1, sl 1 yif) twice, * k1, sl 1 yif, sl 1 yib, p1, (k1, sl 1 yif) 3 times, rep from *. Turn.

Row 2: with light rep row 1. Slide.

Row 3: dark—(sl 1 yib, p1) twice, * k1, sl 1 yif, sl 1 yib, p1, k1, sl 1 yif, (sl 1 yib, p1) twice, rep from *. Turn.

Row 4: with light rep row 3. Slide.
        rep Rows 1–4.

CHECKMATE (center and bottom)

opposite reversible

Checkmate belongs to the same family as Argyle Check, Tweed and Solid Bars, Variegated Stripes, Flecked Bands, and Birds-eye Stripes. They should suggest variations to interested pattern designers.

Use of dpn required. Multiple of 18 sts plus 4. Cast on dark, slide.

Row 1: light—* k1, sl 1 yif, rep from *. Turn.

Row 2: with dark rep row 1. Slide.

Row 3: light—* sl 1 yib, p1, rep from *. Turn.

Row 4: with dark rep row 3. Slide.

Row 5: light—(k1, sl 1 yif) twice, * (sl 1 yib, p1, k1, sl 1 yif) 4 times, k1, sl 1 yif, rep from *. Turn.

Row 6: with dark rep row 5. Slide.

Row 7: light—(sl 1 yib, p1) twice, * (sl 1 yib, p1, k1, sl 1 yif) 3 times, (sl 1 yib, p1) 3 times, rep from *. Turn.

Row 8: with dark rep row 7. Slide.

Rows 9–12: rep rows 5–8.

Rows 13–16: rep rows 5–8.

Rows 17–20: rep rows 5–8.

Rows 21 and 22: rep rows 5 and 6.

Rows 23 and 24: rep rows 3 and 4.
        rep Rows 1–24.

VARIEGATED STRIPES

opposite reversible

This pattern is rather precise, yet the tweed effect gives it a sporty look. It is especially attractive in uses where part folds over to show the opposite side.

Use of dpn required. Multiple of 10 sts. Cast on light, slide.

Row 1: dark—* k1, sl 1 yif, sl 1 yib, p1 (k1, sl 1 yif) twice, sl 1 yib, p1, rep from *. Turn.

Row 2: light—* sl 1 yib, p1, (k1, sl 1 yif) twice, sl 1 yib, p1, k1, sl 1 yif, rep from *. Slide.

Row 3: dark—* k1, sl 1 yif, sl 1 yib, p1, k1, sl 1 yif, (sl 1 yib, p1) twice, rep from *. Turn.

Row 4: light—* (sl 1 yib, p1) twice, k1, sl 1 yif, sl 1 yib, p1, k1, sl 1 yif, rep from *. Slide.
rep Rows 1–4.

MOTIFS

A motif is a figure or design which can be repeated as needed. This section gives a variety of examples, all worked in the "spot form." In most cases only one repeat of the motif will be formed by following the directions given. It is up to the knitter to arrange one or more of the motifs so as to make an over-all fabric or to highlight the garment being designed. Some of the designs are already scattered about to make a sort of "print" fabric, and at least one (Ogee Pattern) can be used as a single motif, a border, or an overall design.

All of the designs given here are opposite reversibles which are made by working light- and dark-colored rows alternately. They may be used on a background of any pattern which is done in the same way. The illustration shows a Heart Motif used on a background pattern called Block Party. When working a motif in this way it is helpful to use stitch markers to set off the area where the motif appears. Some knitters may prefer to work from a graphed design rather than written directions.

The heart motif sample shown here also illustrates **Trapunto Knitting,** a form in which motifs are stuffed and raised. Compare it with the plain Heart Motif on page 142. Trapunto Knitting uses solid color motifs (Wreaths would not adapt well). Work a motif, or a row of them, nearly to the top. On the next row knit up to the motif, slip the stitches of the motif alternately onto two needles (slip a knit stitch to one needle, a purl to the other, a knit to the first, etc.). All dark-colored stitches will then be on one needle, light ones on the other, and there will be an opening between with the motifs forming a pocket. Stuff this pocket with fiberfill, cotton, snippets of yarn, or cut-up pieces of clean, old stockings. The idea is to make it pleasingly plump without stretching too much. Replace the stitches on one needle in their original order and work the final row or two of the design, closing it off.

In the colored pictures of this book are shown Christmas Tree Coasters. Directions for making them are in Chapter Five. Any of the larger motifs may be used for coasters; a set of clubs, diamonds, hearts, and spades for example. Help in adapting a motif to a coaster design is given following the Christmas Tree Coaster directions.

The creative knitter who enjoys designing her own pattern can surely think of many other possible motifs. A few suggestions are miniature crowns, shields or houses, monograms, triangles (every other one upside down). If you graph a design, first allow for the distortion resulting from stitches being wider than tall. Make your figure tall and skinny.

Motif directions are generally given with a few extra stitches on a side. To do plain rows before and after (as shown in the pictures), adapt the Solid Two-Color Opposite Reversible as explained in Chapter Six.

SEGMENTED DIAMOND MOTIF

opposite reversible

If you are not sure of yourself doing Reversible Geometrics, this is not for you. The diamonds actually make a motif, but the pattern directions are written to make an overall design. This could, of course, be enlarged to spread the pieces wider apart.

Use of dpn required. Multiple of 44 sts plus 22. Cast on dark, slide.

Row 1: light—(k1, sl 1 yif) 16 times, * sl 1 yib, p1, (k1, sl 1 yif) 21 times, rep from * but end (k1, sl 1 yif) 16 times. Turn.

Row 2 and all even-numbered rows: with dark, repeat preceeding row. Slide.

Row 3: light (maintain)—(sl 1 yib, p1) 16 times, * k1, sl 1 yif, (sl 1 yib, p1) 21 times, rep from * but end (sl 1 yib, p1) 16 times. Turn.

Row 5: light—(k1, sl 1 yif) 15 times, * (sl 1 yib, p1) 3 times, (k1, sl 1 yif) 19 times, rep from * but end (k1, sl 1 yif) 15 times. Turn.

Row 7: light (maintain)—(sl 1 yib, p1) 15 times, * (k1, sl 1 yif) 3 times, (sl 1 yib, p1) 19 times, rep from * but end (sl 1 yib, p1) 15 times. Turn.

Row 9: light—rep row 1. Turn.

Row 11: light—(sl 1 yib, p1) 14 times, * k1, sl 1 yif, (sl 1 yib, p1, k1, sl 1 yif) twice, (sl 1 yib, p1) 17 times, rep from * but end (sl 1 yib, p1) 14 times. Turn.

Row 13: light—(k1, sl 1 yif) 14 times, * sl 1 yib, p1, (k1, sl 1 yif) 3 times, sl 1 yib, p1, (k1, sl 1 yif) 17 times, rep from * but end (k1, sl 1 yif) 14 times. Turn.

Row 15: light—(sl 1 yib, p1) 13 times, * (k1, sl 1 yif) 3 times, sl 1 yib, p1, (k1, sl 1 yif) 3 times, (sl 1 yib, p1) 15 times, rep from * but end (sl 1 yib, p1) 13 times. Turn.

Row 17: light (maintain)—(k1, sl 1 yif) 13 times, * (sl 1 yib, p1) 3 times, k1, sl 1 yif, (sl 1 yib, p1) 3 times, (k1, sl 1 yif) 15 times, rep from * but end (k1, sl 1 yif) 13 times. Turn.

Row 19: light—(sl 1 yib, p1) 14 times, * k1, sl 1 yif, (sl 1 yib, p1) 3 times, k1, sl 1 yif, (sl 1 yib, p1) 17 times, rep from * but end (sl 1 yib, p1) 14 times. Turn.

Row 21: light—(k1, sl 1 yif) 14 times, * sl 1 yib, p1, (k1, sl 1 yif, sl 1 yib, p1) twice, (k1, sl 1 yif) 17 times, rep from * but end (k1, sl 1 yif) 14 times. Turn.

Row 23: light—rep row 3. Turn.

Row 25: light—rep row 5. Turn.

Row 27: light (maintain)—rep row 7. Turn.

Row 29: light—rep row 1. Turn.

Row 31: light (maintain)—rep row 3. Turn.

Row 33: light—* k1, sl 1 yif, rep from *. Turn.

Row 35: light—* sl 1 yib, p1, rep from *. Turn.

Rows 37, 41, 45, 49: light—rep row 33.

Rows 39, 43, 47: light—rep row 35.

Row 51: light—(sl 1 yib, p1) 5 times, * k1, sl 1 yif, (sl 1 yib, p1) 21 times, rep from * but end (sl 1 yib, p1) 5 times. Turn.

Row 53: light (maintain)—(k1, sl 1 yif) 5 times, * sl 1 yib, p1, (k1, sl 1 yif) 21 times, rep from * but end (k1, sl 1 yif) 5 times. Turn.

Row 55: light—(sl 1 yib, p1) 4 times, * (k1, sl 1 yif) 3 times, (sl 1 yib, p1) 19 times, rep from * but end (sl 1 yib, p1) 4 times. Turn.

Row 57: light (maintain)—(k1, sl 1 yif) 4 times, * (sl 1 yib, p1) 3 times, (k1, sl 1 yif) 19 times, rep from * but end (k1, sl 1 yif) 4 times. Turn.

Row 59: light—rep row 51. Turn.

Row 61: light—(k1, sl 1 yif) 3 times, * sl 1 yib, p1, (k1, sl 1 yif, sl 1 yib, p1) twice, (k1, sl 1 yif) 17 times, rep from * but end (k1, sl 1 yif) 3 times. Turn.

Row 63: light—(sl 1 yib, p1) 3 times, * k1, sl 1 yif, (sl 1 yib, p1) 3 times, k1, sl 1 yif, (sl 1 yib, p1) 17 times, rep from * but end (sl 1 yib, p1) 3 times. Turn.

Row 65: light—(k1, sl 1 yif) twice, * (sl 1 yib, p1) 3 times, k1, sl 1 yif, (sl 1 yib, p1) 3 times, (k1, sl 1 yif) 15 times, rep from * but end (k1, sl 1 yif) twice. Turn.

Row 67: light (maintain)—(sl 1 yib, p1) twice, * (k1, sl 1 yif) 3 times, sl 1 yib, p1, (k1, sl 1 yif) 3 times, (sl 1 yib, p1) 15 times, rep from * but end (sl 1 yib, p1) twice. Turn.

Row 69: light—(k1, sl 1 yif) 3 times, * sl 1 yib, p1, (k1, sl 1 yif) 3 times, sl 1 yib, p1, (k1, sl 1 yif) 17 times, rep from * but end (k1, sl 1 yif) 3 times. Turn.

Row 71: light—(sl 1 yib, p1) 3 times, * k1, sl 1 yif, (sl 1 yib, p1, k1, sl 1 yif) twice, (sl 1 yib, p1) 17 times, rep from * but end (sl 1 yib, p1) 3 times. Turn.

Row 73: light—rep row 53. Turn.

Row 75: light—rep row 55. Turn.

Row 77: light (maintain)—rep row 57. Turn.

Row 79: light—rep row 51. Turn.

Row 81: light (maintain)—rep row 53. Turn.

Rows 83, 87, 91, 95, 99: light—rep row 35. Turn.

Rows 85, 89, 93, 97: light—rep row 33. Turn.

rep Rows 1–100.

OGEE PATTERN OR BORDER

opposite reversible

As this is actually a motif, the pattern may be enlarged. It may also be adapted as a border. If rows 7–24 are used, you will start and end on the side with the light-colored s-curve; or use 1–30 and start on the other side. As written, it makes a lovely, intricate overall design. Since the pattern is symmetrical, each repeat begins with the same unit it ended with. That is, a repeat of row 1 ends sl 1 yib, p1, then the next repeat in that row will begin again sl 1 yib, p1. It is easy to become confused and forget one of them if you are not careful.

Use of dpn required. Multiple of 28 sts. Cast on dark, slide. Even numbered rows rep, with dark, the previous row.

Row 1: light—* sl 1 yib, p1, (k1, sl 1 yif) 12 times, sl 1 yib, p1, rep from *. Turn.

Row 3: light—* (k1, sl 1 yif) twice, (sl 1 yib, p1) twice, k1, sl 1 yif, (sl 1 yib, p1) 4 times, k1, sl 1 yif, (sl 1 yib, p1) twice, (k1, sl 1 yif) twice, rep from *. Turn.

Row 5: light—rep row 1. Turn.

Row 7: light—* (sl 1 yib, p1) 3 times, (k1, sl 1 yif) 3 times, (sl 1 yib, p1) twice, (k1, sl 1 yif) 3 times, (sl 1 yib, p1) 3 times, rep from *. Turn.

Row 9: light—* (k1, sl 1 yif) twice, (sl 1 yib, p1) 3 times, k1, sl 1 yif, (sl 1 yib, p1) twice, k1, sl 1 yif, (sl 1 yib, p1) 3 times, (k1, sl 1 yif) twice, rep from *. Turn.

Row 11: light—* (sl 1 yib, p1) twice, (k1, sl 1 yif) twice, (sl 1 yib, p1) 6 times, (k1, sl 1 yif) twice, (sl 1 yib, p1) twice, rep from *. Turn.

Row 13: light—* k1, sl 1 yif, (sl 1 yib, p1) 4 times, (k1, sl 1 yif) 4 times, (sl 1 yib, p1) 4 times, k1, sl 1 yif, rep from *. Turn.

Row 15: light—* (sl 1 yib, p1) twice, (k1, sl 1 yif) 3 times, (sl 1 yib, p1) 4 times, (k1, sl 1 yif) 3 times, (sl 1 yib, p1) twice, rep from *. Turn.

Row 17: light—* (k1, sl 1 yif) twice, (sl 1 yib, p1) 4 times, (k1, sl 1 yif) twice, (sl 1 yib, p1) 4 times, (k1, sl 1 yif) twice, rep from *. Turn.

Row 19: light—* (sl 1 yib, p1) 3 times, (k1, sl 1 yif) twice, (sl 1 yib, p1) 4 times, (k1, sl 1 yif) twice, (sl 1 yib, p1) 3 times, rep from *. Turn.

Row 21: light—* sl 1 yib, p1, k1, sl 1 yif, (sl 1 yib, p1) 3 times, (k1, sl 1 yif) 4 times, (sl 1 yib, p1) 3 times, k1, sl 1 yif, sl 1 yib, p1, rep from *. Turn.

Row 23: light—* sl 1 yib, p1, (k1, sl 1 yif) 3 times, (sl 1 yib, p1) 6 times, (k1, sl 1 yif) 3 times, sl 1 yib, p1, rep from *. Turn.

Row 25: light—* (k1, sl 1 yif) 6 times, (sl 1 yib, p1) twice, (k1, sl 1 yif) 6 times, rep from *. Turn.

Row 27: light—* (sl 1 yib, p1) twice, k1, sl 1 yif, (sl 1 yib, p1) twice, (k1, sl 1 yif) 4 times, (sl 1 yib, p1) twice, k1, sl 1 yif, (sl 1 yib, p1) twice, rep from *. Turn.

Rows 29-48: Work these rows, following each with a dark rep row as before—25, 23, 21, 19, 17, 15, 13, 11, 9, 7.

rep Rows 1–48.

WINDOW MOTIF

opposite reversible

If you are using this as a single motif, first do solid color rows of opposite reversible, as explained in Chapter Six, and continue in solid colors after the motif. If you wish to do an overall pattern, that is explained in the next stitch pattern.

Use of dpn required. 22 sts (allows 2 sts left and right of motif on each surface). For all even-numbered rows: with dark rep previous row, slide.

Rows 3, 7, 11, 15, 19, 23: light—(sl 1 yib, p1) twice, (k1, sl 1 yif) 3 times, sl 1 yib, p1, (k1, sl 1 yif) 3 times, (sl 1 yib, p1) twice, Turn.

Rows 3, 7, 11, 15, 19, 23: light—(sl 1 yib, p1) twice, (k1, sl 1 yif) 3 times, sl 1 yib, p1, (k1, sl 1 yif) 3 times, (sl 1 yib, p1) twice. Turn.

Row 13: light—* k1, sl 1 yif, rep from *. Turn.

Overall Window Pattern

opposite reversible

This will arrange the window motifs approximately as the Segmented Diamonds are in that pattern (page 128). Even-numbered rows rep with dark, as before.

Use of dpn required. Multiple of 52 sts plus 22. Cast on dark, slide.

Rows 1, 5, 9, 17, 21, 25: light—(k1, sl 1 yif) twice, * (sl 1 yib, p1) 3 times, k1, sl 1 yif, (sl 1 yib, p1) 3 times, (k1, sl 1 yif) 19 times, rep from * but end (k1, sl 1 yif) twice. Turn.

Rows 3, 7, 11, 15, 19, 23: light—(sl 1 yib, p1) twice, * (k1, sl 1 yif) 3 times, sl 1 yib, p1, (k1, sl 1 yif) 3 times, (sl 1 yib, p1) 19 times, rep from * but end (sl 1 yib, p1) twice. Turn.

Rows 13, 29, 33, 37, 41, 45, 61, 77, 81, 85, 89, 93: light—* k1, sl 1 yif, rep from *. Turn.

Rows 27, 31, 35, 39, 43, 47, 75, 79, 83, 87, 91: light—* sl 1 yib, p1, rep from *. Turn.

Rows 49, 53, 57, 65, 69, 73: light—(k1, sl 1 yif) 15 times, * (sl 1 yib, p1) 3 times, k1, sl 1 yif, (sl 1 yib, p1) 3 times, (k1, sl 1 yif) 19 times, rep from * but end (k1, sl 1 yif) 15 times. Turn.

Rows 51, 55, 59, 63, 67, 71: light—(sl 1 yib, p1) 15 times, * (k1, sl 1 yif) 3 times, sl 1 yib, p1, (k1, sl 1 yif) 3 times, (sl 1 yib, p1) 19 times, rep from * but end (sl 1 yib, p1) 15 times. Turn. rep Rows 1–94.

SPADE MOTIF

opposite reversible

Use of dpn required. 42 sts (allows 3 sts left and right of motif on each surface). Cast on dark, slide. Each even row is a rep with dark of previous row.

Row 1: light—(k1, sl 1 yif) 8 times, (sl 1 yib, p1) 5 times, (k1, sl 1 yif) 8 times. Turn.

Row 3: light—(sl 1 yib, p1) 9 times, (k1, sl 1 yif) 3 times, (sl 1 yib, p1) 9 times. Turn.

Row 5: light (maintain)—(k1, sl 1 yif) 9 times, (sl 1 yib, p1) 3 times, (k1, sl 1 yif) 9 times. Turn.

Row 7: light—(sl 1 yib, p1) 5 times, (k1, sl 1 yif) 3 times, (sl 1 yib, p1) twice, k1, sl 1 yif, (sl 1 yib, p1) twice, (k1, sl 1 yif) 3 times, (sl 1 yib, p1) 5 times. Turn.

Row 9: light—(k1, sl 1 yif) 4 times, (sl 1 yib, p1) 5 times, k1, sl 1 yif, sl 1 yib, p1, k1, sl 1 yif, (sl 1 yib, p1) 5 times, (k1, sl 1 yif) 4 times. Turn.

Row 11: light—(sl 1 yib, p1) 3 times, (k1, sl 1 yif) 15 times, (sl 1 yib, p1) 3 times. Turn.

Row 13: light (maintain)—(k1, sl 1 yif) 3 times, (sl 1 yib, p1) 15 times, (k1, sl 1 yif) 3 times. Turn.

Row 15: light (maintain)—rep row 11. Turn.

Row 17: light (maintain)—rep row 13. Turn.

Row 19: light—(sl 1 yib, p1) 4 times, (k1, sl 1 yif) 13 times, (sl 1 yib, p1) 4 times. Turn.

Row 21: light—(k1, sl 1 yif) 5 times, (sl 1 yib, p1) 11 times, (k1, sl 1 yif) 5 times. Turn.

Row 23: light (maintain)—(sl 1 yib, p1) 5 times, (k1, sl 1 yif) 11 times, (sl 1 yib, p1) 5 times. Turn.

Row 25: light—(k1, sl 1 yif) 6 times, (sl 1 yib, p1) 9 times, (k1, sl 1 yif) 6 times. Turn.

Row 27: light—(sl 1 yib, p1) 7 times, (k1, sl 1 yif) 7 times, (sl 1 yib, p1) 7 times. Turn.

Row 29: light (maintain)—(k1, sl 1 yif) 7 times, (sl 1 yib, p1) 7 times, (k1, sl 1 yif) 7 times.

Row 31: light—(sl 1 yib, p1) 8 times, (k1, sl 1 yif) 5 times, (sl 1 yib, p1) 8 times. Turn.

Row 33: light (maintain)—(k1, sl 1 yif) 8 times, (sl 1 yib, p1) 5 times, (k1, sl 1 yif) 8 times. Turn.

Row 35: light—rep row 3. Turn.

Row 37: light (maintain)—rep row 5. Turn.

Row 39: light—(sl 1 yib, p1) 10 times, k1, sl 1 yif, (sl 1 yib, p1) 10 times. Turn.

Row 41: light (maintain)—(k1, sl 1 yif) 10 times, sl 1 yib, p1, (k1, sl 1 yif) 10 times. Turn.

Follow with Solid Two-Color Opposite Reversible, starting with row 3.

DIAMOND MOTIF

opposite reversible

Use of dpn required. 38 sts (allows 3 extra sts left and right of motif on each surface). Cast on dark, slide. Each even row is a rep with dark of previous row.

Row 1:   light—(k1, sl 1 yif) 9 times, sl 1 yib, p1, (k1, sl 1 yif) 9 times. Turn.

Row 3:   light (maintain)—(sl 1 yib, p1) 9 times, k1, sl 1 yif, (sl 1 yib, p1) 9 times. Turn.

Row 5:   light—(k1, sl 1 yif) 8 times, (sl 1 yib, p1) 3 times, (k1, sl 1 yif) 8 times. Turn.

Row 7:   light (maintain)—(sl 1 yib, p1) 8 times, (k1, sl 1 yif) 3 times, (sl 1 yib, p1) 8 times. Turn.

Row 9:   light—(k1, sl 1 yif) 7 times, (sl 1 yib, p1) 5 times, (k1, sl 1 yif) 7 times. Turn.

Row 11: light (maintain)—(sl 1 yib, p1) 7 times, (k1, sl 1 yif) 5 times, (sl 1 yib, p1) 7 times. Turn.

Row 13: light—(k1, sl 1 yif) 6 times, (sl 1 yib, p1) 7 times, (k1, sl 1 yif) 6 times. Turn.

Row 15: light (maintain)—(sl 1 yib, p1) 6 times, (k1, sl 1 yif) 7 times, (sl 1 yib, p1) 6 times. Turn.

Row 17: light—(k1, sl 1 yif) 5 times, (sl 1 yib, p1) 9 times, (k1, sl 1 yif) 5 times. Turn.

Row 19: light—(sl 1 yib, p1) 4 times, (k1, sl 1 yif) 11 times, (sl 1 yib, p1) 4 times. Turn.

Row 21: light—(k1, sl 1 yif) 3 times, (sl 1 yib, p1) 13 times, (k1, sl 1 yif) 3 times. Turn.

Rows 23–41: rep rows 19, 17, 15, 13, 11, 9, 7, 5, 3, 1, each followed by a rep with dark. Note: "maintain" rows will not be the same.

Follow with Solid Two-Color Opposite Reversible, starting with row 3.

CLUB MOTIF

opposite reversible

Use of dpn required. 42 sts (allows 3 sts left and right of motif on each surface). Cast on dark, slide. Work Solid Two-Color Opposite Reversible first, as required. In motif, even-numbered rows are rep with dark of previous row. (Row 2 is "with dark rep row 1", etc.)

Row 1: light—(k1, sl 1 yif) 8 times, (sl 1 yib, p1) 5 times, (k1, sl 1 yif) 8 times. Turn.

Row 3: light—(sl 1 yib, p1) 9 times, (k1, sl 1 yif) 3 times, (sl 1 yib, p1) 9 times. Turn.

Row 5: light (maintain)—(k1, sl 1 yif) 9 times, (sl 1 yib, p1) 3 times, (k1, sl 1 yif) 9 times. Turn.

Row 7: light—(sl 1 yib, p1) 5 times, (k1, sl 1 yif) 3 times, (sl 1 yib, p1) twice, k1, sl 1 yif, (sl 1 yib, p1) twice, (k1, sl 1 yif) 3 times, (sl 1 yib, p1) 5 times. Turn.

Row 9: light—(k1, sl 1 yif) 4 times, (sl 1 yib, p1) 5 times, k1, sl 1 yif, sl 1 yib, p1, k1, sl 1 yif, (sl 1 yib, p1) 5 times, (k1, sl 1 yif) 4 times. Turn.

Row 11: light—(sl 1 yib, p1) 4 times, (k1, sl 1 yif) 13 times, (sl 1 yib, p1) 4 times. Turn.

Row 13: light—(k1, sl 1 yif) 3 times, (sl 1 yib, p1) 15 times, (k1, sl 1 yif) 3 times. Turn.

Row 15: light (maintain)—(sl 1 yib, p1) 3 times, (k1, sl 1 yif) 15 times, (sl 1 yib, p1) 3 times. Turn.

Row 17: light (maintain)—rep row 13. Turn.

Row 19: light (maintain)—rep row 15. Turn.

Row 21: light (maintain)—rep row 13. Turn.

Row 23: light—(sl 1 yib, p1) 4 times, (k1, sl 1 yif) 13 times, (sl 1 yib, p1) 4 times. Turn.

Row 25: light—(k1, sl 1 yif) 4 times, (sl 1 yib, p1) 3 times, k1, sl 1 yif, (sl 1 yib, p1) 5 times, k1, sl 1 yif, (sl 1 yib, p1) 3 times, (k1, sl 1 yif) 4 times. Turn.

Row 27: light—(sl 1 yib, p1) 7 times, (k1, sl 1 yif) 7 times, (sl 1 yib, p1) 7 times. Turn.

Row 29: light (maintain)—(k1, sl 1 yif) 7 times, (sl 1 yib, p1) 7 times, (k1, sl 1 yif) 7 times. Turn.

Row 31: light (maintain)—rep row 27. Turn.

Row 33: light (maintain)—rep row 29. Turn.

Row 35: light (maintain)—rep row 27. Turn.

Row 37: light—(k1, sl 1 yif) 8 times, (sl 1 yib, p1) 5 times, (k1, sl 1 yif) 8 times. Turn.

Row 39: light—rep row 3. Turn.

Row 41: light—(k1, sl 1 yif) 10 times, sl 1 yib, p1, (k1, sl 1 yif) 10 times. Turn.

Follow with Solid Two-Color Opposite Reversible, starting with row 3.

WREATH MOTIF

opposite reversible

This pattern creates a polka-dot effect. The advanced knitter, if she wishes, can open up or enlarge the design so there won't be so many wreaths in a given area. If you try to work this pattern without referring to the directions after you have done a set, certain slip stitches may give you trouble. They are slipped only to give a rounder effect (circles being very difficult to achieve in knitting). These stitches are printed in italics to guide you.

Use of dpn required. Multiple of 24 stitches plus 2. Cast on dark, slide.

Preparatory row A: light—* p1, sl 1 yib, rep from *. Turn.

Preparatory row B: with dark rep row A. Slide.

Row 1:   light—sl 1 yif, * (k1, sl 1 yif) 3 times, sl 1 yib, p1, (k1, sl 1 yif) 8 times, rep from *, k last st of row. Turn.

Row 2:   dark—sl 1 yif, * (k1, sl 1 yif) 8 times, sl 1 yib, p1, (k1, sl 1 yif) 3 times, rep from *, k last st. Slide.

Row 3:   light—p1, * (sl 1 yib, p1) 7 times, k1, sl 1 yif, *sl 1 yib,* sl 1 yif, k1, sl 1 yif, (sl 1 yib, p1) twice, rep from *, sl last st. Turn.

Row 4:   dark—p1, * (sl 1 yib, p1) twice, k1, sl 1 yif, *sl 1 yib,* sl 1 yif, k1, sl 1 yif, (sl 1 yib, p1) 7 times, rep from *, sl last st. Slide.

Row 5:   light—sl 1 yif, * k1, sl 1 yif, sl 1 yib, p1, (k1, sl 1 yif) 3 times, sl 1 yib, p1, (k1, sl 1 yif) 6 times, rep from *, k last st. Turn.

Row 6:   dark—sl 1 yif, * (k1, sl 1 yif) 6 times, sl 1 yib, p1, (k1, sl 1 yif) 3 times, sl 1 yib, p1, k1, sl 1 yif, rep from *, k last st. Slide.

Row 7:   light—p1, * (sl 1 yib, p1) 6 times, k1, sl 1 yif, (sl 1 yib, p1) 3 times, k1, sl 1 yif, sl 1 yib, p1, rep from *, sl last st. Turn.

Row 8:   dark—p1, * sl 1 yib, p1, k1, sl 1 yif, (sl 1 yib, p1) 3 times, k1, sl 1 yif, (sl 1 yib, p1) 6 times, rep from *, sl last st. Slide.

Row 9: light—sl 1, * k1, sl 1 yif, *sl 1 yib, sl 1 yif,* (k1, sl 1 yif) 3 times, *sl 1 yib, sl 1 yif,* (k1, sl 1 yif) 6 times, rep from *, k last st. Turn.

Row 10: dark—sl 1 yif, * (k1, sl 1 yif) 6 times, sl 1 yib, *sl 1 yif,* (k1, sl 1 yif) 3 times, sl 1 yib, *sl 1 yif,* k1, sl 1 yif, rep from *, k last st. Slide.

Row 11: light—rep row 7. Turn.

Row 12: dark—rep row 8. Slide.

Row 13: light—sl 1 yif, * (k1, sl 1 yif) twice, (sl 1 yib, p1) 3 times, (k1, sl 1 yif) 7 times, rep from *, k last st. Turn.

Row 14: dark—sl 1 yif, * (k1, sl 1 yif) 7 times, (sl 1 yib, p1) 3 times, (k1, sl 1 yif) twice, rep from *, k last st. Slide.

Row 15: light—p1, * (sl 1 yib, p1) 8 times, *sl 1 yib,* sl 1 yif, (sl 1 yib, p1) 3 times, rep from *, sl last st. Turn.

Row 16: dark—p1, * (sl 1 yib, p1) 3 times, *sl 1 yib,* sl 1 yif, (sl 1 yib, p1) 8 times, rep from *, sl last st. Slide.

Row 17: light—sl 1, * (k1, sl 1 yif) 9 times, sl 1 yib, p1, (k1, sl 1 yif) twice, rep from *, k last st. Turn.

Row 18: dark—sl 1, * (k1, sl 1 yif) twice, sl 1 yib, p1, (k1, sl 1 yif) 9 times, rep from *, k last st. Slide.

Row 19: light—p1, * sl 1 yib, p1, k1, sl 1 yif, *sl 1 yib,* sl 1 yif, k1, sl 1 yif, (sl 1 yib, p1) 8 times, rep from *, sl last st. Turn.

Row 20: dark—p1, * (sl 1 yib, p1) 8 times, k1, sl 1 yif, *sl 1 yib,* sl 1 yif, k1, sl 1 yif, sl 1 yib, p1, rep from *, k last st. Slide.

Row 21: light—sl 1, * (k1, sl 1 yif) 7 times, sl 1 yib, p1, (k1, sl 1 yif) 3 times, sl 1 yib, p1, rep from *, k last st. Turn.

Row 22: dark—sl 1, * sl 1 yib, p1 (k1, sl 1 yif) 3 times, sl 1 yib, p1, (k1, sl 1 yif) 7 times, rep from *, k last st. Slide.

Row 23: light—p1, * k1, sl 1 yif, (sl 1 yib, p1) 3 times, k1, sl 1 yif, (sl 1 yib, p1) 7 times, rep from *, sl last st. Turn.

Row 24: dark—p1, * (sl 1 yib, p1) 7 times, k1, sl 1 yif, (sl 1 yib, p1) 3 times, k1, sl 1 yif, rep from *, sl last st. Slide.

Row 25: light—sl 1, * (k1, sl 1 yif) 7 times, sl 1 yib, *sl 1 yif,* (k1, sl 1 yif) 3 times, sl 1 yib, *sl 1 yif,* rep from *, k last st. Turn.

Row 26: dark—sl 1, * sl 1 yib, *sl 1 yif,* (k1 sl 1 yif) 3 times, sl 1 yib, *sl 1 yif,* (k1 sl 1 yif) 7 times, rep from *, k last st. Slide.

Row 27: light—rep row 23. Turn.

Row 28: dark—rep row 24. Slide.

Row 29: light—sl 1, * (k1, sl 1 yif) 8 times, (sl 1 yib, p1) 3 times, k1, sl 1 yif, rep from *, k last st. Turn.

Row 30: dark—sl 1, * k1, sl 1 yif, (sl 1 yib, p1) 3 times, (k1, sl 1 yif) 8 times, rep from *, k last st. Slide.

Row 31: light—p1, * (sl 1 yib, p1) twice, *sl 1 yib,* sl 1 yif, (sl 1 yib, p1) 9 times, rep from *, sl last st. Turn.

Row 32: dark—p1, * (sl 1 yib, p1) 9 times, *sl 1 yib,* sl 1 yif, (sl 1 yib, p1) twice, rep from *, sl last st. Slide.

rep rows 1–32.

At end, work—

Finishing Row I: light—* sl 1 yif, k1, rep from *. Turn.

Finishing Row II: with dark rep Finishing Row I. Slide.

CANADIAN MAPLE LEAF MOTIF

opposite reversible

Work Solid Two-Color Opposite Reversible, as many rows as needed, before and after the motif. Even rows of pattern rep, with dark, the previous light row.

Use of dpn required. 42 sts (allows 2 sts left and right of motif on each surface). Cast on dark, slide.

Row 1: light—(k1, sl 1 yif) 10 times, sl 1 yib, p1, (k1, sl 1 yif) 10 times. Turn.

Row 3: light (maintain)—(sl 1 yib, p1) 10 times, k1, sl 1 yif, (sl 1 yib, p1) 10 times. Turn.

Row 5: light (maintain)—rep row 1. Turn.

Row 7: light—(sl 1 yib, p1) 6 times, (k1, sl 1 yif) twice, (sl 1 yib, p1) twice, k1, sl 1 yif, (sl 1 yib, p1) twice, (k1, sl 1 yif) twice, (sl 1 yib, p1) 6 times. Turn.

Row 9: light—(k1, sl 1 yif) 6 times, (sl 1 yib, p1) 3 times, k1, sl 1 yif, sl 1 yib, p1, k1, sl 1 yif, (sl 1 yib, p1) 3 times, (k1, sl 1 yif) 6 times. Turn.

Row 11: light—(sl 1 yib, p1) 7 times, (k1, sl 1 yif) 7 times, (sl 1 yib, p1) 7 times. Turn.

Row 13: light—(k1, sl 1 yif) 6 times, (sl 1 yib, p1) 9 times, (k1, sl 1 yif) 6 times. Turn.

Row 15: light—(sl 1 yib, p1) 5 times, (k1, sl 1 yif) 11 times, (sl 1 yib, p1) 5 times. Turn.

Row 17: light—(k1, sl 1 yif) 3 times, (sl 1 yib, p1) 15 times, (k1, sl 1 yif) 3 times. Turn.

Row 19: light—(sl 1 yib, p1) twice, (k1, sl 1 yif) 17 times, (sl 1 yib, p1) twice. Turn.

Row 21: light (maintain)—(k1, sl 1 yif) twice, (sl 1 yib, p1) 17 times, (k1, sl 1 yif) twice. Turn.

Row 23: light—(sl 1 yib, p1) 3 times, (k1, sl 1 yif) 15 times, (sl 1 yib, p1) 3 times. Turn.

Row 25: light—(k1, sl 1 yif) 3 times, (sl 1 yib, p1) 4 times, k1, sl 1 yif, (sl 1 yib, p1) 5 times, k1, sl 1 yif, (sl 1 yib, p1) 4 times, (k1, sl 1 yif) 3 times. Turn.

Row 27: light—(sl 1 yib, p1) 3 times, (k1, sl 1 yif) 3 times, (sl 1 yib, p1) twice, (k1, sl 1 yif) 5 times, (sl 1 yib, p1) twice, (k1, sl 1 yif) 3 times, (sl 1 yib, p1) 3 times. Turn.

Row 29: light—(k1, sl 1 yif) 5 times, sl 1 yib, p1, k1, sl 1 yif, (sl 1 yib, p1) 7 times, k1, sl 1 yif, sl 1 yib, p1 (k1, sl 1 yif) 5 times. Turn.

Row 31: light—rep row 11. Turn.

Row 33: light (maintain)—(k1, sl 1 yif) 7 times, (sl 1 yib, p1) 7 times, (k1, sl 1 yif) 7 times. Turn.

Row 35: light—(sl 1 yib, p1) 7 times, k1, sl 1 yif, sl 1 yib, p1, (k1, sl 1 yif) 3 times, sl 1 yib, p1, k1, sl 1 yif, (sl 1 yib, p1) 7 times. Turn.

Row 37: light—(k1, sl 1 yif) 9 times, (sl 1 yib, p1) 3 times, (k1, sl 1 yif) 9 times. Turn.

Row 39: light—(sl 1 yib, p1) 10 times, k1, sl 1 yif, (sl 1 yib, p1) 10 times. Turn.

LARGE STAR MOTIF

opposite reversible

Work as many rows as required of Solid Two-Color Opposite Reversible before and after the motif. Directions are given only for odd-numbered rows. Even-numbered rows repeat, with dark, the previous row (2 repeats 1, 4 repeats 3, etc.)

Use of dpn required. 46 sts (allows two extra stitches left and right of motif on each surface). Cast on dark, slide.

Row 1: light—(k1, sl 1 yif) 5 times, sl 1 yib, p1, (k1, sl 1 yif) 11 times, sl 1 yib, p1, (k1, sl 1 yif) 5 times. Turn.

Row 3: light—(sl 1 yib, p1) 5 times, (k1, sl 1 yif) twice, (sl 1 yib, p1) 9 times, (k1, sl 1 yif) twice, (sl 1 yib, p1) 5 times. Turn.

Row 5: light—(k1, sl 1 yif) 5 times, (sl 1 yib, p1) 3 times, (k1, sl 1 yif) 7 times, (sl 1 yib, p1) 3 times, (k1, sl 1 yif) 5 times. Turn.

Row 7: light—(sl 1 yib, p1) 6 times, (k1, sl 1 yif) 3 times, (sl 1 yib, p1) 5 times, (k1, sl 1 yif) 3 times, (sl 1 yib, p1) 6 times. Turn.

Row 9: light—(k1, sl 1 yif) 6 times, (sl 1 yib, p1) 4 times, (k1, sl 1 yif) 3 times, (sl 1 yib, p1) 4 times, (k1, sl 1 yif) 6 times. Turn.

Row 11: light—(sl 1 yib, p1) 7 times, (k1, sl 1 yif) 4 times, sl 1 yib, p1, (k1, sl 1 yif) 4 times, (sl 1 yib, p1) 7 times. Turn.

Row 13: light—(k1, sl 1 yif) 7 times, (sl 1 yib, p1) 9 times, (k1, sl 1 yif) 7 times. Turn.

Row 15: light—(sl 1 yib, p1) 8 times, (k1, sl 1 yif) 7 times, (sl 1 yib, p1) 8 times. Turn.

Row 17: light (maintain)—(k1, sl 1 yif) 8 times, (sl 1 yib, p1) 7 times, (k1, sl 1 yif) 8 times. Turn.

Row 19: light—(sl 1 yib, p1) 7 times, (k1, sl 1 yif) 9 times, (sl 1 yib, p1) 7 times. Turn.

Row 21: light—(k1, sl yif) 5 times, (sl 1 yib, p1) 13 times, (k1, sl 1 yif) 5 times. Turn.

Row 23: light—(sl 1 yib, p1) 4 times, (k1, sl 1 yif) 15 times, (sl 1 yib, p1) 4 times. Turn.

Row 25: light—(k1, sl 1 yif) 3 times, (sl 1 yib, p1) 17 times, (k1, sl 1 yif) 3 times. Turn.

Row 27: light—(sl 1 yib, p1) twice, (k1, sl 1 yif) 19 times, (sl 1 yib, p1) twice. Turn.

Row 29: light—(k1, sl 1 yif) 9 times, (sl 1 yib, p1) 5 times, (k1, sl 1 yif) 9 times. Turn.

Row 31: light (maintain)—(sl 1 yib, p1) 9 times, (k1, sl 1 yif) 5 times, (sl 1 yib, p1) 9 times. Turn.

Row 33: light—(k1, sl 1 yif) 10 times, (sl 1 yib, p1) 3 times, (k1, sl 1 yif) 10 times. Turn.

Row 35: light (maintain)—(sl 1 yib, p1) 10 times, (k1, sl 1 yif) 3 times, (sl 1 yib, p1) 10 times. Turn.

Row 37: light (maintain) rep row 33. Turn.

Row 39: light—(sl 1 yib, p1) 11 times, k1, sl 1 yif, (sl 1 yib, p1) 11 times. Turn.

Row 41: light (maintain)—(k1, sl 1 yif) 11 times, sl 1 yib, p1, (k1, sl 1 yif) 11 times. Turn.

Medium Star Motif

All preparatory information same as Large Star except: uses 30 sts.

Row 1: light—(k1, sl 1 yif) 3 times, sl 1 yib, p1, (k1, sl 1 yif) 7 times, sl 1 yib, p1, (k1, sl 1 yif) 3 times. Turn.

Row 3: light—(sl 1 yib, p1) 3 times, (k1, sl 1 yif) twice, (sl 1 yib, p1) 5 times, (k1, sl 1 yif) twice, (sl 1 yib, p1) 3 times. Turn.

Row 5: light—(k1, sl 1 yif) 4 times, (sl 1 yib, p1) twice, (k1, sl 1 yif) 3 times, (sl 1 yib, p1) twice, (k1, sl 1 yif) 4 times. Turn.

Row 7: light—(sl 1 yib, p1) 4 times, (k1, sl 1 yif) 3 times, sl 1 yib, p1, (k1, sl 1 yif) 3 times, (sl 1 yib, p1) 4 times. Turn.

Row 9: light—(k1, sl 1 yif) 5 times, (sl 1 yib, p1) 5 times, (k1, sl 1 yif) 5 times. Turn.

Row 11: light (maintain)—(sl 1 yib, p1) 5 times, (k1, sl 1 yif) 5 times, (sl 1 yib, p1) 5 times. Turn.

Row 13: light—(k1, sl 1 yif) 4 times, (sl 1 yib, p1) 7 times, (k1, sl 1 yif) 4 times. Turn.

Row 15: light—(sl 1 yib, p1) 3 times, (k1, sl 1 yif) 9 times, (sl 1 yib, p1) 3 times. Turn.

Row 17: light—(k1, sl 1 yif) twice, (sl 1 yib, p1) 11 times, (k1, sl 1 yif) twice. Turn.

Row 19: light—(sl 1 yib, p1) 6 times, (k1, sl 1 yif) 3 times, (sl 1 yib, p1) 6 times. Turn.

Row 21: light—(k1, sl 1 yif) 7 times, sl 1 yib, p1, (k1, sl 1 yif) 7 times. Turn.

Row 23: light (maintain)—(sl 1 yib, p1) 7 times, k1, sl 1 yif, (sl 1 yib, p1) 7 times. Turn.

Row 25: light (maintain)—rep row 21. Turn.

Finish with Solid Two-Color Opposite Reversible, starting with row 3.

Small Star Motif

Like Large Star except uses 22 sts.

Row 1: light—(k1, sl 1 yif) 3 times, sl 1 yib, p1, (k1, sl 1 yif) 3 times, sl 1 yib, p1, (k1, sl 1 yif) 3 times. Turn.

Row 3: light—(sl 1 yib, p1) 3 times, (k1, sl 1 yif) twice, sl 1 yib, p1, (k1, sl 1 yif) twice, (sl 1 yib, p1) 3 times. Turn.

Row 5: light—(k1, sl 1 yif) 4 times, (sl 1 yib, p1) 3 times, (k1, sl 1 yif) 4 times. Turn.

Row 7: light (maintain)—(sl 1 yib, p1) 4 times, (k1, sl 1 yif) 3 times, (sl 1 yib, p1) 4 times. Turn.

Row 9: light—(k1, sl 1 yif) 3 times, (sl 1 yib, p1) 5 times, (k1, sl 1 yif) 3 times. Turn.

Row 11: light—(sl 1 yib, p1) twice, (k1, sl 1 yif) 7 times, (sl 1 yib, p1) twice. Turn.

Row 13: light (k1, sl 1 yif) 5 times, sl 1 yib, p1, (k1, sl 1 yif) 5 times. Turn.

Row 15: light (maintain)—(sl 1 yib, p1) 5 times, k1, sl 1 yif, (sl 1 yib, p1) 5 times. Turn.

HEART MOTIF

opposite reversible

Use of dpn required. 42 sts (allows 3 extra sts left and right of motif on each surface). Cast on dark, slide. Each even row is a rep with dark of previous row.

Row 1: light—(k1, sl 1 yif) 10 times, sl 1 yib, p1, (k1, sl 1 yif) 10 times. Turn.

Row 3: light (maintain)—(sl 1 yib, p1) 10 times, k1, sl 1 yif, (sl 1 yib, p1) 10 times. Turn.

Row 5: light—(k1, sl 1 yif) 9 times, (sl 1 yib, p1) 3 times, (k1, sl 1 yif) 9 times. Turn.

Row 7: light (maintain)—(sl 1 yib, p1) 9 times, (k1, sl 1 yif) 3 times, (sl 1 yib, p1) 9 times. Turn.

Row 9: light—(k1, sl 1 yif) 8 times, (sl 1 yib, p1) 5 times, (k1, sl 1 yif) 8 times. Turn.

Row 11: light—(sl 1 yib, p1) 7 times, (k1, sl 1 yif) 7 times, (sl 1 yib, p1) 7 times. Turn.

Row 13: light (maintain)—(k1, sl 1 yif) 7 times, (sl 1 yib, p1) 7 times, (k1, sl 1 yif) 7 times. Turn.

Row 15: light—(sl 1 yib, p1) 6 times, (k1, sl 1 yif) 9 times, (sl 1 yib, p1) 6 times. Turn.

Row 17: light—(k1, sl 1 yif) 5 times, (sl 1 yib, p1) 11 times, (k1, sl 1 yif) 5 times. Turn.

Row 19: light (maintain)—(sl 1 yib, p1) 5 times, (k1, sl 1 yif) 11 times, (sl 1 yib, p1) 5 times. Turn.

Row 21: light—(k1, sl 1 yif) 4 times, (sl 1 yib, p1) 13 times, (k1, sl 1 yif) 4 times. Turn.

Row 23: light (maintain)—(sl 1 yib, p1) 4 times, (k1, sl 1 yif) 13 times, (sl 1 yib, p1) 4 times. Turn.

Row 25: light—(k1, sl 1 yif) 3 times, (sl 1 yib, p1) 15 times, (k1, sl 1 yif) 3 times. Turn.

Row 27: light (maintain)—(sl 1 yib, p1) 3 times. (k1, sl 1 yif) 15 times, (sl 1 yib, p1) 3 times. Turn.

Rows 29–32 (all maintain): rep rows 25–28.

Rows 33 and 34 (maintain): rep rows 25 and 26.

Row 35: light—(sl 1 yib, p1) 3 times, (k1, sl 1 yif) 7 times, sl 1 yib, p1, (k1, sl 1 yif) 7 times, (sl 1 yib, p1) 3 times. Turn.

Row 37: light—(k1, sl 1 yif) 4 times, (sl 1 yib, p1) 6 times, k1, sl 1 yif, (sl 1 yib, p1) 6 times, (k1, sl 1 yif) 4 times. Turn.

Row 39: light—(sl 1 yib, p1) 4 times, (k1, sl1 yif) 5 times, (sl 1 yib, p1) 3 times, (k1, sl 1 yif) 5 times, (sl 1 yib, p1) 4 times. Turn.

Row 41: light—(k1, sl 1 yif) 5 times, (sl 1 yib, p1) 3 times, (k1, sl 1 yif) 5 times, (sl 1 yib, p1) 3 times, (k1, sl 1 yif) 5 times. Turn.

Work Solid Two-Color Opposite Reversible as needed, starting with row 3.

DARYL'S DAISIES

opposite and mirror reversible

This is a prime example of why the "spot form" of reversible geometric is seldom used. While it makes an unusually pretty fabric, the directions are long and complicated without even a "maintain" row along the way. However, it is worth the effort for an occasional special article.

Use of dpn required. Multiple of 36 sts plus 2. Cast on dark, slide.

Row 1: light—sl 1 * (k1, sl 1 yif) twice, (sl 1 yib, p1) 3 times, (k1, sl 1 yif) 9 times, (sl 1 yib, p1) twice, (k1, sl 1 yif) twice, rep from *, k last st. Turn.

Row 2: dark—sl 1 * (k1, sl 1 yif) twice, (sl 1 yib, p1) twice, (k1, sl 1 yif) 9 times, (sl 1 yib, p1) 3 times, (k1, sl 1 yif) twice, rep from *, k last st. Slide.

Row 3: light—p1, * sl 1 yib, p1, (k1, sl 1 yif) twice, (sl 1 yib, p1) 11 times, (k1, sl 1 yif) 3 times, sl 1 yib, p1, rep from *, sl last st. Turn.

Row 4: dark—p1, * sl 1 yib, p1, (k1, sl 1 yif) 3 times, (sl 1 yib, p1) 11 times, (k1, sl 1 yif) twice, sl 1 yib, p1, rep from *, sl last st. Slide.

Row 5: light—sl 1, * (sl 1 yib, p1) twice, (k1, sl 1 yif) 12 times, (sl 1 yib, p1) 4 times, rep from *, k last st. Turn.

Row 6: dark—sl 1, * (sl 1 yib, p1) 4 times, (k1, sl 1 yif) 12 times, (sl 1 yib, p1) twice, rep from *, k last. Slide.

Row 7: light—p1, * sl 1 yib, p1 (k1, sl 1 yif) 3 times, (sl 1 yib, p1) 11 times, (k1, sl 1 yif) 3 times, rep from *, sl last st. Turn.

Row 8: dark—p1, * (k1, sl 1 yif) 3 times, (sl 1 yib, p1) 11 times, (k1, sl 1 yif) 3 times, sl 1 yib, p1, rep from *, sl last st. Slide.

Row 9: light—sl 1 * (sl 1 yib, p1) 3 times, (k1, sl 1 yif) 12 times, sl 1 yib, p1, (k1, sl 1 yif) twice, rep from *, k last. Turn.

Row 10: dark—sl 1 * (k1, sl 1 yif) twice, sl 1 yib, p1, (k1, sl 1 yif) 12 times, (sl 1 yib, p1) 3 times, rep from *, k last st. Slide.

Row 11: light—p1, * (sl 1 yib, p1) 10 times, k1, sl 1 yif, (sl 1 yib, p1) 5 times, k1, sl 1 yif, sl 1 yib, p1, rep from *, sl last st. Turn.

Row 12: dark—p1, * sl 1 yib, p1, k1, sl 1 yif, (sl 1 yib, p1) 5 times, k1, sl 1 yif, (sl 1 yib, p1) 10 times, rep from *, sl last st. Slide.

Row 13: light—sl 1, * (k1, sl 1 yif) 6 times, (sl 1 yib, p1) 3 times, (k1, sl 1 yif) twice, sl 1 yib, p1, (k1, sl 1 yif) 6 times, rep from *, k last st. Turn.

Row 14: dark—sl 1, * (k1, sl 1 yif) 6 times, sl 1 yib, p1 (k1, sl 1 yif) twice, (sl 1 yib, p1) 3 times, (k1, sl 1 yif) 6 times, rep from *, k last st. Slide.

Row 15: light—p1, * (sl 1 yib, p1) 5 times, (k1, sl 1 yif) 3 times, sl 1 yib, p1, (k1, sl 1 yif) 3 times, (sl 1 yib, p1) 6 times, rep from *, sl last st. Turn.

Row 16: dark—p1, * (sl 1 yib, p1) 6 times, (k1, sl 1 yif) 3 times, sl 1 yib, p1, (k1, sl 1 yif) 3 times, (sl 1 yib, p1) 5 times, rep from *, sl last st. Slide.

Row 17: light—sl 1 * (k1, sl 1 yif) 7 times, (sl 1 yib, p1) 6 times, (k1, sl 1 yif) 5 times, rep from *, k last st. Turn.

Row 18: dark—sl 1, * (k1, sl 1 yif) 5 times, (sl 1 yib, p1) 6 times, (k1, sl 1 yif) 7 times, rep from *, k last st. Slide.

Row 19: light—p1, * (sl 1 yib, p1) 6 times, (k1, sl 1 yif) twice, (sl 1 yib, p1) twice, (k1, sl 1 yif) 3 times, (sl 1 yib, p1) 5 times, rep from *, sl last st. Turn.

Row 20: dark—p1, * (sl 1 yib, p1) 5 times, (k1, sl yif) 3 times, (sl 1 yib, p1) twice, (k1, sl 1 yif) twice, (sl 1 yib, p1) 6 times, rep from *, sl last st. Slide.

Row 21: light—sl 1 * (k1, sl 1 yif) 4 times, (sl 1 yib, p1) 3 times, (k1, sl 1 yif) 4 times, (sl 1 yib, p1) twice, (k1, sl 1 yif) 5 times, rep from *, k last st. Turn.

Row 22: dark—sl 1, * (k1, sl 1 yif) 5 times, (sl 1 yib, p1) twice, (k1, sl 1 yif) 4 times, (sl 1 yib, p1) 3 times, (k1, sl 1 yif) 4 times, rep from *, k last st. Slide.

Row 23: light—p1, * (sl 1 yib, p1) 4 times, (k1, sl 1 yif) 3 times, (sl 1 yib, p1) 4 times, (k1, sl 1 yif) twice, (sl 1 yib, p1) 5 times, rep from *, sl last st. Turn.

Row 24: dark—p1, * (sl 1 yib, p1) 5 times, (k1, sl 1 yif) twice, (sl 1 yib, p1) 4 times, (k1, sl 1 yif) 3 times, (sl 1 yib, p1) 4 times, rep from *, sl last st. Slide.

Row 25: light—sl 1, * (k1, sl 1 yif) 6 times, (sl 1 yib, p1) twice, (k1, sl 1 yif) twice, (sl 1 yib, p1) 3 times, (k1, sl 1 yif) 5 times, rep from *, k last st. Turn.

Row 26: dark—sl 1, * (k1, sl 1 yif) 5 times, (sl 1 yib, p1) 3 times, (k1, sl 1 yif) twice, (sl 1 yib, p1) twice, (k1, sl 1 yif) 6 times, rep from *, k last st. Slide.

Row 27: light—p1, * (sl 1 yib, p1) 7 times, (k1, sl 1 yif) 6 times, (sl 1 yib, p1) 5 times, rep from *, sl last st. Turn.

Row 28: dark—p1, * (sl 1 yib, p1) 5 times, (k1, sl 1 yif) 6 times, (sl 1 yib, p1) 7 times, rep from *, sl last st. Slide.

Row 29: light—sl 1, * (k1, sl 1 yif) 5 times, (sl 1 yib, p1) 3 times, k1, sl 1 yif, (sl 1 yib, p1) 3 times, (k1, sl 1 yif) 6 times, rep from *, k last st. Turn.

Row 30: dark—sl 1, * (k1, sl 1 yif) 6 times, (sl 1 yib, p1) 3 times, k1, sl 1 yif, (sl 1 yib, p1) 3 times, (k1, sl 1 yif) 5 times, rep from *, k last st. Slide.

Row 31: light—p1, * (sl 1 yib, p1) 6 times, (k1, sl 1 yif) 3 times, (sl 1 yib, p1) twice, k1, sl 1 yif, (sl 1 yib, p1) 6 times, rep from *, sl last st. Turn.

Row 32: dark—p1, * (sl 1 yib, p1) 6 times, k1, sl 1 yif, (sl 1 yib, p1) twice, (k1, sl 1 yif), 3 times, (sl 1 yib, p1) 6 times, rep from *, sl last st. Slide.

Row 33: light—sl 1, * (k1, sl 1 yif) 10 times, sl 1 yib, p1, (k1, sl 1 yif) 5 times, sl 1 yib, p1, k1, sl 1 yif, rep from *, k last st. Turn.

Row 34: dark—sl 1, * k1, sl 1 yif, sl 1 yib, p1, (k1, sl 1 yif) 5 times, sl 1 yib, p1, (k1, sl 1 yif) 10 times, rep from *, k last st. Slide.

Row 35: light—p1, * (k1, sl 1 yif) 3 times, (sl 1 yib, p1) 12 times, k1, sl 1 yif, (sl 1 yib, p1) twice, rep from *, sl last st. Turn.

Row 36: dark—p1, * (sl 1 yib, p1) twice, k1, sl 1 yif, (sl 1 yib, p1) 12 times, (k1, sl 1 yif) 3 times, rep from *, sl last st. Slide.

Row 37: light—sl 1, * k1, sl 1 yif, (sl 1 yib, p1) 3 times, (k1, sl 1 yif) 11 times, (sl 1 yib, p1) 3 times, rep from *, k last st. Turn.

Row 38: dark—sl 1, * (sl 1 yib, p1) 3 times, (k1, sl 1 yif) 11 times, (sl 1 yib, p1) 3 times, k1, sl 1 yif, rep from *, k last st. Slide.

Row 39: light—p1, * (k1, sl 1 yif) twice, (sl 1 yib, p1) 12 times, (k1, sl 1 yif) 4 times, rep from *, sl last st. Turn.

Row 40: dark—p1, * (k1, sl 1 yif) 4 times, (sl 1 yib, p1) 12 times, (k1, sl 1 yif) twice, rep from *, sl last st. Slide.

Row 41: light—sl 1, * k1, sl 1 yif, (sl 1 yib, p1) twice, (k1, sl 1 yif) 11 times, (sl 1 yib, p1) 3 times, k1, sl 1 yif, rep from *, k last st. Turn.

Row 42: dark—sl 1, * k1, sl 1 yif, (sl 1 yib, p1) 3 times, (k1, sl 1 yif) 11 times, (sl 1 yib, p1) twice, k1, sl 1 yif, rep from *, k last st. Slide.

Row 43: light—p1, * (sl 1 yib, p1) twice, (k1, sl 1 yif) 3 times, (sl 1 yib, p1) 9 times, (k1, sl 1 yif) twice, (sl 1 yib, p1) twice, rep from *, sl last st. Turn.

Row 44: dark—p1, * (sl 1 yib, p1) twice, (k1, sl 1 yif) twice, (sl 1 yib, p1) 9 times, (k1, sl 1 yif) 3 times, (sl 1 yib, p1) twice, rep from *, sl last st. Slide.

rep Rows 1–44.

COAT OF ARMS

opposite reversible

This is a complicated motif. Of course, you could design your own. It is an interesting motif for use on a pocket.

Use of dpn required. 42 sts (allows 2 sts right and left of motif on each surface). Cast on dark, slide.

Row 1: light—(k1, sl 1 yif) 10 times, sl 1 yib, p1, (k1, sl 1 yif) 10 times. Turn.

Row 2: with dark rep row 1. Slide.

Row 3: light—(sl 1 yib, p1) 9 times, (k1, sl 1 yif) 3 times, (sl 1 yib, p1) 9 times. Turn.

Row 4: with dark rep row 3. Slide.

Row 5: light—(k1, sl 1 yif) 6 times, (sl 1 yib, p1) 9 times, (k1, sl 1 yif) 6 times. Turn.

Row 6: with dark rep row 5. Slide.

Row 7: light—(sl 1 yib, p1) 4 times, (k1, sl 1 yif) 7 times, (sl 1 yib, p1) twice, (k1, sl 1 yif) 4 times, (sl 1 yib, p1) 4 times. Turn.

Row 8: dark—(sl 1 yib, p1) 4 times, (k1, sl 1 yif) 4 times, (sl 1 yib, p1) twice, (k1, sl 1 yif) 7 times, (sl 1 yib, p1) 4 times. Slide.

Row 9: light—(k1, sl 1 yif) 3 times, (sl 1 yib, p1) 3 times, (k1, sl 1 yif) 4 times, (sl 1 yib, p1) 4 times, k1, sl 1 yif, (sl 1 yib, p1) 3 times, (k1, sl 1 yif) 3 times. Turn.

Row 10: dark—(k1, sl 1 yif) 3 times, (sl 1 yib, p1) 3 times, k1, sl 1 yif, (sl 1 yib, p1) 4 times, (k1, sl 1 yif) 4 times, (sl 1 yib, p1) 3 times, (k1, sl 1 yif) 3 times. Slide.

Row 11: light—(sl 1 yib, p1) twice, (k1, sl 1 yif) twice, (sl 1 yib, p1) 5 times, * (k1, sl 1 yif) twice, (sl 1 yib, p1) twice, rep from *. Turn.

Row 12: dark—* (sl 1 yib, p1) twice, (k1, sl 1 yif) twice, rep from * twice more, then end (sl 1 yib, p1) 5 times, (k1, sl 1 yif) twice, (sl 1 yib, p1) twice. Slide.

Row 13: light—(k1, sl 1 yif) twice, sl 1 yib, p1, k1, sl 1 yif, (sl 1 yib, p1) 5 times, k1, sl 1 yif, (sl 1 yib, p1) 4 times, k1, sl 1 yif, (sl 1 yib, p1) 4 times, (k1, sl 1 yif) twice. Turn.

Row 14: dark—(k1, sl 1 yif) twice, (sl 1 yib, p1) 4 times, k1, sl 1 yif, (sl 1 yib, p1) 4 times, k1, sl 1 yif, (sl 1 yib, p1) 5 times, k1, sl 1 yif, sl 1 yib, p1, (k1, sl 1 yif) twice. Slide.

Row 15: light—(sl 1 yib, p1) twice, (k1, sl 1 yif) 3 times, (sl 1 yib, p1) 3 times, (k1, sl 1 yif) 3 times, sl 1 yib, p1, (k1, sl 1 yif) 5 times, sl 1 yib, p1, k1, sl 1 yif, (sl 1 yib, p1) twice. Turn.

Row 16: dark—(sl 1 yib, p1) twice, k1, sl 1 yif, sl 1 yib, p1, (k1, sl 1 yif) 5 times, sl 1 yib, p1, (k1, sl 1 yif) 3 times, (sl 1 yib, p1) 3 times, (k1, sl 1 yif) 3 times, (sl 1 yib, p1) twice. Slide.

Row 17: light—(k1, sl 1 yif) twice, sl 1 yib, p1, (k1, sl 1 yif) twice, sl 1 yib, p1, k1, sl 1 yif, (sl 1 yib, p1) twice, k1, sl 1 yif, sl 1 yib, p1, (k1, sl 1 yif) 7 times, sl 1 yib, p1, (k1, sl 1 yif) twice. Turn.

Row 18: dark—(k1, sl 1 yif) twice, sl 1 yib, p1, (k1, sl 1 yif) 7 times, sl 1 yib, p1, k1, sl 1 yif, (sl 1 yib, p1) twice, k1, sl 1 yif, sl 1 yib, p1, (k1, sl 1 yif) twice, sl 1 yib, p1, (k1, sl 1 yif) twice. Slide.

Row 19: light—(sl 1 yib, p1) twice, (k1, sl 1 yif) twice, (sl 1 yib, p1) 5 times, (k1, sl 1 yif) twice, (sl 1 yib, p1) twice, (k1, sl 1 yif) 3 times, (sl 1 yib, p1) twice, k1, sl 1 yif, (sl 1 yib, p1) twice. Turn.

Row 20: dark—(sl 1 yib, p1) twice, k1, sl 1 yif, (sl 1 yib, p1) twice, (k1, sl 1 yif) 3 times, (sl 1 yib, p1) twice, (k1, sl 1 yif) twice, (sl 1 yib, p1) 5 times, (k1, sl 1 yif) twice, (sl 1 yib, p1) twice. Slide.

Row 21: light—(k1, sl 1 yif) twice, sl 1 yib, p1, (k1, sl 1 yif) 4 times, sl 1 yib, p1, (k1, sl 1 yif) twice, (sl 1 yib, p1) twice, (k1, sl 1 yif, sl 1 yib, p1) 3 times, sl 1 yib, p1, (k1, sl 1 yif) twice. Turn.

Row 22: dark—(k1, sl 1 yif) twice, (sl 1 yib, p1) twice, (k1, sl 1 yif, sl 1 yib, p1) 3 times, sl 1 yib, p1, (k1, sl 1 yif) twice, sl 1 yib, p1, (k1, sl 1 yif) 4 times, sl 1 yib, p1, (k1, sl 1 yif) twice. Slide.

Row 23: light—(sl 1 yib, p1) twice, (k1, sl 1 yif) 9 times, (sl 1 yib, p1) 7 times, k1, sl 1 yif, (sl 1 yib, p1) twice. Turn.

Row 24: dark—(sl 1 yib, p1) twice, k1, sl 1 yif, (sl 1 yib, p1) 7 times, (k1, sl 1 yif) 9 times, (k1, sl 1 yif) twice. Slide.

Row 25: light—(k1, sl 1 yif) twice, (sl 1 yib, p1) 9 times, (k1, sl 1 yif) 7 times, sl 1 yib, p1, (k1, sl 1 yif) twice. Turn.

Row 26: dark—(k1, sl 1 yif) twice, sl 1 yib, p1, (k1, sl 1 yif) 7 times, (sl 1 yib, p1) 9 times, (k1, sl 1 yif) twice. Slide.

Row 27: light—(sl 1 yib, p1) twice, (k1, sl 1 yif) twice, (sl 1 yib, p1) twice, k1, sl 1 yif, (sl 1 yib, p1) twice, (k1, sl 1 yif) 3 times, (sl 1 yib, p1) 5 times, (k1, sl 1 yif) twice, (sl 1 yib, p1) twice. Turn.

Row 28: dark—(sl 1 yib, p1) twice, (k1, sl 1 yif) twice, (sl 1 yib, p1) 5 times, (k1, sl 1 yif) 3 times, (sl 1 yib, p1) twice, k1, sl 1 yif, (sl 1 yib, p1) twice, (k1, sl 1 yif) twice, (sl 1 yib, p1) twice. Slide.

Row 29: light—(k1, sl 1 yif) twice, sl 1 yib, p1, (k1, sl 1 yif) twice, (sl 1 yib, p1, k1, sl 1 yif) twice, (k1, sl 1 yif, sl 1 yib, p1) 5 times, (k1, sl 1 yif) twice. Turn.

Row 30: dark—(k1, sl 1 yif) twice, (sl 1 yib, p1, k1, sl 1 yif) 5 times, (k1, sl 1 yif, sl 1 yib, p1) twice, (k1, sl 1 yif) twice, sl 1 yib, p1, (k1, sl 1 yif) twice. Slide.

Row 31: light—(sl 1 yib, p1) twice, k1, sl 1 yif, (sl 1 yib, p1) twice, (k1, sl 1 yif) 3 times, (sl 1 yib, p1) twice, k1, sl 1 yif, sl 1 yib, p1, (k1, sl 1 yif) twice, sl 1 yib, p1, (k1, sl 1 yif) twice, sl 1 yib, p1, k1, sl 1 yif, (sl 1 yib, p1) twice. Turn.

Row 32: dark—(sl 1 yib, p1) twice, k1, sl 1 yif, sl 1 yib, p1, (k1, sl 1 yif) twice, sl 1 yib, p1, (k1, sl 1 yif) twice, sl 1 yib, p1, k1, sl 1 yif, (sl 1 yib, p1) twice, (k1, sl 1 yif) 3 times, (sl 1 yib, p1) twice, k1, sl 1 yif, (sl 1 yib, p1) twice. Slide.

Row 33: light—(k1, sl 1 yif) twice, * (sl 1 yib, p1) 4 times, k1, sl 1 yif, rep from * once, (sl 1 yib, p1) 5 times, k1, sl 1 yif, sl 1 yib, p1, (k1, sl 1 yif) twice. Turn.

Row 34: dark—(k1, sl 1 yif) twice, sl 1 yib, p1, k1, sl 1 yif, (sl 1 yib, p1) 5 times, k1, sl 1 yif, (sl 1 yib, p1) 4 times, k1, sl 1 yif, (sl 1 yib, p1) 4 times, (k1, sl 1 yif) twice. Slide.

Row 35: light—(sl 1 yib, p1) twice, k1, sl 1 yif, (sl 1 yib, p1) twice, (k1, sl 1 yif) 3 times, (sl 1 yib, p1) twice, (k1, sl 1 yif) twice, (sl 1 yib, p1, k1, sl 1 yif) 3 times, k1, sl 1 yif, (sl 1 yib, p1) twice. Turn.

Row 36: dark—(sl 1 yib, p1) twice, (k1, sl 1 yif) twice, (sl 1 yib, p1, k1, sl 1 yif) 3 times, k1, sl 1 yif, (sl 1 yib, p1) twice, (k1, sl 1 yif) 3 times, (sl 1 yib, p1) twice, k1, sl 1 yif, (sl 1 yib, p1) twice. Slide.

Row 37: light—(k1, sl 1 yif) twice, sl 1 yib, p1, (k1, sl 1 yif) 7 times, (sl 1 yib, p1, k1, sl 1 yif) 5 times, k1, sl 1 yif. Turn.

Row 38: dark—(k1, sl 1 yif) twice, (sl 1 yib, p1, k1, sl 1 yif) 5 times, (k1, sl 1 yif) 6 times, sl 1 yib, p1, (k1, sl 1 yif) twice. Slide.

Row 39: light—(sl 1 yib, p1) twice, (k1, sl 1 yif) twice, (sl 1 yib, p1) twice, k1, sl 1 yif, (sl 1 yib, p1) twice, (k1, sl 1 yif) 3 times, (sl 1 yib, p1, k1, sl 1 yif) 3 times, k1, sl 1 yif, (sl 1 yib, p1) twice. Turn.

Row 40: dark—(sl 1 yib, p1) twice, (k1, sl 1 yif) twice, (sl 1 yib, p1, k1, sl 1 yif) 3 times, (k1, sl 1 yif) twice, (sl 1 yib, p1) twice, k1, sl 1 yif, (sl 1 yib, p1) twice, (k1, sl 1 yif) twice, (sl 1 yib, p1) twice. Slide.

Row 41: light—(k1, sl 1 yif) twice, (sl 1 yib, p1) 9 times, (k1, sl 1 yif) twice, (sl 1 yib, p1) 4 times, k1, sl 1 yif, sl 1 yib, p1, (k1, sl 1 yif) twice. Turn.

Row 42: dark—(k1, sl 1 yif) twice, sl 1 yib, p1, k1, sl 1 yif, (sl 1 yib, p1) 4 times, (k1, sl 1 yif) twice, (sl 1 yib, p1) 9 times, (k1, sl 1 yif) twice. Slide.

Work Solid Two-Color Opposite Reversible as desired, starting with row 3.

FOX MOTIF

opposite reversible

The fox head ("mask", to the hunters) is actually 32 sts wide. The directions are written for 40 sts to give a few solid color ones along side it. It is suggested that a few preparatory rows be worked first in Solid Two-Color Opposite Reversible. Since the design is symmetrical, all even numbered rows are repeats, with dark, of the previous light-colored row. These are not written out.

Use of dpn required. 40 sts. Cast on desired color, work preparatory rows starting with light color.

Row 1: light—(k1, sl 1 yif) 9 times, (sl 1 yib, p1) twice, (k1, sl 1 yif) 9 times. Turn.

Row 2 and all even numbered rows: with dark, rep preceding row. Slide.

Row 3: light (maintain)—(sl 1 yib, p1) 9 times, (k1, sl 1 yif) twice, (sl 1 yib, p1) 9 times. Turn.

Row 5: light (maintain)—rep row 1. Turn.

Row 7: light—(sl 1 yib, p1) 8 times, (k1, sl 1 yif) 4 times, (sl 1 yib, p1) 8 times. Turn.

Row 9: light (maintain)—(k1, sl 1 yif) 8 times, (sl 1 yib, p1) 4 times, (k1, sl 1 yif) 8 times. Turn.

Row 11: light—(sl 1 yib, p1) 7 times, (k1, sl 1 yif) 6 times, (sl 1 yib, p1) 7 times. Turn.

Row 13: light—(k1, sl 1 yif) 6 times, (sl 1 yib, p1) 8 times, (k1, sl 1 yif) 6 times. Turn.

Row 15: light—(sl 1 yib, p1) 5 times, (k1, sl 1 yif) 10 times, (sl 1 yib, p1) 5 times. Turn.

Row 17: light—(k1, sl 1 yif) 4 times, (sl 1 yib, p1) 12 times, (k1, sl 1 yif) 4 times. Turn.

Row 19: light—(sl 1 yib, p1) 4 times, (k1, sl 1 yif) 3 times, sl 1 yib, p1, (k1, sl 1 yif) 4 times, sl 1 yib, p1 (k1, sl 1 yif) 3 times, (sl 1 yib, p1) 4 times. Turn.

Row 21: light—(k1, sl 1 yif) 3 times, (sl 1 yib, p1) 3 times, (k1, sl 1 yif) twice, (sl 1 yib, p1) 4 times, (k1, sl 1 yif) twice, (sl 1 yib, p1) 3 times, (k1, sl 1 yif) 3 times. Turn.

Row 23: light—(sl 1 yib, p1) 3 times, (k1, sl 1 yif) 3 times, sl 1 yib, p1, (k1, sl 1 yif) 6 times, sl 1 yib, p1, (k1, sl 1 yif) 3 times, (sl 1 yib, p1) 3 times. Turn.

Row 25: light—(k1, sl 1 yif) 3 times, (sl 1 yib, p1) 14 times, (k1, sl 1 yif) 3 times. Turn.

Row 27: light (maintain)—(sl 1 yib, p1) 3 times, (k1, sl 1 yif) 14 times, (sl 1 yib, p1) 3 times. Turn.

Row 29: light—(k1, sl 1 yif) 4 times, (sl 1 yib, p1) 12 times, (k1, sl 1 yif) 4 times. Turn.

Row 31: light—(sl 1 yib, p1) 4 times, * (k1, sl 1 yif) 4 times, (sl 1 yib, p1) 4 times, rep from *. Turn.

Row 33: light—(k1, sl 1 yif) 3 times, (sl 1 yib, p1) 4 times, (k1, sl 1 yif) 6 times, (sl 1 yib, p1) 4 times, (k1, sl 1 yif) 3 times. Turn.

Row 35: light (maintain)—(sl 1 yib, p1) 3 times, (k1, sl 1 yif) 4 times, (sl 1 yib, p1) 6 times, (k1, sl 1 yif) 4 times, (sl 1 yib, p1) 3 times. Turn.

Row 37: light—(k1, sl 1 yif) 3 times, (sl 1 yib, p1) 3 times, (k1, sl 1 yif) 8 times, (sl 1 yib, p1) 3 times, (k1, sl 1 yif) 3 times. Turn.

Row 39: light—(sl 1 yib, p1) 3 times, (k1, sl 1 yif) twice, (sl 1 yib, p1) 10 times, (k1, sl 1 yif) twice, (sl 1 yib, p1) 3 times. Turn.

Row 41: light—(k1, sl 1 yif) 3 times, sl 1 yib, p1, (k1, sl 1 yif) 12 times, sl 1 yib, p1 (k1, sl 1 yif) 3 times. Turn.

Row 43: light (maintain)—(sl 1 yib, p1) 3 times, k1, sl 1 yif, (sl 1 yib, p1) 12 times k1, sl 1 yif, (sl 1 yib, p1) 3 times. Turn.

Finish by doing more Solid Two-Color Opposite Reversible.

CHAPTER FIVE

SOME ARTICLES TO MAKE

The whole point of knitting is to make something pretty and useful. None of the stitch patterns in this book is worth anything until it is used for some knitted article. This chapter will give a few suggestions of places to start.

One advantage of two-color knitting is the extra firmness gained by the interweaving of two strands of yarn. There are a few items here which are not usually made by knitting but now can be because of this quality. In some of these the reversibility won't even matter. For the more conventional knitter there are also directions for such basics as a sweater, hat, and mittens.

These items are fairly simple to make. The eyeglass cases or belts can each be finished the same day they are started. Simple directions are given to encourage you to try reversible knitting with two colors. If you want to make a major article you will probably prefer to design your own anyway. The color illustrations show not only the articles for which directions are given but several others which may inspire you. Chapter Six will suggest how to proceed.

Since these are mostly small projects, some of them use very little yarn. The directions may call for "$\frac{1}{2}$ oz. of knitting worsted." Yarn companies don't package skeins or balls this size, but if you have a postal or kitchen scale which measures fractions of an ounce you can check whether that bit of yarn left from your last sweater will do the job. In the same vein, have you ever wanted to make a scarf with a different color on the ends to use up some leftover yarn? Simply weigh the yarn first and make a note of the amount. As you work along occasionally weigh again until you have half the original amount left for the other end. You could also weigh and divide the yarn before you start work. The same trick may be used in adding color to a sweater with back and front made separately; for a contrasting band around each sleeve; to divide a color to make even bands across an afghan,

154

etc. You may find yourself using up a lot of yarn leftovers with an assist from a scale. Of course weight gives only a fair estimate. Don't expect it to be accurate down to the exact number of stitches.

Let's return from that digression and try a few reversibles. You will increase the variety of your knitting abilities and possibilities.

REVERSIBLE HAT AND MITTENS

Woven Dot Pattern, adapted for circular knitting:
Rnd 1: white—purl
Rnd 2: double strand red—sl 1 yib, * sl 1 yif, sl 1 yib, rep from *.
Rnd 3: white—knit.
Rnd 4: white—purl.
Rnd 5: double strand red—sl 1 yif, * sl 1 yib, sl 1 yif, rep from *.
Rnd 6: white—knit. Rep these 6 rnds.

Note: always work with a double strand of red yarn. When ending a red rnd, leave yarn where it is (after sl 1 yib, leave yarn in back while working white rnds). (See Plate 4)

HAT

for ages 6–10 years

Materials
2½ oz bulky off-white yarn
less than ½ oz red knitting worsted
1 set (4) size 10 dpn

Gauge
3 sts per inch
10 rnds per inch

Directions
Cast on 71 sts. Divide on three needles, join in a circle, avoiding twisting sts. Put marker on needle at beginning of rnd. Work in pattern, as above, for 13 rnds. Decrease as follows in place of knit rnd: * k2 tog, k7, rep from * but end k6. Continue in pattern on 63 sts until piece measures 4½″ from cast-on. Shape crown: decrease round 1 (instead of k rnd)—* k2 tog, k6, rep from * but end k5. Purl 1 rnd, work 1 rnd red. Decrease rnd 2—* k2 tog, k5, rep from * but end k4. Continue to decr in this fashion every k rnd (next k4 between decrs, then k3, etc.), until 15 sts remain. Last rnd: k2 tog seven times, k1. Pull ends of both colors through last 8 sts. Tuck in ends. Block. (See Plate 4)
Note: continue weaving red strand as before even when decrease rnds seem to upset the established pattern.

MITTENS

for ages 6–8 years (9–10 years in parentheses)

Materials

2 oz (2½ oz) unscoured white fisherman's
    yarn or knitting worsted
1 oz (1 oz) red knitting worsted
1 set (4) size 4 dpn

Gauge

11 sts = 2″
13 rnds = 1″

Directions

With white cast on 32 (36) sts. Divide on 3 needles, join in circle being careful not to twist stitches. Put marker on needle at beginning of rnd. Work in k2, p2 ribbing for 2 (2½) inches, decreasing 1 st in last rnd, giving 31 (35) sts. Work 8 (11) rnds in pattern as above ending with a red rnd.

1st incr rnd: incr 1 in first st, k1, incr 1 in next st, k to end of rnd. Continue pattern on 33 (37) sts. Incr 2 sts in every other k rnd, as: 2nd incr rnd: incr 1 st in first st, k3, incr 1 in next st, k rest of rnd having 35 (39) sts. 3rd incr rnd: k5 between incrs. 4th decr rnd: k7 between incrs. Work even in pattern on 39 (43) sts as follows: * 1 p rnd, 1 red rnd, 1 k rnd, rep from *once (twice). Cast on 3 sts at end of last rnd. Slip to a strand of yarn the 11 thumb sts which come immediately after the marker. Work other 31 (35) sts including the 3 cast on sts in pattern and starting with a p round. Work even until mitten measures 5 (5½) inches above cuff ending with a red rnd.

First decr rnd: * k2 tog, k2, rep from * 8 times (9 times), ending k1. P1 rnd, work 1 rnd red, k1 rnd, p1 rnd, 1 red rnd. 2nd decr rnd: k1, * k2 tog, k1, rep from * 7 (8) times but end k2. 3rd decr rnd: p2 tog 8 (9) times. On 8 (9) sts work 1 rnd red, k1 rnd. Break off both colors. Pull end of white yarn through the 8 (9) remaining sts.

Thumb: Put 11 thumb sts on two needles. With 3rd needle pick up the 3 cast-on sts. P1 rnd, decreasing 1 st. Continue in pattern starting double strand of red in next row. Work even on 13 sts until thumb measures 1½ (1¾) inches above cast-on sts, ending with a red rnd.

1st decr rnd: k1, * k2 tog, k1, rep from *. Work 1 p rnd decreasing 1 st only. Work 1 red rnd. Next rnd, k2 tog four times. Break off yarn pulling white through remaining 4 sts. To finish, work ends of yarn into mitten being especially careful, if you want it to be reversible, that ends do not show on either side. Make second mitten like the first. (See Plate 4)

EYEGLASSES CASES (Plate 5)

Materials, for each case
less than $\frac{1}{2}$ oz knitting worsted
  in dark color
less than $\frac{1}{2}$ oz knitting worsted
  in light color
one pair size 5 dpn
crochet hook

Gauge
8 sts = 1 inch
8 rows = 1 inch

Directions, Dots and Dashes Pattern

Cast on 43 sts and work in pattern as given elsewhere in this book. Note that the case illustrated in color section was made by casting on with white (the light color) and working the first row in red (dark color) which is the opposite of the way the pattern directions are written.

When piece measures approximately 5 inches and you are ready to start a #4 row of the pattern, bind off 22 sts in p1, k1. Continue across remaining 21 sts in established pattern. Break off dark strand of yarn and start new row #1 at end of bind off, being certain to continue pattern. Work 2 dark rows, 2 light, 2 dark, 1 light. Then, with light, bind off remaining sts in p1, k1.

Fold case in half with stripes inside. With light yarn sew across bottom. With light and crochet hook, starting at bottom work single crochet along open side, across top, down to bound-off edge in front. (See Plate 5)

Directions, Stairway Pattern

With light, cast on 50 sts. Work in Stairway pattern for approximately $5\frac{1}{2}$ inches, stopping after an odd-numbered pattern row. Work half (25 sts) of the next row. Put remaining 25 sts on a holder. Start other color and work a half-row over and back with that, continuing in pattern. Next row decrease: put two k sts on needle side by side at each end of the row and k these tog. This will leave 2 p sts side by side at each end. On the next row when they appear as k sts, k2 tog each end. Next row bind off in p1, k1 bind off. Put other 25 sts onto needle, attach yarn and work to compare with side already finished. Fold case in half and sew up open side.

Notes: These two cases are of different design as may be seen in Plate 5. Each will fit average-size glasses but they will have to be enlarged for over-size ones.

If you wish to reinforce the case, cut a piece of plastic approximately $4\frac{1}{2}''$ by $5''$ (from an empty bleach bottle, for example). Fold in half gently (don't crease) making a case about $4\frac{1}{2}''$ tall. Fasten a strip of adhesive tape down the open side. Slip this inside your knitted case. (See Plate 5)

REVERSIBLE BELTS

Materials, for each belt
Knitting worsted, dark and light colors, approx. $\frac{1}{2}$ oz each
one pair dpn, size 6
belt buckle ($1\frac{3}{4}''$ opening for A Cross and Across pattern,
  2″ opening for Nip and Tuck pattern belt)
crochet hook

A CROSS AND ACROSS BELT

Gauge
7 sts = 1 inch

Directions
With size 6 dpn and dark yarn cast on 11 sts. Work in A Cross and Across pattern until belt measures 4 to 6 inches longer than waist (measure with belt slightly stretched). On a number 8 row of pattern, with dark color, * k2 tog, rep from *, end k1. Turn, bind off in dark. Starting at cast-on edge, work sc up side of belt, across end, down other side. Fold cast on edge over buckle and sew on. (See Plate 3)

NIP AND TUCK BELT

Gauge
5 sts = 1 inch

Directions
With size 6 dpn and light yarn cast on 10 sts. Work in Nip and Tuck pattern until belt measures 3″ longer than waist when slightly stretched. Decrease and Bind Off: Row 1: with dark—sl 2 (knitwise), y o, (sl 1, y o) 6 times, sl 2, y o. Row 2: dark—k3 tog in back (that is, the y o and 2 sts), (k2 tog in back) 6 times, k3 tog. Rows 3 and 4: with light, work in pattern on 8 sts. Row 5: with dark—sl 2 y o, (sl 1, y o) 4 times, sl 2, y o. Row 6: dark—k3 tog in back, (k2 tog in back) 4 times, k3 tog. Rows 7 and 8: light—work pattern on 6 sts. Row 9: dark—work pattern on 6 sts. Row 10: dark—k2 tog in back, * k2 tog in back, bind off one, rep from *. Work s c on all edges except cast on. Sew belt to buckle as in previous belt directions. (See Plate 3)

Alternate Method of Working Belts
Work belt until it measures 22 inches longer than waist measurement. Omit decrease and work only bind off (rows 9 and 10 of Nip and Tuck Belt, ordinary bind off on other). Single crochet along both sides. Attach fringe to ends. Wear belt tied with both ends hanging loose.

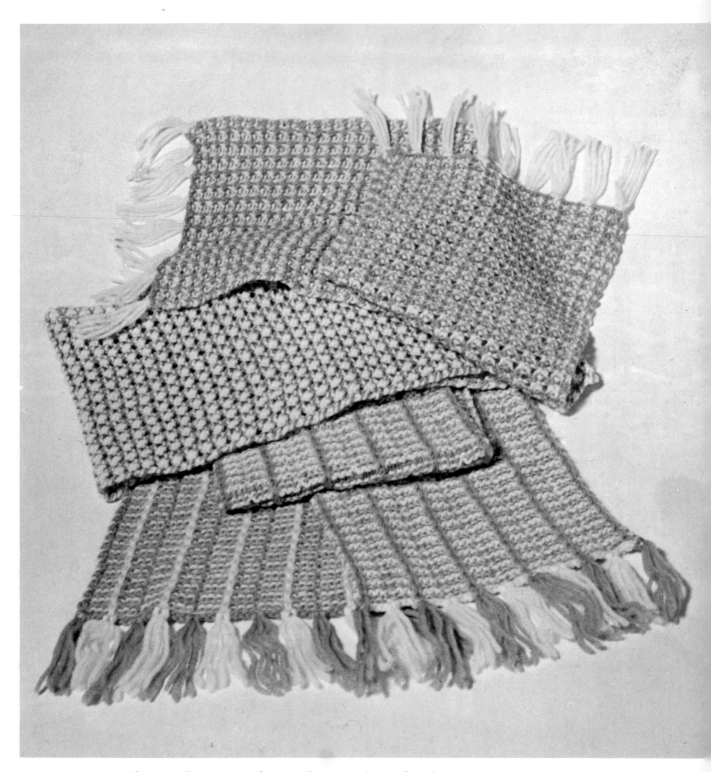

Plate 1. The easiest thing to knit is a fringed stole or cozy
muffler. Two colors can be used without the wearer having
to worry about a wrong side showing. (Patterns: Doubleberry; p. 23 Ripple and Chain p. 38.)

Plate 3. Most knitting isn't firm enough for a belt but these two patterns can handle the job with a little assist from a crocheted edge. The brown one is in the Nip and Tuck pattern, the blue is A Cross and Across. (directions, p. 158).

Plate 2. A larger project, almost as easy as a scarf, is an afghan, either full-sized or baby-sized. This blue and white one is of the thermal Shadow Boxing pattern. P. 24.

Plate 4. This child's hat and mitten set, in Woven Dot pattern, looks essentially the same on both sides. The reversibility can be a great advantage if one side gets dirty before your little imp gets to Grandmother's house. (directions, p. 155).

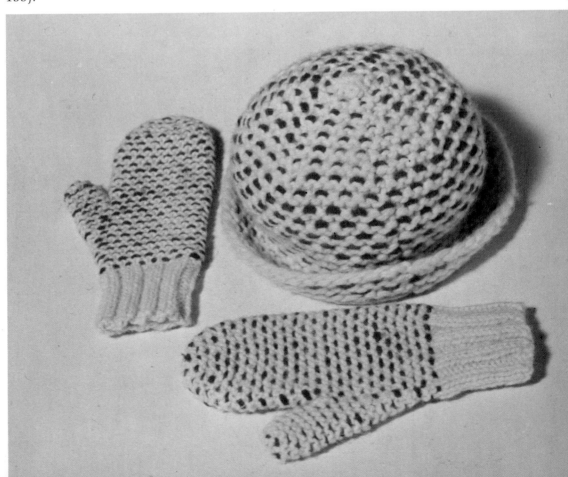

Plate 5. *Reversible geometric patterns are firm enough for eyeglass cases. The brown and gold one, in Stairway pattern, reveals the same effect on the inside. The Dots and Dashes design is striped within. (directions, p. 157).*

Plate 6. *A simple sleeveless v-neck in See the Light pattern looks only slightly different on the two sides. There are no seams to worry about. (directions, p. 160).*

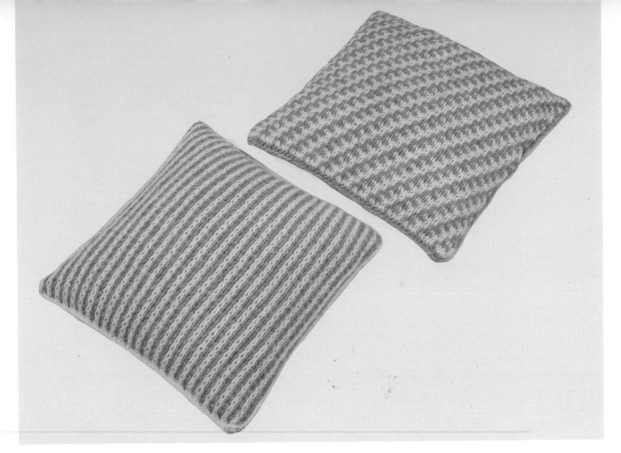

Plate 7. No one will see the reverse of these patterns until they are taken apart and remade after they show signs of wear or spotting. The principal advantages of the patterns are firmness and design. (patterns: Off-set Steps, Two-sided Stripes, variation. Directions, p. 159).

Plate 8. Coasters can be knit from any of the larger motifs. These Christmas Trees have red embroidered decorations. (directions, p. 162).

Plates 9. and 10. This extra-warm ribbed sweater was done in related colors using Shadow Rib, p. 25. It is an ideal sweater for a child. With no front or back, inside or out, it is almost impossible to put on wrong.

Plate 11. This tailored man's vest does double duty. The plain side can be worn with patterned clothing while the argyle side will dress up solid-colored shirt and pants. It was knitted from the top down. (Pattern: enlarged version of Diamond Tweed and Solid, p. 111).

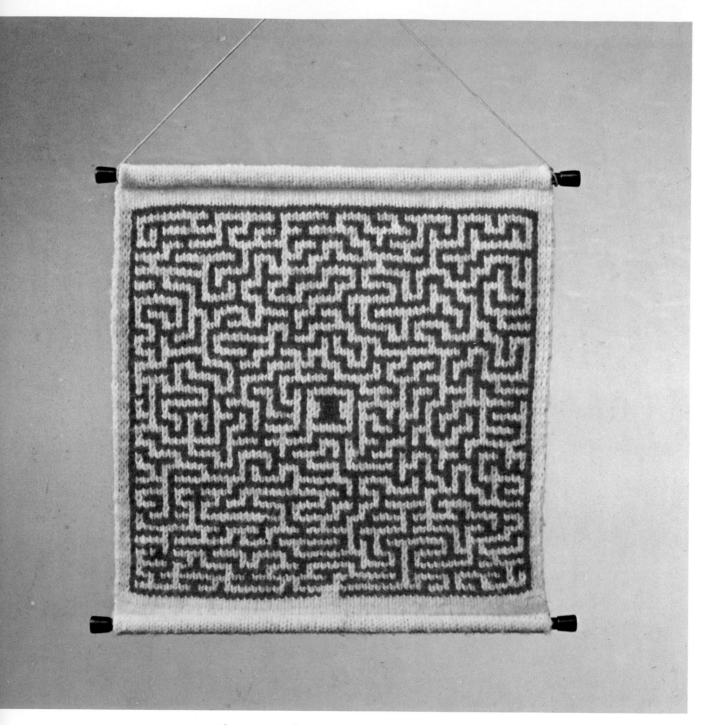

Plate 12. Take another look at this modern design wall-hanging. It is a maze! Reversibility is not the point here (the other side is merely striped). This type of knitting is ideal for complicated patterns and firm enough to hang. The maze is difficult enough to present a real challenge to a puzzle-lover. (directions, p. 166, for making this one or designing your own.)

THROW PILLOWS

These pillows are part of the recycling movement. For a year all the little snippets of yarn, which are cut off any knitting project when it is finished, were saved in a plastic bag. They were more than adequate to stuff these two pillows. Saving snippets for stuffing certainly is better than dropping them in ashtrays where unwary smokers set them afire. Any long leftovers can be wrapped around a ruler, then cut down one side to make small pieces. Of course, foam rubber, fiberfill, cut-up run stockings, etc., can be substituted.

In this case, small (10″ × 10″) pillows were made. The knit part is just a covering for a square made of plain cotton. The backs were made of a solid color dense pattern. The fronts were knit in Reversible Geometrics because of the designs and the firmness of the "fabric." If one side begins to wear a little they will immediately be taken apart and rejoined with the insides out.

Materials, for each pillow front
1 oz green sport yarn
1 oz ecru sport yarn
1 circular needle, size 3 (to be used straight)
1 crochet hook

Directions
One pillow was made in Two-Sided Stripes using 95 sts. The other is Off-set Steps of 106 sts. Simply cast on and work until the piece is square. Work a comparable square in any solid color pattern. Fasten the two together over the prepared pillow by crocheting the edges together. (Plate 7)

REVERSIBLE V-NECKED SLEEVELESS SWEATER

See-the-Light Pattern:
On circular needle, working around
Rnd 1: white—* k1, sl 1 yif, rep from *
Rnd 2: white—* p1, k1, rep from *
Rnd 3: turquoise—* p1, sl 1 yib, rep from *
Rnd 4: turquoise—* k1, p1, rep from *

On circular needle used straight, sliding from one end to the other (be careful to start in same place in pattern as you left off knitting around)
Row 1: white—* k1, sl 1 yif, rep from *. Turn.
Row 2: white—* k1, p1, rep from *. Slide.
Row 3: turquoise—rep row 1. Turn.
Row 4: turquoise—rep row 2. Slide.

Materials
2 skeins (4 oz size) white
   knitting worsted
2 skeins (4 oz size) turquoise
   knitting worsted
1 circular needle, size 5
1 circular needle, size 7

Gauge
13 sts = 2 inches
8 rows = 1 inch

Directions for small size, 32–34 (medium size, 36–38 in parentheses)
With turquoise and size 5 circular needle cast on 204 (228) st, join in circle being careful not to twist, put marker at beginning of round. Work in k2, p2 ribbing for 3″ increasing 18 (22) sts in last rnd. Change to size 7 circular needle and work in pattern, as above, in two colors. When piece measures 12 (13) inches from cast on edge, after round 3 start

Armholes: Bind off 16 (20) sts. Work 95 (105) sts in pattern round 4. Bind off 16 (20) sts. Work 95 (105) more sts. Put front sts on holder.

Back: Following pattern for circular needle used straight, dec 1 st each armhole edge every other row 10 (11) times. Continue in pattern on 75 (83) sts until back measures 6½ (7) inches above bind off.

Neck: On next row work 28 (30) sts, bind off 19 (23) sts, work remaining 28 (30) sts. Attach new balls of yarn and work both sides at the same time decreasing 1 st each neck edge every row 14 times. Work remaining 14 (16) sts until armhole measures 8½ (9) inches. Put sts on holders.

Front: Work armhole decr same as for back *except* when armhole measures 2 inches start *Neck:* Work half way across front, bind off middle st, continue across front. Attach extra balls of yarn and work both sides of neck at same time in pattern, continuing armhole decreases. Also decr 1 st each neck edge every other row 23 (25) times. Continue on 14 (16) sts each shoulder until equal to back.

Shoulder: Shoulders may be carefully sewn together so no seam is apparent on either side. Another possibility is to use an adaptation of weaving (Kitchener stitch). The knitter who is familiar with this method as applied to socks will realize that the stitches on the front needle are knit sts and those on the back are purl. If you will carefully consider each st being worked on this pattern and weave them according to whether they are knit or purl sts the results will be very pleasing.

Ribbings: Pick up 136 (144) sts around neck with size 5 circular needle and turquoise yarn. Work in k2, p2 ribbing for 1″ and bind off in ribbing, loosely. Pick up 124 (132) sts each armhole and work as for neck.

If pattern looks slightly different where worked in rows or in rounds, a few vertical and horizontal tugs on the fabric should correct the situation. (See Plate 6)

CHRISTMAS TREE COASTERS

Materials
sport yarn in green and white. Man-made yarn is preferred because these are certain to get wet and wool may smell. 1 oz. of each color will probably make 8 coasters or more. (See Plate 7)

one pair of size 4 dpn

A few yards of red yarn or thread may be used to embroider decorations on the finished coasters. Sequins may be substituted.

Gauge
23 sts = 2 inches

15 rows = 1 inch

Directions
Cast on 43 sts with green yarn. Slide all sts to other end of needle.

Row 1: white—k1, * sl 1 yif, k1, rep from *. Turn.

Row 2: green (maintain)—sl 1 yif, * k1, sl 1 yif, rep from *. Slide.

Row 3: white (maintain)—p1, * sl 1 yib, p1, rep from *. Turn.

Row 4: green (maintain)—sl 1 yib, * p1, sl 1 yib, rep from *. Slide.

Rows 5–8: rep rows 1–4.

Row 9: white—(k1, sl 1 yif) 9 times, (sl 1 yib, p1) 3 times, sl 1 yib, (sl 1 yif, k1) 9 times. Turn.

Row 10: green—(sl 1 yif, k1) 9 times, (p1, sl 1 yib) 3 times, p1, (k1, sl 1 yif) 9 times. Slide.

Row 11: white (maintain)—(pl, sl 1 yib) 9 times, (sl 1 yif, k1) 3 times, sl 1 yif, (sl 1 yib, p1) 9 times. Turn.

Row 12: green (maintain)—(sl 1 yib, p1) 9 times, (k1, sl 1 yif) 3 times, k1, (p1, sl 1 yib) 9 times. Slide.

Row 13: white—(k1, sl 1 yif) 3 times, (sl 1 yib, sl 1 yif) 3 times, (k1, sl 1 yif) 3 times, (sl 1 yib, p1) 3 times, sl 1 yib, (sl 1 yif, k1) 3 times, (sl 1 yif, sl 1 yib) 3 times, (sl 1 yif, k1) 3 times. Turn.

Row 14: green—(sl 1 yif, k1) 3 times, (p1, sl 1 yib) 3 times, (sl 1 yif, k1) 3 times, (p1, sl 1 yib) 3 times, p1, (k1, sl 1 yif) 3 times, (sl 1 yib, p1) 3 times, (k1, sl 1 yif) 3 times. Slide.

Row 15: white—(p1, sl 1 yib) 3 times, (sl 1 yif, k1) 3 times, (p1, sl 1 yib) 3 times, (sl 1 yif, k1) 3 times, sl 1 yif, (sl 1 yib, p1) 3 times, (k1, sl 1 yif) 3 times, (sl 1 yib, p1) 3 times. Turn.

Row 16: green (maintain)—(sl 1 yib, p1) 3 times, (k1, sl 1 yif) 3 times, (sl 1 yib, p1) 3 times, (k1, sl 1 yif) 3 times, k1, (p1, sl 1 yib) 3 times, (sl 1 yif, k1) 3 times, (p1, sl 1 yib) 3 times. Slide.

Row 17: white—(k1, sl 1 yif) 3 times, (sl 1 yib, p1) 15 times, sl 1 yib, (sl 1 yif, k1) 3 times. Turn.

Row 18: green—(sl 1 yif, k1) 3 times, (p1, sl 1 yib) 15 times, p1, (k1, sl 1 yif) 3 times. Slide.

Row 19: white (maintain)—(p1, sl 1 yib) 3 times, (sl 1 yif, k1) 15 times, sl 1 yif, (sl 1 yib, p1) 3 times. Turn.

Row 20: green (maintain)—(sl 1 yib, p1) 3 times, (k1, sl 1 yif) 15 times, k1, (p1, sl 1 yib) 3 times. Slide.

Row 21: white—(k1, sl 1 yif) 4 times, (sl 1 yib, p1) 13 times, sl 1 yib, (sl 1 yif, k1) 4 times. Turn.

Row 22: green—(sl 1 yif, k1) 4 times, (p1, sl 1 yib) 13 times, p1, (k1, sl 1 yif) 4 times. Slide.

Row 23: white (maintain)—(p1, sl 1 yib) 4 times, (sl 1 yif, k1) 13 times, sl 1 yif, (sl 1 yib, p1) 4 times. Turn.

Row 24: green (maintain)—(sl 1 yib, p1) 4 times, (k1, sl 1 yif) 13 times, k1, (p1, sl 1 yib) 4 times. Slide.

Row 25: white—(k1, sl 1 yif) 5 times, (sl 1 yib, p1) 11 times, sl 1 yib, (sl 1 yif, k1) 5 times. Turn.

Row 26: green—(sl 1 yif, k1) 5 times, (p1, sl 1 yib) 11 times, p1 (k1, sl 1 yif) 5 times. Slide.

Row 27: white (maintain)—(p1, sl 1 yib) 5 times, (sl 1 yif, k1) 11 times, sl 1 yif, (sl 1 yib, p1) 5 times. Turn.

Row 28: green (maintain)—(sl 1 yib, p1) 5 times, (k1, sl 1 yif) 11 times, k1, (p1, sl 1 yib) 5 times. Slide.

Row 29: white—(k1, sl 1 yif) 6 times, (sl 1 yib, p1) 9 times, sl 1 yib, (sl 1 yif, k1) 6 times. Turn.

Row 30: green—(sl 1 yif, k1) 6 times, (p1, sl 1 yib) 9 times, p1 (k1, sl 1 yif) 6 times. Slide.

Row 31: white (maintain)—(p1, sl 1 yib) 6 times, (sl 1 yif, k1) 9 times, sl 1 yif, (sl 1 yib, p1) 6 times. Turn.

Row 32: green (maintain)—(sl 1 yib, p1) 6 times, (k1, sl 1 yif) 9 times, k1, (p1, sl 1 yib) 6 times. Slide.

Row 33: white—(k1, sl 1 yif) 7 times, (sl 1 yib, p1) 7 times, sl 1 yib, (sl 1 yif, k1) 7 times. Turn.

Row 34: green—(sl 1 yif, k1) 7 times, (p1, sl 1 yib) 7 times, p1, (k1, sl 1 yif) 7 times. Slide.

Row 35: white (maintain)—(p1, sl 1 yib) 7 times, (sl 1 yif, k1) 7 times, sl 1 yif, (sl 1 yib, p1) 7 times. Turn.

Row 36: green (maintain)—(sl 1 yib, p1) 7 times, (k1, sl 1 yif) 7 times, k1, (p1, sl 1 yib) 7 times. Slide.

Row 37: white—(k1, sl 1 yif) 8 times, (sl 1 yib, p1) 5 times, sl 1 yib, (sl 1 yif, k1) 8 times. Turn.

Row 38: green—(sl 1 yif, k1) 8 times, (p1, sl 1 yib) 5 times, p1, (k1, sl 1 yif) 8 times. Slide.

Row 39: white (maintain)—(p1, sl 1 yib) 8 times, (sl 1 yif, k1) 5 times, sl 1 yif, (sl 1 yib, p1) 8 times. Turn.

Row 40: green (maintain)—(sl 1 yib, p1) 8 times, (k1, sl 1 yif) 5 times, k1, (p1, sl 1 yib) 8 times. Slide.

Row 41: white—(k1, sl 1 yif) 9 times, (sl 1 yib, p1) 3 times, sl 1 yib, (sl 1 yif, k1) 9 times. Turn.

Row 42: green—(sl 1 yif, k1) 9 times, (p1, sl 1 yib) 3 times, p1, (k1, sl 1 yif) 9 times. Slide.

Row 43: white (maintain)—(p1, sl 1 yib) 9 times, (sl 1 yif, k1) 3 times, sl 1 yif, (sl 1 yib, p1) 9 times. Turn.

Row 44: green (maintain)—(sl 1 yib, p1) 9 times, (k1, sl 1 yif) 3 times, k1, (p1, sl 1 yib) 9 times. Slide.

Row 45: white—(k1, sl 1 yif) 10 times, sl 1 yib, p1, sl 1 yib, (sl 1 yif, k1) 10 times. Turn.

Row 46: green—(sl 1 yif, k1) 10 times, p1, sl 1 yib, p1, (k1, sl 1 yif) 10 times. Slide.

Row 47: white (maintain)—(p1, sl 1 yib) 10 times, sl 1 yif, k1, sl 1 yif, (sl 1 yib, p1) 10 times. Turn.

Row 48: green (maintain)—(sl 1 yib, p1) 10 times, k1, sl 1 yif, k1, (p1, sl 1 yib) 10 times. Slide.

Rows 49–52: rep rows 1–4 (row 2 will not maintain).

Rows 53–55: rep rows 1–3.

Row 56: green—* k1, p1, rep from *. Turn.

Bind off: with green—k2 tog, * k2 tog, bind off 1, rep from *, ending k1, bind off 1. Cut end and pull through last st. Tuck in ends.

Embroider decorations on tree if desired. (See Plate 8)

Block to approx. $3\frac{3}{4}''$ by $3\frac{3}{4}''$ square.

DESIGNING COASTERS FROM A MOTIF

Any large, solid color motif (star, playing card design, etc.) given in Chapter Four may be adapted to make a coaster by overcoming one problem.

Suppose you want to make a blue and yellow coaster. Put your two hands flat together with the fingers straight and the finger-tips *barely* interlaced or alternating. Make believe your right hand is blue and your left hand yellow. Your fingers represent the stitches which will make up the two faces of the coaster. Do you see that the blue face will have one yellow edge stitch and the yellow face will have one blue edge stitch? Let's make both edges blue by adding an extra finger (stitch) to the blue face.

Since the motif patterns have the same number of stitches in each face, you must add a stitch to one side. Ideally it will be in the middle of the design although this means that the picture on one side will not precisely match the other. Sometimes it is best to subtract a stitch from the center line of one side. Occasionally the only way to avoid destroying the appearance of the design is to add the stitch at one edge or the other (as you just did with your fingers). Although that results in a coaster with one motif slightly off-center, chances are that one stitch-worth won't be apparent.

Your own stitch gauge will determine how many edge (solid color) stitches you will want on either side of the motif to make an appropriate sized coaster. Your row gauge will determine how many plain rows will be needed to make it square. Divide these so you do half before and half after the motif. *Remember* when looking at one side of a sample swatch that you will only see half the stitches and half the rows which were actually worked.

MAZE WALL-HANGING

Directions are given for making the wall-hanging in Plate 12 followed by directions for designing an original maze for those who prefer to do so.

Materials

2 pieces $\frac{3}{8}''$ dowel, each 1″ longer than width of completed hanging
4 rubber tips, $\frac{3}{8}''$ size (these are used for chair legs, usually)
2 feet (or as required) gold cord
2 oz. red lightweight orlon knitting worsted (such as Spinnerin Wintuk Featherlon)
2 oz. white lightweight knitting worsted
1 pr 14″ straight needles, size 7
1 circular needle size 3

Gauge

To check the gauge, work a swatch of stockinette st with the larger size needles. Then make another swatch of *twice as many* stitches with the smaller needle and work that in k1, p1 ribbing. The two swatches should be the same width (that is, there should be twice as many sts per inch with the smaller needles).

Directions

With white yarn and straight needles, cast on 67 sts. Work in stockinette st for $1\frac{1}{2}''$. On the next right side row, knit each stitch from the needle together with a st from the cast on edge. This turns up a "hem" or "casing" into which the dowel will be inserted. Change to circular needle which will be used straight (do *not* join work in a circle). Increase to 133 sts by purling into each stitch twice (purl into front then purl into back) *except* do *not* increase in the last st. Next row: k1, * p1, k1, rep from *. Following row: p1, * k1, p1, rep from *. Rep these two rows until piece measures 1″ above casing, finishing after a right-side row. Slide all sts to other end of needle.

At this point you will start the Maze pattern. It will be worked as a "short form" reversible geometric. First you will start at the right edge of the graph (page 167) and work 1 row of red across followed by a row of red coming back. Next will be two rows of white, across and back, but starting at the left edge of the graph. You will continue to alternate 2 rows of red and 2 of white. It will be much easier in the long run to work directly from the graph, but six rows of pattern are written out below so you can check if you understand what to do. There are only a few concepts to understand. Only half the sts show on the

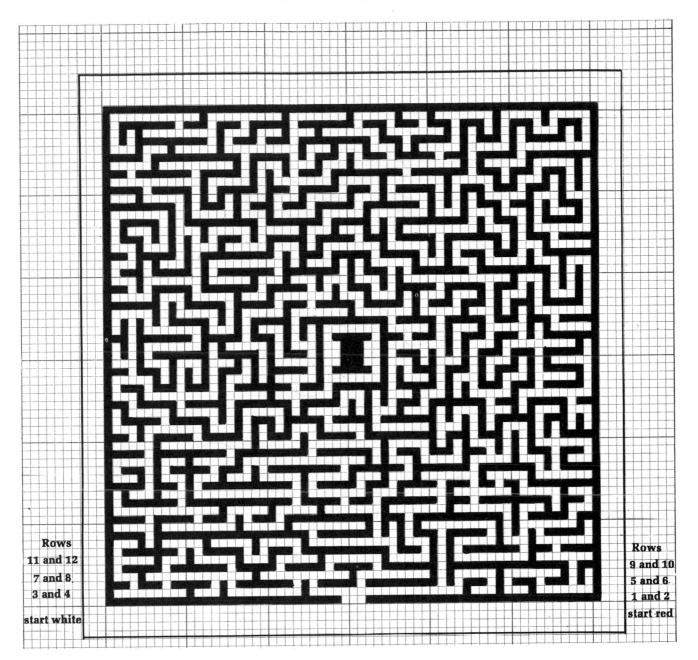

Rows
11 and 12
7 and 8
3 and 4

start white

Rows
9 and 10
5 and 6
1 and 2

start red

right-side of the wall hanging. All the wrong-side sts will be worked in whatever color is being used, thus forming stripes on the reverse side. The pattern will be determined by whether you work or slip the intervening right-side sts. They will be worked if you want them to be the color you are using and slipped if you want them to remain the color of the previous row.

The first pair of red rows will start at the right edge, and the first st will be a knit (right-side) st. Slip it with the yarn in back because the first three edge sts will always be white. Second is a purl (wrong-side) st. Purl it because you always work wrong-side sts. Slip the next st, purl the next, slip another, purl another. You have now worked the three edge sts (and their partners which make up the wrong side). The next st is a right-side one and you want it to be red, so knit it. Purl the next (wrong-side). You will want to knit and purl the next 28 *pairs* of sts to make a total of 29 red sts for the bottom of the maze, as far as the entrance. The three entrance sts are white. Work these three pairs of sts: (sl 1 yib, p1) 3 times. Next come 29 red sts so (k1, p1) 29 times. There are now 5 sts left. The last one is single and does not make a pair. Work (sl 1 yib, p1) twice, sl the last st. This gives you the three white sts on the left edge of the graph.

Remember always to work wrong-side sts. Turn the wall-hanging around and start back with red yarn. Wrong side sts are now k sts. Fortunately each time you work a second row with a color it is a "maintain" row. Row 2 will therefore start by slipping a purl (right-side) st to leave it white and knitting the wrong side st which makes a pair with it. Repeat this twice more for the three edge sts. Next you come to the bottom edge of the maze where you must work 29 sets of red sts as (p1, k1) 29 times up to the entrance. Continue across the row in this way, working *all* wrong-side sts but working only such right-side sts as you wish to be red.

Row 3 will be worked with white and will start at the left edge of the graph. The wall-hanging will have its reverse side toward you. You will work *all* wrong-side (knit) sts but only those purl sts which you wish to be white. At the end of row 3, turn and work back with white having the right side of the wall-hanging toward you and reading from the right edge of the graph.

Even if the above explanation seems very wordy and confusing, do try the row-directions which follow, continually comparing what you are doing with what you see on the graph. Keep in mind that the first row of boxes on the graph will be made by working rows 1 and 2 with red. The second row of boxes will be made by working rows 3 and 4 with white, and so on. This is indicated on the edge of the graph. Now on to the directions.

Row 1: (with right side of wall-hanging toward you) red—(sl 1 yib, p1) 3 times, (k1, p1) 29 times, (sl 1 yib, p1) 3 times, (k1, p1) 29 times, (sl 1 yib, p1) twice, sl 1 yib. Turn.

Row 2: (with wrong side of wall-hanging toward you) red (maintain)—(sl 1 yif, k1) 3 times, (p1, k1) 29 times, (sl 1 yif, k1) 3 times, (p1, k1) 29 times, (sl 1 yif, k1) twice, sl 1 yif. Slide.

Row 3: (with wrong side toward you) white—(p1, k1) 3 times, sl 1 yif, k1, (p1, k1) 9 times, sl 1 yif, k1, (p1, k1) 3 times, sl 1 yif, k1, (p1, k1) 9 times, sl 1 yif, k1, (p1, k1) 19 times, sl 1 yif, k1, (p1, k1) 3 times, sl 1 yif, k1, (p1, k1) 3 times, sl 1 yif, k1, (p1, k1) 7 times, sl 1 yif, k1, (p1, k1) twice, p1. Turn.

Row 4: (with right side toward you) white (maintain)—(k1, p1) 3 times, sl 1 yib, p1, (k1, p1) 7 times, sl 1 yib, p1, (k1, p1) 3 times, sl 1 yib, p1, (k1, p1) 3 times, sl 1 yib, p1, (k1, p1) 19 times, sl 1 yib, p1, (k1, p1) 9 times, sl 1 yib, p1, (k1, p1) 3 times, sl 1 yib, p1, (k1, p1) 9 times, sl 1 yib, p1, (k1, p1) twice, k1. Slide.

Row 5: (with right side toward you) red—(sl 1 yib, p1) 3 times, k1, p1, sl 1 yib, p1, k1, p1, sl 1 yib, p1, (k1, p1) 3 times, sl 1 yib, p1, (k1, p1) 3 times, sl 1 yib, p1, k1, p1, sl 1 yib, p1, (k1, p1) 3 times, sl 1 yib, p1, k1, p1, sl 1 yib, p1, (k1, p1) 9 times, sl 1 yib, p1, (k1, p1) 5 times, sl 1 yib, p1, k1, p1, sl 1 yib, p1, (k1, p1) 7 times, sl 1 yib, p1, k1, p1, sl 1 yib, p1, (k1, p1) 5 times, sl 1 yib, p1, (k1, p1) 3 times, sl 1 yib, p1, (k1, p1) 3 times, (sl 1 yib, p1) twice, sl 1 yib. Turn.

Row 6: red—(sl 1 yif, k1) 3 times, (p1, k1) 3 times, sl 1 yif, k1, (p1, k1) 3 times, sl 1 yif, k1, (p1, k1) 5 times, sl 1 yif, k1, p1, k1 sl 1 yif, k1, (p1, k1) 7 times, sl 1 yif, k1, p1, k1, sl 1 yif, k1, (p1, k1) 5 times, sl 1 yif, k1, (p1, k1) 9 times, sl 1 yif, k1, p1, k1, sl 1 yif, k1, (p1, k1) 3 times, sl 1 yif, k1, p1, k1, sl 1 yif, k1, (p1, k1) 3 times, sl 1 yif, k1, (p1, k1) 3 times, sl 1 yif, k1, p1, k1, sl 1 yif, k1, p1, k1, (sl 1 yif, k1) twice, sl 1 yif. Slide.

Continue in this manner, working from the graph.

When the maze is completed, discontinue the red yarn. Work in white k1, p1 ribbing, as before, for 1 inch. On a right side row, k1, * k2 tog, rep from *. You will now have 67 sts. Change to larger needles and do $1\frac{1}{2}''$ of stockinette st. To bind off and close top casing, on a right-side row: k tog 1 stitch from needle and 1 st from decrease row; again * k tog 1 st from needle and 1 st from decr row, bind off 1 st, rep from * across row.

Block, insert dowels, fasten on rubber tips, tie on cord, and hang. (See Plate 12)

DESIGNING A MAZE

Mazes are fun to design and not as difficult as you might think, so why not do your own? All you need is some graph paper (squared-off paper) and a pencil. First, outline your maze, either a square one or a rectangle, with a solid dark border. Just *be sure* that you enclose an odd number of rows both vertically and horizontally. Now make a little mark at the top and bottom of every other vertical row of boxes. The first one would be the left border, * skip a row and mark the next, rep from * until you get to the right border. Do the same for horizontal rows—first is the bottom border, skip one, mark next, etc. *These marked rows are the only ones on which you are allowed to make the "walls" of the maze.* They may twist and turn, stop and start, go any way you wish so long as you leave white any squares which are not in rows you have marked. If a square has a mark *either* at the side of the row it is in, *or* at the top and bottom of the column it is in, that square may be part of a wall.

Before starting to make walls, you must do two things. First make HOME or the goal to be reached, preferably in the center. Second, make a hole somewhere in the border for an entrance. Starting from the entrance, make your walls form as intricate a trail as possible to the center. Include plenty of false trails and dead ends to make the puzzle more difficult. Work in pencil so you may erase walls, open up new gates, etc., as you find it appropriate to do so. When you have finished and checked to be certain that your trail *does* lead to the center but none of the dead ends can, then you can go over the whole thing with a felt-tipped pen for added clarity.

To knit the maze, use the directions for the previous one by substituting the appropriate number of sts. The number to cast on for the casing is the number of boxes in a row (including the dark borders) plus 3 on each side for a white edging. (The graphed maze has 61 squares across, so $3 + 61 + 3 = 67$ sts cast on.) This will become twice as many less one after the increase row. ($2 \times 67 = 134 - 1 = 133$ sts.) Other than that, work it just like the one illustrated except, of course, substitute your own ingenious maze.

CHAPTER SIX

USING TWO-COLOR REVERSIBLES

It is really not very difficult to design knitwear with two-color reversibles. Frequently the knitting methods are the same familiar ones used for construction of any knit article. The simple and chain stitches almost never require any special technology. Anyone who has used one-color stitch patterns (ribs, cables, laces, etc.) will know that the knitter almost automatically adapts to the pattern such processes as increasing and decreasing. However, Reversible Geometrics are different from most knitting patterns. To help you feel more comfortable with them, a few comments on technique may be helpful. Occasional reference will be made to the simpler stitches, too.

This chapter will not try to teach you how to make any specific type of garment. It is intended as a reference when making knit articles in general.

YARN

The whole range of available yarns may be used for simple stitches. Chain patterns generally work best with medium weights. When selecting yarn to use for Reversible Geometrics, remember that essentially you will be making a double, or lined, article. If you plan to make something to wear, a light-weight yarn will probably be the best choice in order to have flexibility. Sport yarn would be fine. For other knitted articles, knitting worsted may be effective, especially if you are interested in firmness. The old rule of buying enough yarn of the same dye lot is especially important to remember. The simple stitch patterns may or may not take somewhat more yarn than would stockinette stitch, but Reversible Geometrics can use nearly twice as much. If your chosen pattern is one of the Plain and Fancy ones, approximately two-thirds of the yarn should be in the color used for the solid side. Suppose you are making a jacket using a true or opposite Reversible Geometric. Buy as much of each color as you would get for one jacket. After all, you really are going to make two of them!

171

GAUGE

Along these same lines, be careful when checking gauge. Knit a good-sized swatch in your chosen stitch pattern. Do you then lay on your ruler, count the stitches in, say, three inches, divide by three and have a stitch gauge? WRONG! If this is a Reversible Geometric, don't forget there are twice as many stitches involved as you can see on one side. If you count 15 stitches in a 3-inch segment, you have actually worked 30 stitches and your gauge is 10 sts = 1 inch.

The same sort of thing is true of row gauge, but this is slightly more complicated. On Plain and Fancy patterns, every two rows you see equal three rows knit. With Short Form try to see the "bands" of pattern. Remember you did two rows of dark and two of light, alternately. Counting stitches to ascertain the number of rows may be dangerous because some are slipped over a three-row segment. In Long Form or Spot Form patterns (including Motifs), one visible row indicates two rows knit. Combination Form patterns are sometimes difficult to figure. Scrutinizing the swatch while considering how it was worked is helpful. You may be able to serve the purpose by measuring designs. If there are six "pyramids" to three vertical inches and you know six rows must be worked to make one pyramid, you have it. 6 rows × 6 pyramids = 36 rows per 3 inches. 36 ÷ 3 in. = 12 rows per inch.

CASTING ON

Most methods of casting on will be perfectly acceptable. The "invisible cast-on" will not work. That method allows you to pick up stitches later from the cast-on edge and work in the other direction without showing a break. If the technique is carefully analyzed, however, the new stitches actually come from between two adjoining original ones. Since Reversible Geometrics have knit and purl stitches adjoining, and since one of them is trying to hide because it belongs to the other side, the plan fails. Recommended instead is Picot Ribbing (from *A Second Treasury of Knitting Patterns* by Barbara G. Walker). Picking up the stitches from this edge later is a little more difficult but the results are very pleasing.

There is another way to make a suitable edge for Reversible Geometrics. It is a variation of the Cable Cast-on. In that one, two stitches are first cast on using a short length of yarn and the two-strand method. Place the needle with these two stitches in the left hand. Insert the other needle *between* the two stitches, catch up the yarn as in knitting and bring through a new stitch. Put it on the left needle with the other two. Insert right needle between this and the next stitch and knit up another one. Place it, too, on the left needle. Continue in this way until there are a sufficient number of stitches. You are, of course, doing a variation of "knitting on" by knitting between stitches rather than into them. Now try the adaptation.

k1, p1 Cable Cast on

Once again, start with two stitches on the left needle. This time insert the other needle from the *back* between the two and pick up a purl stitch. Put it on the left needle. Reach in front, now, in the ordinary way between the first two stitches and pick up a knit stitch to place on the needle. Continue alternating purl stitches, by reaching in from the back, and knit stitches, by reaching in from the front. To know which kind to do next, notice that the needle will always be inserted from the side the strand of yarn comes out of.

Casting on an even number of stitches prepares you for rows which begin k1 at either end. If you wish to begin p1 and end k1 (as for Reversible Geometrics with edge stitches), simply insert the needle from the front the first time and alternate from there.

This is an excellent edge for Reversible Geometrics as it holds the stitches together. It can also be used for regular ribbing.

Nearly every knitter knows at least one way to cast on using two strands of yarn. For some stitch patterns, a pretty edge is made by having one strand one color and one the other color when doing this kind of cast on.

STARTING NEW SKEINS

Many writers of knitting books make a great to-do over their favorite ways to tie, splice, or otherwise fasten in new strands of yarn. Anyone who gets so upset at the thought is likely to be horrified to contemplate hiding knots and ends on a garment with no wrong side.

Don't worry! With Reversible Geometrics it is certainly easy. Simply knot or not, as you prefer, and run the ends in between the two layers with a small crochet hook or a so-called "yarn needle." (I dislike that term because whenever I come across it my mind first thinks "knitting needle" then has to correct the concept and picture an oversize sewing needle.)

Simple and Chain patterns don't have such an ideal hiding place but there is still no problem. When joining a new skein, try to do it at a point where two knit or two purl stitches come together. (Not all patterns have such a thing, so do it where you wish.) Work one stitch with the old skein and the next with the new. Simply leave several inches of each dangling and calmly continue for three or four rows, ignoring those ends. Then tie them together and work the ends in opposite directions for several stitches, following a strand of the same color which is already there. If that doesn't fasten them sufficiently, work them back in the opposite direction for a stitch or two. Before cutting off the remainder, flex the knitting so the new yarn adjusts, then clip closely. I don't even tie a real knot to begin with, only a half knot (such as you tie before the bow on shoelaces). Obviously I'm not exempt from pet theories but I have never had a problem with this method and it leaves no unsightly lump.

EDGES

In every stitch pattern here, unused strands of a color are carried up the edge. That is why the colors change every row or two—so there won't be an unused one being dragged a long ways up an edge. It is also the reason single-pointed needles are not recommended, for they make both colors travel up the same edge.

If each color is used for two rows, when both are at the same row-end, the two should be "twisted". This is also done in other forms of two-color knitting. However, don't overdo this twist. Merely pick up the new strand from beneath the one which was formerly used. Actually twisting strands around each other can make an unattractive edge and many edges will show in the finished article. (The man's vest illustrated in color has no extra borders or finishes.) If colors change at the end of every row the twist is probably unnecessary, at least if edge stitches (see below) exist. Experiment in the sample swatch.

EDGE STITCHES

If a pattern has a multiple of stitches "plus 2" that probably indicates the presence of edge stitches. If directions for each row begin "p1, *" and end "k last st" you can be certain you are dealing with edge stitches. They are included principally when some rows end with a couple of slip stitches. Especially if the next row begins with slip stitches, there could be a problem unless a stitch were worked in between to anchor the yarn at the edge.

If you are going to do such a pattern in circular knitting, simply eliminate the edge stitches and work the basic design. Edge stitches are only needed in flat knitting.

INCREASES AND DECREASES

These basic techniques should cause little difficulty in simple stitch patterns. In working with chain patterns it may be best to work increases and decreases in a stitch next to the chain, but experiment and decide. Think of Reversible Geometrics as two separate fabrics which back up each other. All increases and decreases are done in pairs. First the change is made in the stitches of one side, then a comparable change is worked in the stitches of the other side.

Let's suppose you are increasing at only one edge. Start a row at that end which will "turn" at the other end. When you reach the second or third *knit* stitch increase one. This will mean your normal flow of alternating k and p stitches is interrupted by an extra k. When you get to the far end, turn the work and pick up the other color or continue with the same one as required. Work almost all the way back, to the k stitch before the double purl stitches made by the former increase. Increase again, in such a way that the new stitch will come between those two purl stitches. With some kinds of increase it may be necessary to do a little rearranging of stitches after increasing to achieve this. Or k the stitch, p1, then increase, and p the next st. Whatever way you work the increase, the main thing is to get back to a k, p, k, p pattern.

Decreases are done similarly on consecutive rows. When you get to the proper place, rearrange the stitches. From p, k, p, k, p change the second and third stitches so as to have p, p, k, k, p. Then k together the adjoining k sts (or sl 1 k1, psso; or ssk, as you prefer). Again, two purl stitches will be left adjoining. On the next row, when they are k stitches, decrease with them.

Here is a handy way to make decreases in a hurry for a sharply slanting edge. Again choose a time when the first of two rows ends "turn." To do the decreases at the far edge, work to 4 sts from the end. Rearrange these so you have 2 purl stitches, then 2 knit stitches. Decrease with the purl stitches. Leaving the remaining 2 stitches on the left needle, turn work. Slip the last stitch worked from the left needle to the right. Pass the 2 stitches previously on the right needle over the one just slipped (thus, a double bind off). Now p1 with the appropriate color for the next row and then bind off 1 more stitch. Four stitches have been decreased. If you want the other edge to decrease, too, work to the last 4 stitches and rearrange to k, k, p, p. Do a knit decrease; turn work. Slip last-worked stitch onto the right needle and bind off both other stitches over it at the same time. K1 and bind off 1 in the appropriate color. All these increases and decreases may be done in Plain and Fancy patterns. Start at the beginning of the first of a pair of solid-color rows.

SEAMS

There is no doubt that seams can cause problems in reversible knitting simply because there is no wrong side. One of the best ways to avoid seams is to use circular knitting. If you are serious about making reversible *garments* (sweaters and jackets as opposed to afghans and stoles), the book, *Knitting From the Top,* by Barbara G. Walker, can be a great help. The construction methods are ideal because they almost never make a seam. In some places the book recommends the "invisible cast on". With Reversible Geometrics a picot ribbing works better, as mentioned in the section on casting on, above. Other than that very little has to be done to adapt to reversible knitting. It is also a marvellous book for conventional knitting.

You will have to face the seam problem at some time. For the stitches in Chapters Two and Three the best method is to butt the edges directly against each other and sew back and forth from one edge to the other. Chains can be embroidered over seams of Ripple and Chain articles. Kitchener stitch (weaving or grafting) can be used, too.

Seaming Reversible Geometrics can be done by the flap method. The pattern must first be changed to create the flap. To start, eliminate any edge stitches (cross out "p1," from beginning and "k last st" from end). Insert at the start of each row the stitch which is ordinarily the *next to last* of that row. It will be either k1 or sl 1 yib. Also remove that same stitch (next to last) from the end of the row. One stitch has now been moved from the end of each row to its beginning. It is very important to realize this is done only at the beginning and end of each *row,* not each pattern repeat. Other pattern repeats remain the same.

Knitting in this way, you will have rows which begin with two knit stitches and end with two purl stitches, whereas the rest of the time you will be working on a k1, p1 base. This creates a tiny flap at each edge of the work. The right-hand edge has a flap which is part of the front surface pattern while the left-hand flap belongs to the back surface. Two pieces of this kind of knitting can be carefully placed next to each other with a top (right edge) flap resting on a bottom (left edge) flap and then sewn together. You may want to sew them with a single ply of the yarn you are using.

Remember that one of the best solutions is to use circular needles and avoid most seams.

CIRCULAR KNITTING

All stitch patterns in this book are written for flat knitting, although they use double-pointed or circular needles. We can easily use the same equipment to knit around and around. All patterns can be thus adapted, even those which can never be done on single-pointed needles.

Of course, some changes must be made. First, all rows must work in the same direction. With the exception of Plain and Fancy and a few others, patterns divide into four-row segments. Since two and six-row patterns must be repeated to get both colors back to the edge where they started, all may be considered as being based on a number of rows divisible by four.

Make a scheme of your chosen pattern showing the direction in which the rows are worked for flat knitting. Start with row 1 at the lower right, as it does in knitting. Since you then turn, row 2 starts at left, and so on. In writing the steps of each row proceed in the direction of the arrows and put each stitch over the same one from the row before.

slide	(k	p	k	p	k	p	k	p	k	⟵		4th row
⟶	p	k	p	k	p	k	p	k	p		turn	3rd row
⟶	p	k	yif	k	p	k	yif	k	p		slide	2nd row
turn	(k	p	yib	p	k	p	yib	p	k	⟵		1st row

Figure 1

Figure 1 shows how this is done for "Lattice." This shows exactly how the stitches "stack up" on top of each other. Understand that they are called "k" or "p" as they are in the directions. If you were looking at one side of the knitted fabric you would not see the stitches this way. Some of the ones called "k" would appear purled and vice versa. Lattice has one extra stitch which was added to center the design. This can be seen from the "multiple of 4 sts plus 1." A close look at any row of the pattern will show that one end stitch must be removed. Otherwise, in repeating it over and over there would be a place where two k or p stitches came together and interrupted the pattern. One stitch may be removed from either end, but that *same* stitch must be removed from every row. The left column is circled to show those stitches will not be used in circular knitting. If this were a pattern with edge stitches, you would have to cross off both first and last stitches of each row.

Next we must reverse the direction of rows 2 and 3 so they can go round and round in the same way as 1 and 4. Since we are going to begin work at the opposite end of the row from the former start, we will have the other face of the work toward us and every stitch will be worked backwards of the former way.

p	k	p	k	p	k	p	k	⟵	4th row
p	k	p	k	p	k	p	k	⟵	3rd row
p	yib	p	k	p	yib	p	k	⟵	2nd row
p	yib	p	k	p	yib	p	k	⟵	1st row

Figure 2

Figure 2 shows how they will now be done for Lattice. Simply follow the arrows to write up directions for doing the pattern on a circular needle. Lattice becomes:

Rnd 1: light—* k1, p1, sl 1 yib, p1, rep from *.

Rnd 2: light—rep round 1.

Rnd 3: dark—* k1, p1, rep from *.

Rnd 4: dark—rep round 3.

　　rep Rounds 1–4.

By the way, in working patterns circularly, always leave a strand of yarn where it occurs at the end of a round. That is, if the last stitch of a dark-colored round is sl 1 yif, leave the yarn in front when you start the light color even though you know that the next time it is used it will be for a knit stitch. When you actually get ready to do that knit stitch, *then* move the yarn to the back to knit. Do not bother to twist the colors, either. This will usually give the best appearance with little indication of the place where rounds change. It is still advisable to keep the row change in an unobtrusive spot. On a sweater, down the side is certainly preferable to center front.

REVERSING KNITTING PROCESSES

In changing the direction in which a row is worked, all processes must be reversed. "K" becomes "p" and "p" becomes "k". "Sl 1 yif" becomes "sl 1 yib"; "KRT" becomes "PRT"; "KLT" becomes "PLT". "k2 tog" becomes "p2 tog" and vice versa.

"KPRT" and "PKLT" do not change; "y o" will still be "y o." Stitches will still be slipped purl-wise, even though yif changes to yib. You will discover as you reverse process and direction that (k1, p1) 3 times will still be the same. However, (k1, sl 1 yif) 3 times would become (sl 1 yib, p1) 3 times.

This information is useful not only when changing to circular knitting, but in our next topic, too.

ADAPTING TO SPN

Any four-row pattern (or multiple of four rows) which uses dark, dark, light, light (or vice versa) can be adapted for the use of single-pointed needles. This includes Short Form Reversible Geometrics, Ripple and Chain I stitches and many of the patterns in Chapter Two. These patterns state "use dpn or adapt to spn."

Look at Figure 1 again, this time to adapt Lattice to back-and-forth knitting for the use of single-pointed needles. Rows 3 and 4 will have to reverse their direction now. Do not remove the extra stitch or any edge stitches since the result will still be in flat knitting.

⟶	p	k	p	k	p	k	p	k	p	turn	4th row
turn	k	p	k	p	k	p	k	p	k	⟵	3rd row
⟶	p	k	yif	k	p	k	yif	k	p	turn	2nd row
turn	k	p	yib	p	k	p	yib	p	k	⟵	1st row

Figure 3

Figure 3 shows how the stitches will be worked when the rows and knitting processes are reversed. Therefore, following the arrows, here are directions for Lattice using spn:

Row 1: light—k1, * p1, sl 1 yib, p1, k1, rep from *.
Row 2: light—p1, * k1, sl 1 yif, k1, p1, rep from *.
Row 3: dark—k1, * p1, k1, rep from *.
Row 4: dark—p1, * k1, p1, rep from *.
    rep Rows 1–4.

The disadvantage of using single-pointed needles is that the two colors always twist on the same edge. The two edges will not look comparable and one will be more untidy. If seaming will hide this it may be acceptable. For an afghan or scarf it would be undesirable.

FINISHING HEMS AND EDGES

Many two-color reversibles make fine edges which need no further treatment. Refer also to the sections on casting on and binding off. Ribbing may be used for cuffs, necklines and bottoms of sweaters, especially with the simple patterns. A solid color may be your choice, or one of the ribbed patterns in Chapter Two. Crocheted edges may be applied if desired. Use any conventional edging method which will not interfere with the reversibility of the finished article.

COMBINING SOLIDS AND PATTERNS

There will be times when you want to use Reversible Geometrics on only part of an article. You may be using a border design only, or a motif, or bands of various patterns with solid colors between. You may easily do this and have the solid color knitting be either the same color on both sides or reverse from light to dark. Directions for both will be given but please keep in mind that they cannot be followed slavishly. If the design you are using calls for rows which always start with a purl stitch or uses an odd number of stitches, make a minor adjustment so that knit stitches are always knit (or slipped yib) and purl stitches are always purled (or slipped yif).

SOLID ONE-COLOR REVERSIBLE

Use dpn, or spn without adapting. Even number of sts.
Pattern: * k1, sl 1 yif, rep from *.
Repeat this row as many times as desired. Two rows knit will look like one row per side.

Variation:
Pattern: * k1, p1, rep from *.
Repeat as needed. Not recommended for more than an inch or so between Reversible Geometric designs. Two rows knit look like two rows on each side.

SOLID TWO-COLOR OPPOSITE REVERSIBLE

Use of dpn required. Even number of sts.
Row 1: light—* k1, sl 1 yif, rep from *. Turn.
Row 2: with dark rep row 1. Slide.
Row 3: light * sl 1 yib, p1, rep from *. Turn.
Row 4: with dark rep row 3. Slide.
          rep Rows 1–4 as required.
Two rows knit appear as one row each side. When using with a pattern in which row 1 is "dark", reverse above colors.

Variation, if using spn
Use same directions as above but change order of rows to 1, 3, 4, 2.

CENTERING DESIGNS

The designs for Simple Reversibles and Ripple and Chain Stitches are usually written so they are "centered." To explain, if a Ripple and Chain pattern has a chain two stitches from the right edge on one side, there will be a chain two stitches from the left edge on that side, too. This is as you would want it for scarves, afghans, etc. If you want to put two panels together (for a wide afghan) you may have to remove some stitches from one edge. Be sure you remove the same number from the same edge on each row. That is, the beginning of rows 1 and 4 make the same edge as the end of rows 2 and 3.

Not all Reversible Geometrics are centered. They are easier to adapt to circular knitting if they are not, and circular knitting is recommended for garment construction. Since a sample swatch must be made before any knitwear is started, you will soon see if the design is centered. If not, and you want it to be, proceed as follows.

Look at the swatch as if you were about to start at row number one. Decide which edge you want to add onto and how many stitches (remember to double the number needed for one surface). If you are adding to the right edge, the first and fourth rows will have that many extra stitches at the beginning. The second and third rows will get them at the end. To add to the left edge reverse the process. The stitches will come after the first edge stitch (if any) and before the last one.

The extra stitches must now be put into the pattern design. If they come before the start of a row, look to the end to see how they will be worked. If you are adding four stitches at the beginning do exactly what the last four stitches (excluding edge stitch) do. To add at the end of the row, see what that number of stitches does at the beginning.

BINDING OFF

Nearly any binding off method will be fine for simple and chain reversibles. Try out your favorite method on your sample swatch. There is a fascinating "cast-off in outline stitch" in Elizabeth Zimmerman's delightful book, *Knitting Without Tears*.

Reversible Geometrics should be handled carefully. Too tight a bind-off will restrict flexibility. More likely to cause problems is a too-loose bind-off which allows the k1, p1 base to open up, revealing its parentage and ruining the pattern at that point. Here are some recommended bind-offs with which you may experiment to determine the best for any given use. It is assumed they will be used for patterns of an even number of stitches starting with a knit stitch. If there is a purl edge stitch first or an odd number per row, that is easily allowed for.

BIND-OFF I

K1, * p1, bind off 1, k1, b o 1, rep from *.
This is a regular k1, p1 bind-off and is usually too loose for these patterns, although using a smaller needle helps.

BIND-OFF II

K2 tog, * p2 tog, b o 1, k2 tog, b o 1, rep from *.
Be careful not to work this one too tightly.

BIND-OFF III

K1, p1, * k1, b o first st over next 2, p1, b o 1 over 2, rep from *.
When 2 sts remain, draw the yarn end through both. This makes a firm edge.

BIND-OFF IV

Preparatory row A: * k1, sl 1 yif, rep from *. Turn.
Preparatory row B: with same color rep row A (so all sts formerly slipped are knit and those formerly knit are slipped).
Follow with Bind-off I, II, or III. Even with I, the edge will not spread.

BIND-OFF V

Prep rows: the same as in IV. Turn.
Bind-off row: k1, * sl 1 yif, b o 1, k1, b o 1, rep from *.

BIND-OFF VI

Prep rows: the same as in Bind-off IV. Then slip the stitches alternately onto two double-pointed needles so that all k sts are on one, all p sts on the other. Holding these needles parallel, finish with Kitchener Stitch (weaving or grafting).

BIND-OFF VII

Row 1: * k1, p1, b o 1, rep from *. (When row is completed, half the original number of sts remains.) Turn.
Row 2: (no knitting)—starting where you left off, sl 2 sts, b o 1, * sl 1, b o 1, rep from *.
The final st will have to be fastened (sewn) down. This makes an unusual edge. It is useful for fringing.

CHAPTER SEVEN

DESIGNING REVERSIBLE GEOMETRIC PATTERNS

Now that you have worked with Reversible Geometrics, if you feel comfortable with them you may want to develop patterns of your own. This chapter will discuss all but the Plain and Fancy type. That particular one is specialized, is often designed without graphing, and is covered in its own section of Chapter Four.

The fact that these patterns are geometric makes them very adaptable to graphing. Not all have to be graphed first, but that is the method to be covered here. You may design some merely by experimenting with lines and shapes on graph paper. Or you may see a specific design you admire and deliberately put it down on graph paper for future knitting. American Indian designs, Oriental rugs, graphic art, or the forms of everyday objects may be your inspiration.

Whether you use some of the designs suggested here or your own, it will be necessary to understand how a graphed design is developed by the various Geometric Reversible forms. Refer to the Table of Forms on the next page as you work.

DESIGNING A SHORT FORM PATTERN

A good starting place is the simple pattern graphed on page 185. It is called Fretwork, and you can learn to write the directions for it. It also immediately inspires a variation but the discussion will cover only the simpler form. Here and elsewhere "line" will refer to a horizontal line of squares on the graph; "row" will indicate a row of knitting.

This pattern seems to meet the description of Short Form in the Table of Forms. It is a maze-like pattern of bands. Notice that line **a** is mostly dark, **b** uses light, **c** is mostly dark, **d** is all light, etc.

One pattern "repeat" is marked. There is a box of thin lines around a portion of the pattern. If you look left of it, you will see the next portion is identical. To the right, above, or below, the same is true. The box encloses one pattern repeat. It is a complete unit of the design but contains nothing twice. The repeat for the variation is no wider but must be taller to encompass a complete unit.

TABLE OF REVERSIBLE GEOMETRIC FORMS

TYPE	HOW WORKED	COMMENTS
Short Form	1 line of graph = 2 rows knit; first line do two dark rows, second line do two light rows.	Use for alternating bands of mostly dark and mostly light; maze types (see Key and Snake Walk). Can only be used if, in each dark row, all light squares were light in previous row and vice versa. Makes true or mirror reverse. One-row variation makes tweed effects (see Feather Stripes).
Long Form	1 line of graph = 4 rows knit; 1 dark row, 1 light row to fill in, 2nd dark row and 2nd light row "maintain".	Useful for opposite reversibles. If Short Form fails, try Long. Any Short Form may be done Long Form. Results truest to graph form. Most versatile (can be used for most graphed designs). Smooth—no st is slipped through 2 rows.
Combination	Uses Short Form where possible. When colors must change substitute Long Form or Spot Form.	Useful for rows of small block shapes (see Pyramids). Makes a pattern in fewer rows than Long Form.
Spot Form	1 line of graph = 1 row of dark, 1 row light.	Useful for "spotty" patterns and irregular shapes. Really is 2-row Long Form. Can be opposite reversible or true, sometimes mirror. Used for Motifs.

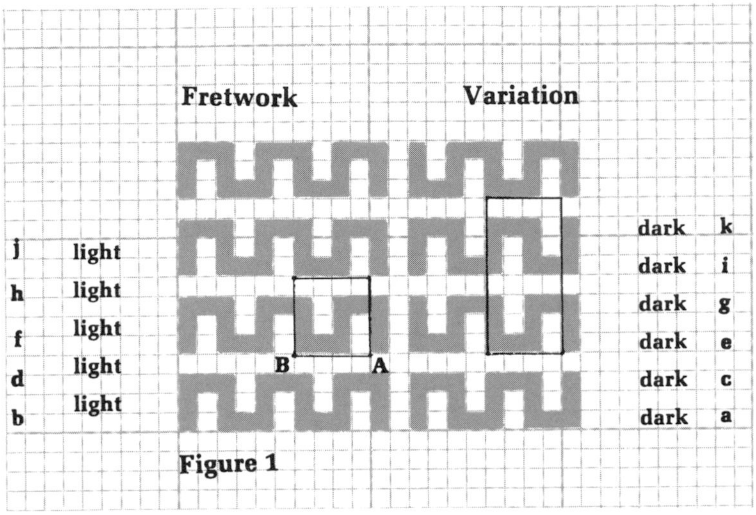

Figure 1

Check for Short Form

To be sure this can be done by Short Form, check in the repeat that all contrast color stitches will appear in the row below.

Line **e** will be done with dark yarn but has one light square in the repeat. This was light in line **d** below so is all right. **f** will be light but has two dark squares, both acceptable because they were dark in **e**. **g** will be dark and its one light square was light in **f**. **h** will be worked in light and has no dark squares to bother with. You can definitely work this in Short Form.

The directions for the pattern will be analyzed step by step. Elements explained here will not be rediscussed in later patterns.

FRETWORK, Short Form

Use dpn or adapt to spn. Multiple of 8 sts plus 2. Cast on light, slide.

e {
Row 1: dark—p1, * sl 1 yib, sl 1 yif, (k1, p1) 3 times, rep from *, k last st. Turn.

Row 2: dark (maintain)—p1, * (k1, p1) 3 times, sl 1 yib, sl 1 yif, rep from *, k last st. Slide.
}

f {
Row 3: light—p1, * sl 1 yib, sl 1 yif, k1, p1, rep from *, k last st. Turn.

Row 4: light (maintain)—p1, * k1, p1, sl 1 yib, sl 1 yif, rep from *. Slide.
}

g {
Row 5: dark—p1, * (k1, p1) twice, sl 1 yib, sl 1 yif, k1, p1, rep from *, k last st. Turn.

Row 6: dark (maintain)—p1, * k1, p1, sl 1 yib, sl 1 yif, (k1, p1) twice, rep from *, k last st. Slide.
}

h {
Row 7: light—* p1, k1, rep from *. Turn.

Row 8: light (maintain)—rep row 7. Slide.
}

rep Rows 1–8.

Multiples

"8 sts" are needed because each square of the repeat represents 1 st on this face and there must be a comparable st on the other face. 4 squares per repeat × 2 = 8. "Plus 2" more sts because some rows will end with two slip sts and they will "unwind" when you turn around and go back. Therefore start each row with an extra "p" and end with an extra "k" to fasten the yarn.

Cast On

Since the first row will be dark, "cast on light". This maintains the alternating colors and also gives light sts to slip where needed in the first row. "Slide" because it is preferable to have dark start at the other end from light. This also determines the use of "dpn", but since it is a pattern in which colors alternate every two rows, it *could* "adapt to spn" (see introduction to Short Form Reversibles on page 54).

Knitting Directions

Stitches should be considered in pairs. Each square represents a "k" st for this side of the knitted fabric and a "p" st for the other. If a square is not the color being used those sts will be slipped. A "k" st would be "sl 1 yib" and a "p" becomes "sl 1 yif". In this way the unused strand moves between the sts of the two faces. In short form a "k" is always followed by a "p" and sl sts always go together. This is because both sides will be made the same. Later pattern forms may follow a different rule which will be discussed then.

Rows 1 and 2

Remember always to begin at the bottom line of the graph. Dark starts at the right edge of the repeat box. After the first p st (discussed above) the * indicates the start of a repeat. The first pair of sts is slipped to remain light. Next come three pairs of k and p sts. Bracket these "(k1, p1) 3 times" rather than write k1, p1, k1, p1, k1, p1. "Rep from *" is used because the directions for one repeat are complete. Then "Turn" because the knitter will continue with dark in the next row. Row 2 will "maintain" because it will be identical to Row 1 and will not change the color of a single st. It is merely worked in a different direction. Note that pairs of sts still go "k1, p1" as former p sts become k sts because the work was turned around. At the end the sts must "slide" to the other end of the needle so that the light strand of yarn becomes available next.

Rows 3 and 4
Remember row 3 starts at the left edge of the repeat box. After writing the directions for the first 2 squares you will discover the next two are identical so immediately go to "rep from *." Row 4 starts at the right and "maintains."

Rows 5 and 6 are done in the same manner.

Rows 7 and 8
Don't make the mistake of writing p1, * k1, p1, rep from *, k last st, as that is unnecessary.

Repeat
You have written directions for one pattern repeat. Everything beyond that point will proceed in the exact same way, so "rep Rows 1–8."

Striped Reverse
You may wish to have this pattern or another Short Form reverse to stripes (see A Cross and Across). All you have to do is work all sts on one side in pattern but always knit or purl the sts on the other side. Never slip them no matter what color you are using. The Maze Wall-Hanging (page 166) gives a more detailed description of this process.

DESIGNING A LONG FORM PATTERN

Do you recognize Figure 2? It is merely an "opposite" reversible of Fretwork. To use it as the other side you will have to design a Long Form. If the repeat looks different, it is! It is backwards, to show how it would look if you turn the original over. That is, the left edge (B) of the Fig. 1 repeat is the right edge of the Fig. 2 repeat. We shall call the side shown in Fig. 2 the "back" although there is no right or wrong side. Be careful in analyzing the directions that you know which side (the "front", Fig. 1, or the "back" Fig. 2) you have toward you on each row, *and* whether you start at edge A or B.

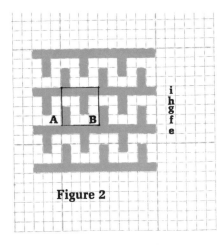

Figure 2

OPPOSITE REVERSIBLE FRETWORK

Use of dpn required. Multiple of 8 sts. Cast on light, slide.

e
> Row 1: dark—* sl 1 yib, p1, (k1, sl 1 yif) 3 times, rep from *. Turn.
> Row 2: light—* (k1, sl 1 yif) 3 times, sl 1 yib, p1, rep from *. Slide.
> Row 3: dark (maintain)—* (sl 1 yib, p1) 3 times, k1, sl 1 yif, rep from *. Turn.
> Row 4: light (maintain)—* k1, sl 1 yif, (sl 1 yib, p1) 3 times, rep from *. Slide.

f
> Row 5: dark—* sl 1 yib, p1, k1, sl 1 yif, rep from *. Turn.
> Row 6: light—* k1, sl 1 yif, sl 1 yib, p1, rep from *. Slide.
> Row 7: dark (maintain)—rep row 5. Turn.
> Row 8: light (maintain)—rep row 6. Slide.

g
> Row 9: dark—* (k1, sl 1 yif) twice, sl 1 yib, p1, k1, sl 1 yif, rep from *. Turn.
> Row 10: light—* k1, sl 1 yif, sl 1 yib, p1, (k1, sl 1 yif) twice, rep from *. Slide.
> Row 11: dark (maintain)—* sl 1 yib, p1, k1, sl 1 yif, (sl 1 yib, p1) twice, rep from *. Turn.
> Row 12: light (maintain)—* (sl 1 yib, p1) twice, k1, sl 1 yif, sl 1 yib, p1, rep from *. Slide.

h
> Row 13: dark—* sl 1 yib, p1, rep from *. Turn.
> Row 14: with light rep row 13. Slide.
> Row 15: dark (maintain)—* k1, sl 1 yif, rep from *. Turn.
> Row 16: with light (maintain) rep row 15. Slide.
> rep Rows 1–16.

Beginning

"Use of dpn required" because in Long Form Colors alternate from row to row. This makes a smoother finish but necessitates sliding the sts from one end of the needle to the other. No edge sts are used (there is no "plus something" after the multiple) because there is never more than a single sl st on the edge due to the way sts are paired in Long Form opposite reversibles. Each "k1" pairs with a "sl 1 yif" and "p1" pairs with "sl 1 yib" to make opposite colors on opposite sides.

Line e

This time four rows must be used to do a line. Each 4-row set will appear as 2 rows per side. First a row of dark is used, slipping the partners of those sts which are worked for the design. Then light comes along and works those which had been slipped and slips those which were done with dark. The same thing is done again in Rows 3 and 4 (maintaining) because single rows of each color do not show up well. Row 2 does not maintain, it completes the design which Row 1 started.

Where Rows Start

Note carefully that Row 1 is worked with the front (Fig. 1) toward you, starting at edge A. Row 2 is done with the back (Fig. 2) toward you, starting at B. Row 3 starts from Fig. 2 B; Row 4 from Fig. 1 A. *This is the normal order for each 4-row segment of a Long Form.*

Row 1

Look at line **e**. Start at Fig. 1, edge A and think "dark". You will have to slip the first st so it can be light, but its pair will be dark so purl that one. The next 3 pairs will have the first st knit in dark and the second slipped yif so as to be light. Therefore, "(k1, sl 1 yif) 3 times."

Row 2

Think "line e, Fig. 2, B, light". The first three pairs will be k1, sl 1 yif; the last pair shows a dark st on this side and needs a light one opposite it, so "sl 1 yib, p1."

Convert the rest of the graph to directions in the same way.

DESIGNING A COMBINATION FORM PATTERN

Figure 3 shows a simple pattern called Peaks and Valleys. There is also a staggered variation for future use if you so desire. We shall make a true reversible version of the simpler form. As a point of interest, don't forget to look at the light, as well as the dark, part of a pattern. In this, the dark design below is inverted as white above.

Remember the rule for Short Form? If not, reread that section (page 184). This pattern works for Short Form in line **a** if you use dark, and in line **d** if you use light, but **b** and **c** will give you trouble. If you use dark for **b** there would be no way to make the light sts by slipping and

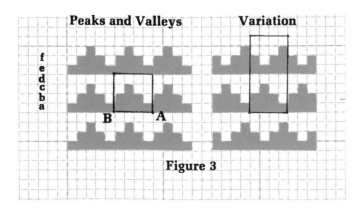

Figure 3

you would have to do four consecutive rows of dark, which is un-desirable. If you use light, what will you use for **c**? Light for two rows? Followed by two more of light in line **d**? Obviously that is unreasonable. Well, you could work the pattern in Long Form, but do you want a 16-row pattern? Perhaps it could be done in less. Line **a** would use only dark (two rows, of course). And line **d** would use only light (another 2 rows). Only lines **b** and **c** would be done long form. The whole pattern would have twelve rows. Wonderful—that's Combination Form!

Do remember when using graphed designs that they will not be reproduced exactly in knitting because sts are not square. Keep that in mind as you consider that it would be possible to work only *one* row of light and *one* of dark in lines **b** and **c**. Now you are down to eight rows per repeat. However, lines **a** and **d** will appear in the knitted version as two rows tall while **b** and **c** will each appear as one row tall. The distortion will be greater so that the jagged peaks of the graph will become gentle swells in the knitting.

If you want to work out directions for this design you will have to do it yourself. Here are some hints to help with both the 12-row and 8-row versions. They tell what color will be used in a row and whether it will be worked from the A edge to the B edge of the repeat or in the other direction. Don't worry about which face is toward you this time because you are doing a true reversible. Just work across a line in the correct direction using pairs of either k and p or sl 1 yib and sl 1 yif.

PEAKS AND VALLEYS

Use of dpn required. Multiple of 8 sts plus 2. Cast on light, slide.

12-row Version

a { Row 1: dark—A to B
{ Row 2: dark—B to A

b { Row 3: light—B to A
{ Row 4: dark—A to B
{ Row 5: light—A to B
{ Row 6: dark—B to A

c { Row 7: light—B to A
{ Row 8: dark—A to B
{ Row 9: light—A to B
{ Row 10: dark—B to A

d { Row 11: light—B to A
{ Row 12: light—A to B

8-row Version

a { Row 1: dark—A to B
{ Row 2: dark—B to A

b { Row 3: light—B to A
{ Row 4: dark—A to B

c { Row 5: light—A to B
{ Row 6: dark—B to A

d { Row 7: light—B to A
{ Row 8: light—A to B

At this point, some knitters may find it easier to knit directly from the graph. If you prefer to write down the directions, here is a sample row to check with.

Row 3: light—p1, * (sl 1 yib, sl 1 yif) 3 times, k1, p1, rep from *, k last st. Turn.

Do you have difficulty understanding why a color goes in a certain direction at a certain time? Since you slide after the cast on, light will be left at B while you start dark at A. Each time you want to use a color, check the last time it was used. If it went from A to B before, it will obviously have to start at B and go to A next.

Luckily, in both these versions both colors end where they started. They are then ready to start another repeat. If they ended at the wrong edge, you would have to continue writing directions until they ended a repeat, ready to begin again as they did originally. That problem does not often arise except in an occasional Plain and Fancy Reversible Geometric.

Before you write up the directions, an observant eye may save you some work. Rows 1 and 2 are the same in both versions because they use the same color, starting in the same place, to create the same line of graph. Do you see any similar comparisons? Rows 3 and 4 are the same in both. Rows 5 and 6 of the 8-row version are the same as Rows 9 and 10 of the 12-row version. And Rows 7 and 8 of the 8-row are the same as 11 and 12 of the 12-row.

Now go ahead and write up the 12-row version. You will have built-in directions for the 8-row version, too. If you are daring, you may then try an opposite reversible version.

DESIGNING A SPOT FORM PATTERN

If you have mastered the preceding methods, Spot Form will give you no trouble. You have already done some in the last pattern without even knowing it. Spot Form opens a new field for it is the method used for Motifs. We shall work, now, on a short and simple pattern. When doing a Motif, allow for distortion. Graph vertical parts taller and thinner than would seem appropriate. Any horizontal parts should be thickened. For example, a plain letter "H" should have tall, thin side pieces and a short, thick cross piece on the graph.

Spot Form Reversible Geometrics use one row of light and one row of dark for each line of graph. That is the method used in lines **b** and **c** of the 8-row Combination Form just completed. Look at Fig. 4 on the next page, Broken Lines. This could be done by Long Form, but Spot Form is simply a shorter version. It does require more care in knowing what edge each color starts from in any given line.

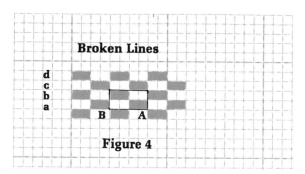

Figure 4

BROKEN LINES

Use of dpn required. Multiple of 8 sts plus 2. Cast on light, slide.

Line	Row	Color	Direction
a	1:	dark	A to B
	2:	light	B to A
b	3:	dark	B to A
	4:	light	A to B

Pair k and p; pair sl sts. Thus you need not worry about looking at the other face as you write directions. Merely work along this face in the required direction. There are no maintain rows.

This is a simple pattern, so you are on your own with it. Again, consider the idea of working directly from the graph. If you want a deeper analysis, there are some other points which can be considered. This was worked by the "true reversible" method of having each st backed up with its own color. However, if you have knit up a swatch, look at each side and you will discover you have a mirror reversible. It would be only slightly more difficult to work an opposite reversible (pairing k1 with sl 1 yif, p1 with sl 1 yib). But the result would be a true reversible!

Many variations are possible from this simple beginning. For instance, you could work lines a-c, then two rows light, then repeat a-c and two more rows of light. That might be more attractive in Long Form. By this time you should be seeing designs and variations of them everywhere. Do you have your graph paper handy?

CENTERING

You may want to center your designs by doing more than a repeat. For instance, in Figures 1, 2, and 3 you could add one more st beyond edge B. This would appear before the * in directions for rows beginning at B and after "rep from *" in rows ending at B ("rep from * but end k1, p1"). In Fig. 4 it would be necessary to add 2 sts outside the B edge to center the design.

Now you are ready to invent your own Reversible Geometric patterns and then design garments from them. You will have the most original knitwear you ever made.

INDEX

INDEX

746.43
N397r

Neighbors.

Reversible two-color knitting.

April 1975